Praise for *Understanding Friendship*

"Gary Chartier's new book, *Understanding Friendship*, is the most exciting and profound study on the topic that we have seen in three decades, since the youthful days of Gilbert Meilaender, Stanley Hauerwas, and Paul Wadell. Chartier presents the most diligent and comprehensive discussion that I have ever read, and he takes us to new levels of analysis throughout. His engagement with politics and economics breaks new ground and makes friendship the most important heuristic key for solving the problems of our modern times. Bravo. A sure classic from the get-go."

—Stephen G. Post, *Stony Brook University*

"Wide-ranging in its exploration of the literature of friendship, Gary Chartier's *Understanding Friendship* invites serious reflection about how we ought to live. Chartier examines the nature, the importance, and the limits of friendship from ethical, political, and theological perspectives. Few readers are likely to agree with every claim he makes, but through engaging his discussion, any reader can come to appreciate more fully the ways in which friendship enriches human life."

—Gilbert C. Meilaender, *Valparaiso University*

"Gary Chartier offers a rich set of reflections about the most essential of human relationships—friendship. His insights are rooted in the classical Western ethical tradition and at the same time creatively addressed to our culture today. At a time when true friendship has been more and more replaced by transactional relationships, Chartier offers ancient wisdom that speaks to our deepest longings as 'social animals.' His poignant reflections on vulnerability and contingency need to be heard by every thoughtful person."

—Stephen J. Pope, *Boston College*

"In *Understanding Friendship*, Gary Chartier invites the reader on a journey to explore the mystery, richness, and blessed possibilities of relationships we frequently take for granted but clearly cannot live well without. He is a most trustworthy and insightful guide who, along the way, deftly demonstrates not only why the love, acceptance, and support that are given and received in friendships are integral to a flourishing and fulfilling life, but also why affirming, protecting, and celebrating good friendships help create and sustain healthy and just societies. Drawing upon theology and philosophy as well as psychology, economics, and social and political theory, Chartier gives a compelling and inspiring account for why friendship matters and deserves greater scholarly attention. Best of all, in opening up the many dimensions of friendship, Chartier, like a good friend, makes *Understanding Friendship* a gift to a most grateful reader."

—Paul Wadell, *St. Norbert College*

"In this wise, wide-ranging, and philosophically astute treatment of friendship, Gary Chartier offers what precious few theologians have dared in the modern period: an account of friendship that does not begin by trying to update Aristotle. We are offered instead a marvelously stimulating proposal: that friendship is 'vulnerable co-creation,' an opening of oneself to embrace life with beloved people one cannot control."

—Brian Brock, *University of Aberdeen*

Understanding Friendship

Understanding Friendship

On the Moral, Political, and Spiritual Meaning of Love

Gary Chartier

Fortress Press
Minneapolis

UNDERSTANDING FRIENDSHIP
On the Moral, Political, and Spiritual Meaning of Love

Portions of chapters 4, 5, and 6 are adapted from Gary Chartier, "Loving Friends and Loving God," *Spectrum* 27.4 (Aut. 1999): 11–22, and from Gary Chartier, *The Analogy of Love* (New York: Griffin 2017, 2020). Used by permission.

Cover image: "A Perch of Birds" (1880) by Hector Giacomelli (1822-1904). Digitally enhanced by rawpixel.
Cover design: Brice Hemmer

Print ISBN: 978-1-5064-7908-8
eBook ISBN: 978-1-5064-7909-5

For Alicia

A degree of simplicity, and of undisguised confidence, which, to uninterested observers, would almost border on weakness, is the charm, nay the essence of love or friendship, all the bewitching graces of childhood again appearing.

—Mary Wollstonecraft, *Letters Written during a Short Residence in Sweden, Norway, and Denmark*

Having a multitude of friends causes disunion, separation, and divergence, since, by calling one hither and thither, and transferring one's attention now to this person, now to that, it does not permit any blending or close attachment of goodwill to take place in the intimacy which moulds itself about friendship and takes enduring form.

—Plutarch, *On Having Many Friends*

Perhaps the greatest element of friendship is faithfulness. To know that there is some one who will be always the same to us, who has a deep and abiding affection for us, to whom in time of trial we may turn for advice or help, adds greatly to the security and happiness of life.

—Benjamin Jowett, *Sermons on Faith and Doctrine*

I hate the idea of causes, and if I had to choose between betraying my country and betraying my friend I hope I should have the guts to betray my country.

—E. M. Forster, *What I Believe*

There is nothing contrary to the spirit of the Gospel, nothing inconsistent with the fulness of Christian love, in having our affections directed in an especial way towards certain objects, towards those whom the circumstances of our past life, or some peculiarities of character, have endeared to us.

—John Henry Newman, *Parochial and Plain Sermons*

Contents

Acknowledgments

I've managed to complete *Understanding Friendship* thanks to innumerable conversations and connections.

Thanks are due, as always, to the usual suspects—A. Ligia Radoias, Aena Prakash, Annette Bryson, Alexander Lian, Alicia Homer, Andrew Howe, Carole Pateman, Charles Teel Jr., Craig R. Kinzer, David B. Hoppe, David Gordon, David R. Larson, Deborah K. Dunn, Donna Carlson, Eddy Palacios, Elaine Claire von Keudell, Elenor L. Webb, Eva Pascal, Fritz Guy, Gen Mensale, Jeffrey Cassidy, Joel Wilson, John Thomas, Julio C. Muñoz, Kenneth A. Dickey, Lalé Welsh, Lawrence T. Geraty, Linn Marie Tonstad, Maria Zlateva, Melissa Cushman, Michael Orlando, Nabil Abu-Assal, Nicole Regina, Patricia M. Cabrera, Roderick Tracy Long, Roger E. Rustad Jr., Ronel Harvey, Ruth E. E. Burke, Sel J. Hwahng, Sheldon Richman, Stephanie Burns, W. Kent Rogers, Wonil Kim, and Xavier Alasdhair Kenneth Doran—for the usual reasons. I want to honor Nabil, in particular, for serving as the nucleus of an array of friends, an urban tribe before anyone was talking about urban tribes, that occasioned my earliest reflections on the nature of friendship and the dynamics of the friendship circle as community.

This book began life as my Cambridge PhD dissertation.[1] Reorganization, deletion, rewriting, editing, and the introduction of a great deal of entirely new material have rendered it a substantially different work in a variety of ways. Stanley Hauerwas prompted me, directly and indirectly, to take friendship seriously as a research topic. Brian Hebblethwaite supervised the preparation of my dissertation through its various twists and turns; I am grateful for his patient willingness to accommodate my shifts in focus. Dave Larson read the entire dissertation in draft and made a vast number of amusing and

1. Gary Chartier, "Toward a Theology and Ethics of Friendship" (PhD diss., University of Cambridge 1991).

enlightening remarks. Nicholas Lash, Rennie Schoepflin, and Jim Fodor, among others, provided helpful comments as the dissertation was developing. Gene Outka thoughtfully discussed my developing research with me during a welcome conversation at the University Centre at Cambridge. Julius Moravcsik stimulated my thinking at a crucial point and offered me what may still be the most important academic insight I gained in graduate school. Delmer Ross, Heather Hessel, Ileana Prado, Marvin Karlow, and Steve Daily offered various kinds of support and stimulation while I was writing. Stephen R. L. Clark and Michael Banner examined what I'd written on behalf of the university, offering useful observations, which are reflected here at more than one point.

Brent Bradley was a predictable source of useful insights when I first laid the groundwork for a book version of the dissertation. Oliver O'Donovan carefully reviewed a prospectus and sample chapter as the book's development continued. Material I intended for use in the book as initially conceived appeared elsewhere in print after progress toward the book's publication slowed; I happily acknowledge authorization for my use (in modified form) of that material here.[2] David Gordon provided characteristically incisive criticisms of the entire manuscript. Suggestions offered by Kevin Carson and Roderick Long improved the book in a variety of ways. Liz Carmichael's work called my attention to a variety of salient texts, and Liz herself made a range of thoughtful suggestions for the improvement of the manuscript. Alexander Nehamas prompted me to engage in some crucial last-minute reflection and clarification. Alicia Homer's diligent scrutiny, exceptional patience, and willingness to think carefully about my phrasing and argumentation alike ensured that what I'd written was more readable and plausible than it would otherwise have been.

The members of the La Sierra University Library faculty and staff managed to be good humored even when I requested obscure information and submitted endless interlibrary loan requests. Jon Hardt and Heather Hessel deserve particular thanks in this regard.

2. The relevant publications, each modified for use here, are "Loving Friends and Loving God," *Spectrum* 27.4 (Aut. 1999): 11–22; and two segments of *The Analogy of Love: Divine and Human Love at the Center of Christian Theology* (New York: Griffin 2017, 2020): "Loving God in Creation," from chapter 5, and "Religious Disagreement with People We Love," from chapter 11. I've drawn on this material almost exclusively in chapter 6 of *Understanding Friendship*, apart from three paragraphs in chapters 4 and 5.

The Committee of Vice-Chancellors and Principals of the Universities of the United Kingdom supported two years of my study at Cambridge with Overseas Research Studentships. And the University of Cambridge presented me with an award from the Burney Fund and a Crosse Studentship that helped significantly to defray the expenses of my final year of study.

Neera Badhwar played an important role in pioneering the contemporary philosophical study of friendship. It was a pleasure to read her important early articles and to interact with them in my dissertation. And it has been a greater pleasure latterly to become her friend. While my interactions with him have been much more limited, Robert Merrihew Adams provided me with a tremendous amount of intellectual stimulation by means of his 1989 Wilde Lectures, which he graciously shared with me well before their publication and on which I reflected repeatedly over the years after I first heard him deliver the lecture about the idea of vocation.

Ryan Hemmer at Fortress Press has been an excellent editor, for whose support I am very grateful. I am thankful to Elvis Ramirez and the team at Scribe Inc. for help throughout this book's production and to Brian Brock, Gilbert C. Meilaender, Paul Wadell, Stephen G. Post, and Stephen J. Pope for their willingness to endorse it.

John Thomas has been an exceptional friend during the twenty-one years I have been associated with what is now the Tom and Vi Zapara School of Business at La Sierra University. I am deeply appreciative of his loyalty, his confidence, and his willingness to welcome and support my scholarly endeavors. Thanks, too, to Joy Fehr and April Summitt for their commitment to keeping the university thriving in challenging times and to Lovelyn Razzouk for aiding me on a variety of fronts.

My parents shared their love unstintingly with me during my sojourn in England, calling and writing frequently—and providing welcome tangible and intangible support. They ensured that, even during lonely periods of isolation, I was sure of love. Parental affection, like the care of one's friends, is surely a means by which God's love is mediated to us, and I am exceedingly grateful for it.

Alicia Homer and I met in England while I was studying at Cambridge. I'm thankful for Sandra Ingram's willingness to welcome me at Newbold College, as a result of which I gained a variety of friends, including Alicia. I enthusiastically celebrate Alicia's willingness to marry me in one of Riverside's few remaining independent bookstores, to set off on a roller coaster of a journey from Canada to California, and to enrich my life with her intellect, charm, wit, warmth, and literary voraciousness.

I hope that through all of the people I've mentioned God's grace has been at work in my life. I will not presume to trace the movements of divine providence; but I thank God for touching my life (and the lives of those who will, I hope, profit from this research in the future) through all of those whose generosity I have acknowledged, through others I have failed to name, and in divers other—doubtless unfathomable—ways.

Introduction

Close friendship is a basic aspect of our flourishing. It is a vital element of our essentially social existence. Friendship is morally weighty, politically significant, and spiritually central. Safeguarding and celebrating friendship's importance and our opportunities to form and nourish intimate ties are crucial parts of welcoming the uniqueness of our lives and the rich variety and flexibility of our social worlds.

We face a variety of intellectual and practical challenges as we seek to understand, navigate, and treasure our friendships. Among them are the following:

- Conceptions of persons as essentially detached make it easy to see friends as optional extras and to treat particular friendships as dispensable at will.
- Notions of friendship as essentially *focused* on topics or activities distinct from the friends themselves to the (relative or complete) exclusion of intimate connection and self-disclosure can tend to undermine vulnerability, self-exposure, and intimate connection between friends.
- Theories of friendship as centered on a friend's character or on the mutual development of virtue by the friends can prompt us to ignore or resist the possibility of friendship with people who don't measure up to our moral expectations.
- Understandings of ethics as essentially a matter of impartiality make it hard to understand the moral importance of identity-constitutive ties to particular people—as sources of special obligation, as objects of focused care, as arenas of personal self-investment and flourishing—and the positive moral significance of the personal projects in which friends often participate.

- Moral theories in accordance with which interpersonal responsibilities flow only from explicit promises or participation in formal social structures obscure the moral heft of tacit institutions, like friendship, in which imprecise responsibilities evolve in subtle ways.
- Friendship involves obligations, and choosing friendship, and therefore obligation, might seem to mean opting for questionable constraints on autonomy. In the name of the autonomous self, then, the claims of special relationships are often minimized or rejected.[1]
- Friendship and other intimate ties are often seen as potential sites of domination,[2] rendering us subject to the whims of others and therefore worth evading.
- Pressures to sit lightly to our intimate ties in the interests of professional advancement, geographic mobility, or sheer economic survival make it harder to remain loyal to our friends.
- Visions of politics as all-consuming prompt us both to subordinate personal to political ties and to subject our relationships to tests of political purity and expediency.
- Relatedly, conceptions of states as deserving our loyalty may encourage us to think that, in case of conflict, we must choose our governments over our friends.
- Notions of politics as concerned with the structures and policies of large states governing mass populations make it difficult to see how to make sense of the classical conviction that friendship is a significant feature of political life.
- Understandings of politics that legitimate aggression and undermine peace impede human flourishing generally and friendship specifically.
- Models of spirituality rooted in contrastive accounts of God's relationship with the world can urge us to turn away from creaturely loves like friendship.
- Similarly, approaches to spirituality that emphasize purity and that see those who do not share our religious beliefs as impure or threatening can urge us to choose our friends only from among those who agree with us.

1. Richard John Bondi, "Fidelity and the Good Life: Special Relations in Christian Ethics" (PhD diss., University of Notre Dame 1981) 15, 88.

2. Agnes Heller, *Beyond Justice* (London: Blackwell 1987) 320.

- Special relationships like friendship can render us vulnerable. The contingencies of history, circumstance, and feeling can limit our options and make us liable to debilitating loss. We might think, then, that we should shun friendship in order to avoid vulnerability.

My goal in this book is to make a case for friendship that responds to these challenges and leaves us free to recognize and affirm the value of friendship.

I begin, in chapter 1, by examining the nature and dynamics of friendship. I explore some central characteristics of this relationship and evaluate some proposals regarding the shape friendship should take.

In chapter 2, I reflect on the significance of our interactions—our interactions with other persons and with God—for our friendships. A conception of the self as socially shaped and relationally constituted helps us understand friendship's role in our lives. After examining such a conception, I turn to the significance of theology for our understanding of selfhood. Then, I consider our freedom in relation to friendship and the contribution a relational understanding of selfhood might make to the process of addressing conflict and loss in friendship. I ask, finally, what it might mean to think of friendship as a gift resulting from our interactions with God.

Some people seem to treat friendship as the site of something like a moral holiday, free of all confining responsibilities. For others, we should resist the thought of obligation in friendship because genuine friendship involves an unconstrained kind of love that is inconsistent with obligation or because obligations to friends compromise our autonomy. However, I argue in chapter 3, attempts to rule out talk of moral responsibility in friendship for the kinds of reasons I've broached here are unsuccessful. Friendship is, indeed, I'm inclined to say, *constituted* in part by friends' obligations to each other.

It is difficult for interpretations of Christian love as a kind of impartial benevolence to make room for our various focused loves—in particular, for obligation in friendship or to acknowledge the positive moral value of commitments to friendship. I begin chapter 4 by noting difficulties with impartialist accounts of love—in principle and as regards their implications for friendship. Then, I attempt to show how a range of alternate conceptions of love might understand friendship and provide support for friends' moral claims and for our self-investment in friendship. I assess the options I've discussed before considering the notion that we should reject as actual or potential friends those who fail to exhibit the right moral qualities and offering a brief portrait of Christian love as a complex, multifaceted phenomenon, one incorporating all our particular loves.

The classical emphasis on friendship as the ground and goal of political life sounds foreign to those of us who inhabit mass societies. But the classical view remains valuable. In chapter 5, I examine friendship's connection with liberalism. Then, I point to ways in which contemporary culture, especially in today's workplace, can pose challenges to friendship and how liberal politics might reduce the seriousness of these challenges. I challenge calls for universal friendship as inconsistent with friendship's particular and preferential character. I stress friendship's capacity to enhance political action, before going on to highlight the ways in which a deterritorialized, network-based conception of politics could help to restore friendship's classical political significance. I reflect on E. M. Forster's famous declaration that he would prefer to betray his country than to betray a friend. And I consider the significance for friendship of a tendency to turn politics into a substitute religion.

Different spiritualities embody different responses to friendship. Arguing for a friendship-positive spirituality, I maintain in chapter 6 that friendship is not a distraction from or a competitor with the love of God. I seek to show that religious disagreement need not be a barrier to friendship. Loving friends, I suggest, is a way in which we love God; and friendship can, in fact, serve as a basis for spiritual growth and for discerning the reality of God while fostering the kind of interpersonal communication that makes reflection on the question of God realistically possible. Finally, I try to make clear in what way we can usefully speak of friendship with God.

In the conclusion, I briefly sum up the book's responses to the challenges I noted above. Then, I emphasize the link between acknowledging and embracing human contingency and vulnerability on the one hand and a satisfactory view of friendship on the other.

Even on a view that assumes that there can be correct answers to moral questions, it might be easy, in theory, to treat friendship as a consumption good for the detached self, to be embraced or rejected in virtue of its contribution to meeting the self's preferences. Modern morality's concern with harmonizing the interests of generic citizens of the moral commonwealth blinds it to the reality of sometimes irreducibly tragic conflict between diverse loyalties and desires. The impartial standpoint it represents may, if consistently adopted, alienate the moral actor from identity-constituting relationships like friendship. And its focus on the interests of the members of large-scale communities—most of whom are necessarily strangers—makes it at best unconcerned with particular connections. I hope that my explication of Christian love will serve as a helpful counter to moral views that seem to have no place for friendship.

Conceptions of the self play crucial roles at multiple places in this book. To view friendship as a conduit for divine grace or as a prerequisite for the existence of a "disclosure situation" in which God's presence might be discerned is to take sides in a long-standing debate in theological anthropology about the capacity of persons to sense and respond to God's action and the ways in which God communicates with us. And a view of the self as social and permeable, formed in a history of contingent interactions, helps to make sense of our friendship bonds and of the process of moral, spiritual, and political formation.

A social, relational view of the self undercuts metaphysical views that promote isolation and prompt the idealization of invulnerability. It helps to legitimate talk about moral responsibility in friendship and encourages potentially challenging interchange. It fosters the formation of relationships which encourage basic trust and thus help make trust, and perhaps explicit belief, in God a live option. And it opens one to the experience of contingency—an experience that may be for some a pointer to the transcendent.

The flight from such contingency is, in fact, a common theme in discussions of friendship. It is evinced in, among other things, the refusal to take seriously the possibility of loyalty to friends whose characters and circumstances change and in attempts to free friends from difficult changes and devastating losses by urging that the love of friendship focuses on the qualities of the friend in abstraction from the friend herself.

A relationship founded on vulnerability can obviously be a source of disquiet and fear as well as of trust and joy. But the risk of vulnerability is, I believe, a worthwhile one. This profoundly important phenomenon, with its attendant risk and resultant delight, deserves to continue occupying an important place in the thinking, acting, and experiencing of contemporary persons.

I know too much to pretend to any expertise regarding ultimate matters. When I discuss such matters here, I am expressing hope rather than feigning certainty. I thank you, then, for joining me on a journey that I happily acknowledge is exploratory. It wouldn't have happened without you.

1

Contours

Friends share an intimate relationship of trustful and loyal sharing and engagement. The immediate, primary focus of the relationship is on the partners themselves, though the relationship can influence their responses to the wider world in a positive way.

After considering the merits of definition and noting some common features of friendship that strike me as readily acknowledged and uncontroversial, I proceed to examine a set of characteristics that I suspect might deserve more attention, including friendship's particular focus, the tendency of friends to create shared worlds, the embodiment of friends (with implications as regards the importance of propinquity and the relationship between friendship and sexuality and friendship and romantic love), the capacity of friendship to help us move beyond definitions of our identity in terms of our social functions, the role of acceptance in friendship, the tension between union and differentiation in friendship, and relevance of species membership to friendship. I conclude by asking whether concern with some external object should effectively exclude self-disclosure and mutual knowing in friendship, considering the role of reasons in establishing and maintaining friendships, and reflecting on the appropriateness of treating friendship as centrally concerned with the moral characters of the friends.

Defining Friendship?

I want to begin by advancing what I trust will prove to be a reasonably clear and well-worked-out account of friendship—not because no other account is possible but simply to make clear what kind of relationship I want to talk about here.[1]

I hope that what I say will have significant cross-cultural appeal. But I'm very much aware that I am exploring elements of a relationship that presupposes particular cultural features. Among these features is an understanding of people as capable of defining themselves in distinctive and potentially idiosyncratic ways—so that people are not collapsed into their social roles and so that their relationships are not determined simply by family ties or occupational tasks. Also significant for the viability of an account of friendship like the one I'm offering is the existence of a society that provides a background against which people can define their identities and that can thus provide a setting in which friends can interact in ways that presuppose and display their freedom and particularity.[2]

An account applicable across cultures may thus need to be relatively general in nature.[3] However, relationships marked by the trust, intimacy, commitment, and camaraderie that characterize the kinds of relationships on which I concentrate here may find sufficient analogues elsewhere to make my analyses of some interest to people in multiple societies.[4]

Drawing on the work of social and behavioral scientists, I will seek to identify some central features of close friendship. I hope that the vision of friendship that underlies what I say will not prove to be a purely idiosyncratic one but that it will begin with assumptions at least frequently shared by my readers. My intention is to start with existing practices and attitudes but not to stop there. I want to take real people's experiences of friendship seriously even while suggesting ways in which that experience may be enriched and our understanding of it deepened.

1. See Kenneth David Alpern, "The Nature of Friendship: Aristotelian and Kantian Themes" (PhD diss., University of Pittsburgh 1980) 14.

2. On the distinctive dynamics that can give rise to this kind of social environment, see Joseph Henrich, *The WEIRDest People in the World: How the West Became Psychologically Peculiar and Particularly Prosperous* (New York: Farrar 2020).

3. See, *e.g.*, Michael Argyle and Monika Henderson, "The Rules of Friendship," *Journal of Social and Personal Relationships* 1.2 (June 1984): 211–37.

4. See Robert Brain, *Friends and Lovers* (London: Hart-Davis 1976); and Cora DuBois, "The Gratuitous Act: An Introduction to the Comparative Study of Friendship Patterns," *The Compact: Selected Dimensions of Friendship*, ed. Elliott Leyton (St. John's, Newfoundland and Labrador: Institute of Social and Economic Research, Memorial University of Newfoundland 1974) 15–32.

While my focus is on close friendship, I realize that there are not clear dividing lines (especially in a culture in which friendship isn't formalized or solemnized) among categories of friends—close friends, not-so-close friends, friendly acquaintances. Much of what I say about close friendships will be relevant to less intimate relationships. But there are, nonetheless, meaningful distinctions to be drawn.

Friendship's most fundamental characteristic is preferentiality: a friendship is a *chosen* relationship, not one linked automatically with kinship or occupancy of some other social role. The other basic characteristics of a typical relationship between two close friends include mutuality, reciprocity, a disposition on the part of each to enjoy the other's company, trust, mutual assistance, acceptance, respect, spontaneity, understanding, and intimacy.[5] Friends desire to share with each other—physically and emotionally as well as cognitively—and, more fundamentally, to be known by each other. Thus, openness and vulnerability are key elements of friendship's intimacy. Friends care for and are devoted to each other and expect each other to be accessible. And this mutual sharing, commitment, and care lead friends to identify with each other to a significant degree. Theirs is a relationship of mutual liking or "mutual love."[6]

Mutual liking in friendship is a source of validation and a source of reassurance and security in the face of vulnerability.[7] Friends refuse to view or treat each other at arm's length or to prize each other only in virtue of mutual usefulness. Friends need to give "themselves over to this personal relation[ship]" in order to "realize its rich gifts."[8]

Within friendship, there is an ongoing tension between respect for the other as other—as a free and independent center of action—and a desire for a union

5. Keith E. Davis and Michael J. Todd, "Assessing Friendship: Prototypes, Paradigm Cases and Relationship Description," *Understanding Personal Relationships: An Interdisciplinary Approach*, ed. Steve Duck and Daniel Perlman (London: SAGE 1985) 19. See Alpern, "Nature of Friendship" 198–206; David B. Annis, "The Meaning, Value, and Duties of Friendship," *American Philosophical Quarterly* 24.4 (Oct. 1987): 349–56; Julius M. E. Moravcsik, "The Perils of Friendship and Conceptions of the Self," *Human Agency: Language, Duty, and Value—Philosophical Essays in Honor of J. O. Urmson*, ed. Jonathan Dancy, Julius M. E. Moravcsik, and C. C. W. Taylor (Stanford, CA: Stanford University Press 1988) 132–51; and Laurence Thomas, "Friendship," *Synthese* 72 (1987): 217–31.

6. See Carol Becker, "A Phenomenological Explication of the Friendship Relation: As Exemplified by Most Important College Women Friends" (PhD diss., Duquesne University 1973).

7. Rudy Arnold Haapanen, "Close Friendship: The Individualistic Community" (PhD diss., University of California at Davis 1976) 24, 31.

8. Becker, "Phenomenological Explication" 174.

with the other that overcomes difference and distinction.[9] But friendship, like erotic love, requires respect for the difference of the other precisely because of the nature of the ongoing desire for union; for it is *union* with the other that one desires, not her dissolution into oneself.[10] So friendship must be a kind of dance in which connection and differentiation alternate (though, at least in the contemporary West, friendship might be expected to involve a greater emphasis on distance than erotic love).

Several other features of the relationship, less readily characterized in brief words or phrases, require (sometimes argumentative) clarification.

Particularity

Of course people participate in *groups* of friends. But each friendship is still ultimately a pair so that each friendship group consists of clusters of pairs, with the dynamic of the relationship between the members of each pair affected by the dynamics of the ties each friend enjoys with others.

Because friendships do not require the same kind of commitment that marriage does, it is possible to have many of them (and how many of us really want just one?). Introverts will presumably want a limited number of close relationships, the extroverted rather more.[11] But while we are, if we are fortunate, sustained by whole circles made up of close friends and friendly acquaintances, we have distinct relations with each person with whom we're connected. Even as specific interactions take place against the backdrop of a friendship group, the particularity of each interaction and each relationship remains. The self formed in these particular interactions and relationships must itself retain its particularity.[12]

9. See Paul Tillich, *Love, Power, and Justice: Ontological Analyses and Ethical Applications* (New York: Oxford University Press 1953) 25, 31–2.

10. See Alistair I. McFadyen, *The Call to Personhood: A Christian Theory of the Individual in Social Relationships* (Cambridge: Cambridge University Press 1990) 136–8, 151–61; and Tillich, *Love, Power, and Justice* 27.

11. Thanks to Liz Carmichael for highlighting this point.

12. See Karl Barth, *Church Dogmatics*, 4 vols. in 13, ed. Geoffrey W. Bromiley and Thomas F. Torrance, trans. A. T. Mackay *et al.* (Edinburgh: Clark 1938–67) 3.2: 248, 269.

Worlds

It is common for friends to create private systems of communication.[13] More broadly, the creation of a "shared world" can be seen as a distinctive achievement of friendship[14]—one that is especially important as a means of maintaining a friendship's identity when friends are not engaging, or are not engaging face-to-face. This world comprises "shared understandings of important aspects of each's past, present and future involvements and goals." While conditioned by the "objective facts of their histories and present . . . (roles, social class, ethnic background, task commitments) it goes beyond these to the personal meaningfulness of these factual givens in each subject's ongoing life"; and it possesses the capacity to mold the participants' experience of space and time.[15]

The relationship between the external world and that created by and within the friendship is dialectical in nature, shifting in focus from the relationship itself to the world that is its context and back again, seeking a satisfactory equilibrium. Engagement in the wider world is not essential to the friendship, but of course the friends may reach out into the world, separately or together, and their love for each other may empower their activities in the world.[16]

Friendship initially builds on connections that reflect people's attitudes and beliefs about and connections and undertakings in the public world; subsequently, their "shared world expands to include *differences* and to be less dependent on experiences together in objective time and space."[17] The public world provides the horizon for the friends' relationship, but, over time, as they make that world their own, their relationship "is less noticeably molded by the world."[18] The security of their shared world enables it to serve as a context for the stabilization and confirmation of the identities of the friends.[19] And its separateness both permits and encourages them to join in embracing and expressing "a playful attitude toward the [outside] world."[20]

13. Haapanen, "Close Friendship" 75.
14. Becker, "Phenomenological Explication" 131; Haapanen, "Close Friendship" ch. 7.
15. Becker, "Phenomenological Explication" 151–2.
16. Becker 159–60.
17. Becker 202 (my italics).
18. Becker 151.
19. Haapanen, "Close Friendship" 110.
20. Haapanen 136.

Because friends create a shared world in which each lives even when they are apart, because each contributes to the orienting conditions of the other's action, because of one's commitment to the other, and because one expects the other's commitment—for all these reasons, a friendship endures over time. It is not simply an aggregation of discrete interactions. At the same time, because bodies matter, because embodied engagement matters, the face-to-face interchange of the friends remains of primary importance.

Embodiment

The human friends we know are *embodied.* Bodies move closer to or farther away from other bodies. They resist confinement. They can behave in ways that conceal or actively misrepresent our thoughts and attitudes, which are often anything but transparent. And of course they grow ill and die. At the same time, embodiment is a means of connection, an occasion for the cultivation and display of individuality, and a source of pleasure.

Embodiment and Proximity

Friendship is an embodied relationship. Whether or not friends touch each other sexually—whether or not, indeed, they touch each other at all—their bodies matter for their communication. Self-disclosure is easiest when I encounter your bodily movements and facial expressions and changes in tone of voice, not merely your words.[21] Your bodily responses to my words and other actions help me to understand your thoughts and feelings, and I can continually readjust my communicative style to take your reactions into account. In a face-to-face relationship, one is uniquely able to take account of the other's reactions to one's own behavior and her or his awareness that one's actions presuppose and respond to her or his own.[22] A face-to-face dialogue builds upon a common environment. By referring to shared experiences in this environment, I

21. See Alfred Schütz and Thomas Luckmann, *The Structures of the Life-World*, trans. Richard Zaner and H. Tristram Engelhardt (London: Heinemann 1973) 66; Alfred Schütz, *The Phenomenology of the Social World*, intro. George Walsh, trans. George Walsh and Frederick Lehner (Evanston, IL: Northwestern University Press 1967) 169; and Mary Daly, "The Morality of Human Nature" (PhD diss., University of Wisconsin–Madison 1984) 71.

22. Schütz, *Phenomenology of the Social World* 169–70.

can continually recheck my perceptions against the responses of a conversation partner. I can question her about her experience of our common situation to clarify my own understanding.[23]

The uniqueness of the face-to-face encounter resides in the concurrent capacity of each participant to modify her or his understanding of the other on an ongoing basis. And because mutual understandings are constantly changing in such an encounter, each participant not only contributes to the ongoing constitution of the other's motivations, perceptions, and understandings but actually shares with the other the process of their creation in real time. In "the face-to-face situation you and I grow older together, and I can add to my expectation of what you are going to do the actual sight of you making up your mind, and then of your action itself in all its constituent phases. During all this time we are aware of each other's stream of consciousness as contemporaneous with our own."[24]

A friendship need not *begin* with a face-to-face encounter, but face-to-face connection is a powerful source of intimacy. The fully embodied, face-to-face friendship is the paradigmatic friendship, even though people can obviously bond at a distance. A change—albeit an often subtle one—takes place in the dynamics of a relationship when periods of face-to-face interaction (whether or not this kind of interaction *initiated* the friendship) give way to other modes of engagement. While the point at which this transition takes place is difficult to discern, *that* it occurs is clear. We can begin by imagining "a face-to-face conversation, followed by a telephone call, followed by an exchange of letters, and finally messages exchanged through a third party. . . . The total number of the other person's reactions open to my observation is progressively diminished until it reaches a minimum point."[25]

The effects of such a transition are not inconsiderable. Memory allows one to take account of the other when she or he is not actually present; one can continue to presuppose the kind of self-disclosure embodied interaction allows. But now "our conscious processes are not bound in genuine simultaneity."[26] The friend has "a 'new self' now; and, although I am contemporaneous with it, I am cut off from vital contact with it. Since the time we were last together, . . . [she or he has] met with new experiences and . . . [has] looked at them from new

23. Schütz 170–1.
24. Schütz 171–2.
25. Schütz 177; cp. Schütz and Luckmann, *Structures of the Life-World* 69.
26. Schütz and Luckmann, *Structures of the Life-World* 70.

points of view. With each change of experience and outlook . . . [she or he has] become a slightly different person."[27]

Phone calls and video chats can obviously help to bridge the gaps between face-to-face encounters, helping friends stay connected in real time. When I was a graduate student in England, a call to the United States cost roughly £1 each minute. Unsurprisingly, it often made sense to schedule calls in advance; and almost everyone needed to place them from landlines, so staying in touch meant limiting one's movements. Less than a quarter century later, I could find myself, while in California, engaged in a real-time video chat with a friend as she drove through the outskirts of Bangkok, on the other side of the world—effectively for free. Technology has enabled us to nurture friendships, to keep connected, far more effectively than our ancestors could do.

Still, face-to-face encounters matter. Touch matters. A background of events and activities to which we can react matters. While interactions other than face-to-face encounters can keep a relationship alive, its quality will be diminished to the extent that it depends on such encounters or on a limited number of face-to-face interactions: unavoidably, the partners cease to know each other as well as they might.[28]

The importance of embodiment to communication between friends helps to explain Aristotle's dictum that "for friends the most desirable thing is living together."[29] Even if friends don't share the same house, choices that make it easy for them to interact in person can help to solidify their connection and enable them to know each other more fully.

Aristotle seems to have envisioned, at minimum, ongoing interaction in the course of public and private life, shared engagement in whatever activities the friends treat as especially important. He clearly supposed that friends would see each other often, and he recognized how crucial such contact was to the experience of close friendship.

Friends do sometimes say that their communication can be suspended for indefinite periods and then resumed without loss. But insofar as our most intimate connections with our friends are forged in the course of three-dimensional, face-to-face encounters, ones in which we often react to varied environments,

27. Schütz, *Phenomenology of the Social World* 178.

28. Schütz 178. See Schütz and Luckmann, *Structures of the Life-World* 71–2; and Schütz, *Phenomenology of the Social World* 179–80.

29. Aristotle, *Ethica Nicomachea*, trans. W. D. Ross (London: Clarendon-Oxford University Press 1925) 1171b <https://www.sacred-texts.com/cla/ari/nico/nico107.htm>.

the absence of such encounters cannot but make a difference to the nature of the bonds that unite us with them. Without the ongoing, body-based correlation of our thoughts, experiences, and actions with theirs, our ties to our friends grow more diffuse. Of course, a friendship can still exist without regular face-to-face contact, but its intensity and intimacy can be affected. While circumstances unavoidably separate us, on occasion, from those we love, if we accept the maintenance of our friendships as a priority, we will want to minimize our absences from their presence.

Many people will not find it practical to integrate their lives thoroughly with those of their friends. The fragmentation so typical of our society makes it difficult for people to live integrated lives in which economic, political, religious, and social activities all occur within the same context. And the constant presence of the same people on the horizon of one's experience might, in any case, feel oppressive. But for those who do find Aristotle's observation about the value of living together for friends appealing, it is not, I think, too far-fetched to suggest that experiments in shared housing, for instance, might prove rewarding. In any case, whether or not one lives together with one's friends under the same roof, in the same housing complex, in the same neighborhood, in the same community, or in the same region, one's experience of friendship will be deeper and more fulfilling if one has regular access to them as embodied selves.

Friendship, Sexuality, and Romance

That friendship is embodied means that it is at least potentially sexual. Touch is clearly an element of friends' communication, and touch can include sexual touch.

Sometimes, sexual engagement simply augments a friendship, adds a sizzle to it, without propelling it toward romance. There is nothing inherently unreasonable about incorporating an erotic dimension into a friendship.[30] However, erotic interaction predictably generates attachment and romantic desire. And if one of the friends becomes significantly more attached, more desirous, than the other and fails ultimately to woo the other into a romance, the result can be tension, conflict, and heartbreak. Sexual engagement can turn a friendship into something else—a romantic relationship, even a marriage. It can also result, contrary to the friends' own intentions, in the friendship's disruption. That

30. See, *e.g.*, Elizabeth Stuart, *Just Good Friends: Towards a Lesbian and Gay Theology of Relationships* (London: Mowbray 1996).

doesn't mean that it's necessarily wise to avoid taking the risks that arise when a friendship becomes sexual or romantic: the benefits may be substantial.[31] But it would be foolish not to recognize the reality of these risks.

Friendship is an essential element of a relationship people in developed societies today would recognize as a romance, though of course it doesn't follow that friendship will always, or even typically, emerge before other elements of a romantic relationship. Friendship may serve as a springboard to romance, or it may develop after a relationship initially rooted in sheer delight or in erotic desire has solidified itself. A romantic relationship lacks something morally crucial if the partners are not equal in status and dignity, and it seems seriously deficient if the partners don't enjoy genuine intimacy with each other; the presence of genuine friendship means, at least presumptively, the presence of both equality and intimacy and thus seems essential to the long-term flourishing of a romantic relationship.

When it's a matter of unfettered choice and personal preference, marriage is the most definitive example of romance. That doesn't mean, of course, that a marriage can or should be expected to feature the excitement frequently characteristic of newfound romance on an ongoing basis. Passion is in significant part a response to the challenge posed by distance, by barriers to connection; and, as a result, the reduction in distance associated with marital union may yield a relative absence of passion.[32] But marriage can and should be marked by mutual knowing, sharing, and understanding; mutual focus; mutual delight; and friendship.

It is not always possible to rank relationships in virtue of the degrees of intimacy they involve. However, given the goal of ever-deepening personal connection between marriage partners and the importance of friendship as a key element of romantic love, it seems reasonable for spouses to seek to make each the other's closest friend. A further reason for this goal is, of course, that a friendship with someone other than one's spouse that is closer than one's friendship with one's spouse runs the risk of proving alienating, a source of disruption, jealousy, and invidious comparison.

31. For a discussion of relevant background issues, see Gary Chartier, *Public Practice, Private Law: An Essay on Love, Marriage, and the State* (Cambridge: Cambridge University Press 2016) 101–26. Compare Jean-Baptiste Botul, *La vie sexuelle d'Emmanuel Kant* (Paris: Éditions Mille et Une Nuits 1999) 13–24.

32. See Robert C. Solomon, *About Love: Reinventing Romance for Our Time* (Indianapolis: Hackett 2006 [1988]) 80.

This emphatically doesn't mean that one shouldn't have close friends other than one's spouse. Spouses obviously won't share all of each other's interests, experiences, and contexts, and it can be a source of quite unnecessary marital stress for them to expect each other to do so. Friends can provide each other with emotional support of various kinds, as well as with opportunities for shared activities. They can also help each other develop capacities for understanding and communication that can enrich their marriages (and their romantic partnerships of other sorts—these benefits aren't just for married people, of course). Spouses should seek deep friendship with each other even while growing in friendship with others.

Equality

Friends are equal. But of course that doesn't mean they're equivalent.

Equality means that there aren't differences of status or authority *within the relationship*. Whatever other roles people occupy, within a close friendship they are peers. Neither is entitled to dominate the other. Of course, this should be true of all interpersonal relationships, but it's especially important in the context of friendship: friends qua friends can't give each other orders. There are no barriers that prevent one from questioning, probing, even challenging. And there are no differences that make it impossible for each to understand the other.

That doesn't mean that friends must be the same: they needn't share this or that characteristic. People can connect, can instinctively prefer each other, can appeal to each other, for all sorts of reasons, and their attraction to each other needn't involve any particular similarity or the comparable possession of any given quality. There's no Platonic ideal of equality between friends to which they are required to conform: the only similarities that matter are ones that matter to the particular friends.

Of course (*i*) these will likely come to matter less and less as a friendship develops and a shared identity and the shared history that undergirds it become more important than the factors—the characteristics of the friends or of their interactions—that initially occasioned their relationship. And (*ii*) while there's never an obligation to be anyone's friend, treating oneself well and treating another fairly means not letting oneself be prevented by superficial dissimilarities from recognizing a potentially delightful friendship. It's always spiritually important to be open to surprises, including the surprise of finding friendships in unexpected places.

Self-Discovery

Friendship can foster self-discovery, as our friends challenge us to see ourselves or our world differently. A friend's perspective can enable me to see myself much more clearly than I would otherwise be able to do. Because I show myself vulnerably to a friend, confident that I am secure and loved, I enable the friend to develop a nuanced, three-dimensional picture of who I am. And the friend's active engagement can help to bring new features of my character and personality to the surface (and perhaps to bring others into being).

A friend may ask the same questions I do—voicing the same doubts, noting the same kind of puzzlement—and so reinforce my curiosity and my doubts about the status quo. (And of course my response can reinforce my friend's own questions.) On the other hand, a friend may open my eyes by asking questions it's never occurred to me to pose.[33] What's needed here is intimacy and trust. For a friend to foster greater self-understanding on my part, she needn't embrace the same moral, spiritual, cultural, or political perspective on the world that I do.[34] A shared perspective may enable a friend to see some things more clearly and to communicate about them in a way I find accessible. At the same time, however, a friend's thoroughly unfamiliar perspective can be exceptionally illuminating.

Role Transcendence

Characteristically originating not in a social demand but in desire and accident, friendship is a *freely chosen* relationship in which freedom plays an ongoing part—in particular, the freedom to define the relationship's contours and boundaries quite apart from any other social or institutional roles the friends may occupy.[35]

33. See Barbara Lee Kerney, "A Theology of Friendship" (PhD diss., University of Durham 2007) 42.

34. Steve Summers, *Friendship: Exploring Its Implications for the Church in Postmodernity* (London: Clark-Continuum 2009) 83, suggests that self-discovery happens when the friend's "virtuous desire" is "aligned closely with one's own."

35. "Friendship is outside the reach of the law, it produces its own laws, it lacks a formalized status, and it is in this sense that it is an anarchic form of relating." Mihalis Mentinis, "Friendship: Towards a Radical Grammar of Relating," *Theory and Psychology* 25.1 (2014): 74.

The distinction between the friends' tasks and self-conceptions *as friends* and those associated with their occupancy of other social roles enables friendship to foster individuation, as each friend's masks are progressively removed and each one's distinctive overall approach to life becomes more evident.[36] The ability to develop friendships depends on a person's ability to distinguish herself from others and thus at least partially to transcend social expectations.

Because friendship involves appreciation for the other as a particular *other* and because conformity to social expectations frustrates the display of individuality, only when someone, at least to a limited extent, steps outside her social role—stops following a script and chooses to ad-lib—will it be possible to discern the individuality that may evoke a desire for friendship.[37] To the extent that this kind of self-disclosure lies at the root of a particular friendship, friends can be expected to recognize each other as transcending what might otherwise be defining roles and to deepen their independence from those roles.[38]

Acceptance

In friendship, we seek "an affectionate relation which is strong enough to bear the weight of difference."[39] When all is well, friends offer each other acceptance. And of course the acceptance of someone who knows me deeply and in a broad range of contexts, as a close friend does, is particularly validating and powerful.[40] The acceptance of friends applies not only to habits and values and interests and preferences but also to styles of communication and emotional reactions.[41] Acceptance will likely develop as the relationship matures: while people may build a friendship on their commonalities, as it develops they come also to acknowledge and accept the ways in which they are *not* alike.[42]

36. Haapanen, "Close Friendship" 16.

37. See Gerald D. Suttles, "Friendship as a Social Institution," *Social Relationships*, by George J. McCall *et al.* (Chicago: Aldine 1970) 100–16.

38. See Suttles 116. This need not mean the reinforcement of overtly dissenting behavior; though, as I suggest in chapter 5, such reinforcement *may* be among an individual friendship's political functions.

39. Oliver O'Donovan, *Ethics as Theology* 3: *Entering into Rest* (Grand Rapids: Eerdmans 2017) 144.

40. See Haapanen, "Close Friendship" 52.

41. See Haapanen 47–8, 50.

42. Becker, "Phenomenological Explication" 202.

Acceptance of the friend qua friend is empowering and liberating. Knowing that one will be embraced despite differences and, when they're evident, undesirable traits offers a vitally important security.[43] Acceptance means embracing the friend, accepting her as a friend, not agreeing with or endorsing any particular choice, characteristic, or habit.

Acceptance is compatible with at least some efforts to foster change; such efforts may be important expressions of the love that is constitutive of friendship and of which acceptance is an expression.[44] Nonetheless, it needs to be clear that the friend will be accepted as a friend whatever the outcome of those efforts. Otherwise, the practical effect will be to diminish openness between the friends. "Experience has shown that the only predictable result of criticism is the weakening of trust in human relationships."[45]

Sometimes, the only practical response will be to avoid raising certain issues.[46] Barriers to communication are, obviously, impediments to intimacy. And someone may be frustrated at being unable to help a friend past what she recognizes, even as the friend does not, as seriously unreasonable behavior patterns. But it's important to distinguish between the desire simply to vent one's opinions, simply because one wants to know that one has been heard, and the desire actually to make a difference in a friend's life. When one's expressions of disagreement are alienating and ineffective, when they seem unlikely to have any positive impact, they become exercises in self-indulgence rather than expressions of love.

Friendship is driven in part by the desire for union with another. So it may be tempting to think of the need to accept difference as a concession to the regrettable reality of disunion. But to think in this way is to confuse union with sameness or absorption. What makes personal union in friendship (as in romantic love) a powerful possibility for real people is precisely that it *doesn't* require sameness.[47] *Union* needn't—and for genuine persons *shouldn't*—mean *uniformity*.

43. See Elisabeth Young-Bruel and Faith Bethelard, *Cherishment: A Psychology of the Heart* (New York: Free 2002).

44. See McFadyen, *Call to Personhood* 140–1.

45. Thomas W. McKnight and Robert H. Phillips, *Love Tactics: How to Win the One You Want* (Garden City Park, NY: Square One 2002) 89.

46. See Haapanen, "Close Friendship" 159–62.

47. See Hugh Prather, *Love and Courage* (Berkeley: Conari 2001) 90–2; Hugh Prather and Gayle Prather, *I Will Never Leave You: How Couples Can Achieve the Power of Lasting Love* (New York: Bantam 1996) 164; and Chartier, *Analogy of Love* 423–9.

Religion and politics may be particularly significant occasions for disagreement among friends[48] and thus particularly important occasions for acceptance. One cannot expect one's friends to agree with one, even about matters of the most profound importance. Disagreement is a regular feature of life in a pluralistic society. It can provide opportunities for learning and growth. And friendship can help one to embody the virtues required to interact in the wider society with persons and communities whose convictions differ from one's own. Friendship is sustained not by the elimination of diversity but by creative and loyal response to the problem of integrating disagreement into the encompassing pattern of loving community.

Acceptance is about acknowledging the reality of flaws, wrongs, and irritants—while loving despite them. It does not depend at all on ignoring them or pretending that they don't exist. Friends don't benefit when they view each other untruthfully; what each needs from the other is precisely a love that recognizes her in her complexity. A friend does, however, have good reason to want one to view her hopefully and in a way that presumes goodwill: as one seeks to understand a friend's action, it's worth trying to discern potential motives that are compatible with the friend's being reasonable and well intentioned. Perhaps in a given case she's not, of course. However, while a charitable interpretive stance is distinct from and isn't required by acceptance, accepting someone can be easier psychologically when one adopts such a posture.

We often find it all too easy to presume the worst, even about those with whom we're close. So actively seeking more benign interpretations of a friend's behavior may help one to see things one might otherwise have missed, may enable one to see her more accurately. In an ambiguous situation, each of us would like others to seek to read our behavior charitably, so it's reasonable for us to attempt to make sense of our friends' actions in this way. This doesn't mean that we should tell ourselves that actions have meanings we believe they don't. It means only that we should be open to interpretations that reflect well on a friend, looking for alternatives to ones that reflect badly on her, unless it becomes clear that an unfavorable interpretation is correct.[49] If it is, again, this shouldn't itself be a barrier to acceptance.

48. Haapanen, "Close Friendship" 161.

49. Charitable interpretation isn't something we owe only to friends; it's part of engaging fruitfully with everyone. But it's worth highlighting here in particular because we may be especially resistant to charitable interpretations when we find ourselves in conflict with people we love; see

Species

The paradigmatic instance of friendship I have in mind here is, as will be apparent, between conscious, communicative, finite persons. We can talk about friendship more broadly, of course—about friendship with groups, with all of humanity, with God. However, when we do this, we are stretching the language of friendship well beyond its primary meaning.

We are also, in a sense, stretching the meaning of friendship when we talk about friendship with nonhuman animals who are unable to communicate as human persons can. But we are doing so less, I think, than when, for instance, we talk about all members of an ethnic or religious or political group as friends.

A nonhuman animal friend cannot discuss the significance of Marcel Proust or offer a plausible interpretation of Uncle David's unexpected willingness to come to Thanksgiving dinner. But of course human friends can't always do these things either (whether because they lack relevant backgrounds or interests or because illnesses have incapacitated them). A nonhuman animal friend *can*, however, recognize our mental states, interact with us in a variety of ways, deliberately share experiences with us, and take active measures to benefit us.[50] A dog equipped with a panel of sound-emitting buttons, each pegged to a relevant word, can even use the panel to say, "Happy ball want outside!"[51] Nonhuman animals' affection, benevolence, desire for interaction, and capacity for

---

Yasmina Reza, *Art: A Play*, trans. Christopher Hampton (London: Faber 1996). Thanks to Alexander Nehamas, *On Friendship* (New York: Basic 2016) 141–85, for reminding me of *Art* and highlighting its significance.

50. On nonhuman animals and friendship, see, *e.g.*, Stephen R. L. Clark, *The Political Animal: Biology, Ethics and Politics* (London: Routledge 1999) 155–66; Stephen R. L. Clark, *The Moral Status of Animals* (Oxford: Clarendon-Oxford University Press 1977) 24–5; Emma Lock, *Animal Kind: Lessons on Love, Fear and Friendship from the Animals in Our Lives* (Miami: Mango 2020); Elizabeth Hess, *Nim Chimpsky: The Chimp Who Would Be Human* (New York: Bantam 2008); Rachel Bucholz, *True Love: Twenty-Four Surprising Stories of Animal Affection* (Washington, DC: National Geographic 2013); Jennifer S. Holland, *Unlikely Friendship: Forty-Seven Remarkable Stories from the Animal Kingdom* (New York: Workman 2011); and Jennifer S. Holland, *Unlikely Loves: Forty-Three Heartwarming True Stories from the Animal Kingdom* (New York: Workman 2013).

51. See, *e.g.*, Hilary Shenfeld, "Dog Learning to Talk by Using a Custom Soundboard to Speak: 'I'm in Constant Amazement,'" *People*, Nov. 4, 2019 <https://people.com/pets/dog-learning-to-talk-by-using-a-custom-soundboard-to-speak-im-in-constant-amazement/>. Speech therapist Christina Hunger chronicles her ongoing friendship with her dog, Stella, at <https://www.hungerforwords.com/>.

mutual engagement make talk of friendship with them comprehensible and appealing.[52]

Intimacy

Friends doubtless ordinarily value shared activities for their own sake. Still, a close friendship, like a romance, is more about being together than about doing together.[53] It's not, of course, that friends aren't doing things together; they're not, in general, simply sitting silently in each other's presence. But whatever they're doing is an opportunity for greater connection, more extensive discovery, greater self-disclosure, greater intimacy.

C. S. Lewis on Friendship: "Side by Side"

The model C. S. Lewis articulates in *The Four Loves* has exerted a pronounced influence on thought and talk about friendship. According to Lewis, while lovers "are normally face to face, absorbed in each other," friends stand "side by side, absorbed in some common interest."[54] Friendship "must be about something, even if it were only an enthusiasm for dominoes or white mice."[55] And, more baldly still,

> You become a man's Friend without knowing or caring whether he is married or single or how he earns his living. What have all these "unconcerning things, matters of fact," to do with the real question, *Do you see the same truth?* In a circle of true friends[,] . . . no one cares twopence about anyone else's family, profession, class, income, race, or previous history. . . . We meet like sovereign princes of independent states, abroad, on neutral ground, freed from our contexts. This love (essentially) ignores not only our physical bodies but that whole embodiment which consists of our family, job, past and connections.[56]

52. Cora Diamond presupposes and builds on our understanding of at least some animals as friends in "Eating Meat and Eating People," *Philosophy* 53 (Oct. 1979): 465–79, esp. 474–5.
53. This point has been put in similar ways by many people, but its inclusion here reflects in the influence of Nehamas, *On Friendship* 88.
54. C. S. Lewis, *The Four Loves* (London: Bles 1960) 73.
55. Lewis 79.
56. Lewis 83.

Thus, Lewis can say that in the experience of friendship, one is "almost wholly free from jealousy, and free without qualification from the need to be needed."[57]

Many people's friendships don't fit comfortably within the boundaries Lewis draws here. His account doesn't square with a significant aspect of his own practice of friendship. And embracing such an account seems likely to impoverish the experience of friendship. Friendship can enrich our lives when, among things, we are willing to give significant independent weight to increasingly deep mutual knowing, to our intimate connections with our friends.

Lewis's definition would seem to restrict the scope of friendship to intellectual interchange ("*Do you see the same truth?*")—and therefore, seemingly, to those with intellectual inclinations. (Indeed, Lewis underscores his intellectualism by describing friendship as *essentially* disembodied.) However, a relationship in which the friends were primarily or exclusively occupied with some common concerns, whether or not those concerns were intellectual, while not making room for intimate connection would still be importantly, and unfortunately, limited. Self-disclosure and developing mutual discovery would still be lacking, as would attachment for its own sake.

Intimacy is hard to contain. Whatever the reason one lowers one's defenses in relation to another person, there is an impetus toward total security, total acceptance. While at the beginnings of some relationships it may really be the case, as on Lewis's model, that one has no interest in the other's history or current circumstances, the sharing of oneself that eventuates as the relationship develops will not likely be limited to the dimensions of oneself that originally occasioned the relationship. As one grows more comfortable with the other, one seeks the other's acceptance, self-disclosure, and support. So there is something not only unduly limiting but also implausible, impracticable, about Lewis's proposal for truncated intimacy.

Keeping Vulnerability at Bay

An account like Lewis's can be appealing because it can appear to reduce the risk of loss in friendship.

If I need not be directly concerned with a friend as a three-dimensional person, if the friend figures in our friendship only as a contributor to common understanding, then the terrors of contingency have been mitigated. Passion, jealousy, regret, fear, insecurity—all are banished from the relationship. The

57. Lewis 91.

death or departure of the other deprives me of the loss of her perspective on the topic of our common interest, but my relationship with her as such does not contribute to the constitution of my identity, so my friendship with her does not render me vulnerable in the same way as if I first and foremost loved *her* and cared only secondarily for dominoes or white mice.

This emphasis on the good to be achieved through relation to the other rather than on the other herself can be appealing because it is, simply put, safe. Vulnerability can be uncomfortable, even terrifying. And there is, in general, no obligation to expose oneself to loss. But different models of friendship do make different sorts of lives possible.

It is clear that a friendship lived according to the conception Lewis elaborates would be safer than a more all-encompassing relationship. But it would also clearly deprive friends of possibilities for rich experiences that they might otherwise enjoy. Each friend can truly discover the other and discover herself in and through the other only if she is willing to risk.

What Do Friends Value?

Lewis's official view doesn't square with the ways in which people often interpret their experiences of friendship. Intimate personal connection between friends, manifested in considerable emotional warmth, even intensity, is evident in diverse cultural settings.[58] Even if friendship is publicly recognized, treated as a formal institution, intimate connection can still be experienced as central to the relationship.[59]

While people do often note the importance of shared interests for their friendships, they do not seem typically to believe that particular common activities are the sole glue that binds them together with their friends. Wide-ranging "mutual understanding" may be at least as important. As one man observes, what he and a close friend talk about "depends on whatever happens to be going on. Just sitting around drinking beer, watching football or baseball games. Just talking about whatever comes up."[60]

58. Brain, *Friends and Lovers* 41–3.

59. Brain 83.

60. Haapanen, "Close Friendship" 42.

A friendship can thus be seen as an *us* group, in which the focus is on the members rather than on a common goal exterior to them.[61] Friendship happens in the world—the world of events and activities and bodies and ideas. But friends' relationships often enable them to transcend their immediate circumstances. Because it is "essentially a loving relationship, friendship is oriented toward the person of the other rather than toward tasks completed with the other." Not surprisingly, then, for close friends, "interest and concern for the other takes precedence over . . . projects . . . or goals."[62] The public world provides the context within which the friends' activities take place, but concern with the world doesn't render their connection trivial, marginal, or irrelevant; their intimate bond remains independently important.[63] Friendship "is directed toward *being with*, rather than *doing with* the other."[64]

Activity and Intimacy

Friends' intimate engagement can result from shared activities; but the desire for engagement can help to *make* activities common. We can show our interest in our friends in part by becoming aware of and sensitive to the things that concern or delight them. And a topic's or activity's significance for a friend can prompt one to find it appealing. Something may thus figure in friends' interactions just because part of being a close friend is taking an interest in one's friends' interests and personal concerns.[65]

Shared interests may be *occasions for* or *results of* friendship, but they are neither essential foci of friendship nor its constitutive elements. Friends can and should enjoy activities together, and perhaps in some cases there will be activities or topics that are characteristic of the friendship. And of course these can be appreciated for their own sakes. But they're not needed to legitimate the friendship, and they shouldn't get in the way of friends' deepening knowledge of each other.

61. On such groups, see R. D. Laing, *The Politics of Experience* (London: Penguin 1968) 7, ctd. Robert Paine, "An Exploratory Analysis in 'Middle-Class' Culture," Leyton, *Compact* 126.
62. Becker, "Phenomenological Explication" 127.
63. Becker 159–60.
64. Becker 127 (my italics); cp. Becker 159.
65. Haapanen, "Close Friendship" 42–4.

Gender and Vulnerability

Lewis's position does not seem to comport with many people's assumptions about friendship. Insofar as it *is* consistent with such assumptions, those assumptions seem likely to be distinctively male ones.

Men in our society have too frequently shied away from linking friendship with affection and self-disclosure, instead emphasizing the importance of "similar interests and beliefs" and the importance of "common activities."[66] Women, by contrast, have enjoyed "affectively richer" friendships that have stressed interchange over shared activity,[67] ones in which creative disagreement is valued as much as or more than sameness.[68] Men and women both appear to value intimacy as a component of friendship, but their definitions evidently differ, with women expecting a significantly greater degree of self-disclosure than men from their same-sex friends.[69]

Paul Wright employs Lewis's side-by-side/face-to-face distinction as a characterization of divergent male and female styles of friendship.[70] But Wright suggests that such distinctions become less noticeable after friendships have developed for some years.[71] (It's not clear that this is what happened in the case of Lewis's own friendships.) We can expect that they will become less common

66. Lawrence Weiss and Marjorie Fiske Lowenthal, "Life-Course Perspectives on Friendship," *Four Stages of Life*, ed. Marjorie Fiske Lowenthal, Majda Thurnber, and David Chiriboga (San Francisco: Jossey-Bass 1975) 59. See also, *e.g.*, Mayta A. Caldwell and Letitia Anne Peplau, "Sex Differences in Same-Sex Friendship," *Sex Roles* 8.7 (1982): 727; John M. Reisman, "Adult Friendships," *Personal Relationships* 2: *Developing Personal Relationships*, ed. Steve Duck and Robin Gilmour (London: Academic 1981) 216–7; William E. Snell Jr., Sharyn S. Belk, Amy Flowers, and James Warren, "Women's and Men's Willingness to Self-Disclose to Therapists and Friends: The Moderating Influence of Instrumental, Expressive, Masculine, and Feminine Topics," *Sex Roles* 18 (1988): 769–76; and Jack Balswick, *The Inexpressive Male: A Study of Men Who Express Love Too Little* (Lanham, MD: Lexington 1988). See Paul H. Wright, "Interpreting Research on Gender Differences in Friendship: A Case for Moderation and a Plea for Caution," *Journal of Social and Personal Relationships* 5.3 (1988): 367–73 (emphasizing the need for nuance in studies of gender and friendship). Ironically, despite his frequent resistance to intimacy, it may still have been "the femininity in . . . [Lewis that] contributed to the friendships of the Inklings." Humphrey Carpenter, *The Inklings: C. S. Lewis, J. R. R. Tolkien, Charles Williams, and Their Friends* (London: Unwin 1978) 166.

67. Weiss and Lowenthal, "Life-Course Perspectives" 59; cp. Reisman, "Adult Friendships" 216.

68. Paul H. Wright, "Men's Friendships, Women's Friendships, and the Alleged Inferiority of the Latter," *Sex Roles* 8.1 (1982): 8.

69. Caldwell and Peplau, "Sex Differences."

70. Wright, "Men's Friendships" 8.

71. Wright 19.

as men encounter more models of intimate connection and as stoic behaviors and attitudes cease to be valorized.

Lewis's View in Practice

Because he "disliked sharing spoken intimacies with friends," Lewis "never allowed the conversation to develop if [J. R. R.] Tolkien tried to speak of his [marital] troubles."[72] This seems to have "annoyed Tolkien, who often wanted to find a sympathetic ear."[73] Understandably, Lewis's friends seem on occasion to have judged his hostility to discussions regarding personal problems "tiresome."[74]

Lewis's official view of friendship—expressing and reinforcing, I suspect, his own disaffection for vulnerability—may have complicated his interactions with his friends.[75] But his own practice of friendship still seems to have been better than his theory. Even while he evidently wanted to keep intimacy at bay, Lewis certainly appears to have admired and desired his friends for themselves. For those of his friends "who were close to Lewis" (perhaps other than Tolkien?), "friendship with him proved to be a uniquely rich experience. 'He gave a warmth of friendship,' said [R. E.] Havard, 'which I have never met anywhere else.'"[76] And it is not really surprising, therefore, that "several of . . . [Lewis's friends] actually thought the whole essay [on friendship] (in *The Four Loves*) was ill judged."[77]

Humphrey Carpenter's *The Inklings* includes a lengthy discussion of the common bond that united Lewis's friendship group. Lewis once dismissed the quest for features which would justify the identification of his friends as forming a

72. A. N. Wilson, *C. S. Lewis: A Biography* (London: Collins 1990) 159.

73. Carpenter, *Inklings* 166.

74. Carpenter 166.

75. Alister McGrath implies that this official view might have reflected the emotional complexities associated with Lewis's discovery that his lifelong best friend, Arthur Greeves, was gay and that Lewis was "the chief object of Greeves's affection," a realization Lewis evidently met with tolerance and equanimity but not reciprocal desire. McGrath opines that "Lewis's complex relationship with Greeves clearly had an impact on Lewis's reflections on the focus and limits of friendship. It is important for readers of *The Four Loves* (1960) to appreciate that Lewis is here exploring . . . the boundaries of intimacy, affection, and respect within *male* relationships." Alister McGrath, *C. S. Lewis—a Life: Eccentric Genius, Reluctant Prophet* (Carol Stream, IL: Tyndale 2013) 72–3.

76. Carpenter, *Inklings* 171.

77. Carpenter 167.

distinct intellectual or literary movement as a hunt for a "fox that isn't there." After himself joining in the hunt for the fox, Carpenter notes that Tolkien once "referred to the Inklings as 'the Lewis seance,' and there was more than an element of truth in this. . . . The group gathered round . . . [Lewis], and in the end one does not have to look any further than Lewis to see why it came into being. He himself is the fox."[78] Lewis's own practice of friendship evoked more personal attachment than his theory seemed to encourage.

Despite the evident value of the friendship he offered others, the understanding of friendship Lewis advanced, one that treats joint activities as more central to friendship than self-disclosure and intimate connection, seems unhelpful. There's no good reason to keep mutual knowledge, vulnerability, and attachment at bay. Many people do understand intimacy as central to friendship, so Lewis's account hardly captures a general consensus. More than that, however, adopting a model of friendship like his would deprive us of genuinely deep and powerful connections. Sharing activities with friends can deepen and express our bonds with them, and of course the activities can be worthwhile on their own, but friendships are richer when they make room not just for common pursuits but also for intimacy. "Friendship is not itself cooperation, but a sabbath rest that comes to fruition in the moment of pause."[79] Shared activities may matter, but connection matters more.

Reasons

We choose people as friends in the first place for reasons of many sorts. However, once a friendship has been established, we can and should be loyal to a friend primarily on different grounds.

Initial Appeal

Friendship is about more than just the friend as a bare rational agent, for in this case, there would be no reason for me to select one person rather than another as a friend; friendship would seem fundamentally arbitrary.[80] And if social

78. Carpenter 171.

79. O'Donovan, *Ethics as Theology* 3: 144.

80. See Moravcsik, "Perils of Friendship" 138; cp. Bernard Williams, *Problems of the Self: Philosophical Papers, 1956–1972* (Cambridge: Cambridge University Press 1973) 228.

relations play indispensable roles in constructing our unique identities,[81] then the particularity of identity, so far from being an unfortunate impediment to the moral life, is precisely part of the divine creational intent that ought to shape the moral life.

There are innumerable reasons for making a commitment to a particular friendship or for making promises to a particular potential friend or for inviting her reliance in the first place. One may, for instance, find oneself immediately drawn to a potential friend in response to particular qualities and thus inclined to embrace the prospect of friendship enthusiastically. Or one may find oneself thrown together with someone to whom one becomes attached over time. In this case, one's commitment to the friendship may not be rooted in particular qualities so much as in a cumulation of shared experience. It may thus develop slowly, perhaps without ever being consciously ratified at all at any one point or perhaps being explicitly acknowledged and affirmed only when the need for a decision presents itself.

Where qualities prompt initial attraction to a friend, they may be of any sort—developed or conferred, central to the other's own self-conception or peripheral to it. What matters is that one finds the other appealing, whether in a coolly reflective way or in and through a spontaneous uprush of feeling, and opts, deliberately or instinctively, to continue engaging.

Overmoralized conceptions of friendship urge us to pick friends (or lovers) in order to empower the excluded or to expand our own social horizons. And it is surely reasonable—with an eye to our own well-being as well as to the well-being of any potential friend—to be aware of irrational prejudices that might prevent the formation of friendships that might otherwise be appealing. But, as a general matter, there is no *positive* obligation to seek close friendship with anyone in particular. There is no obligation to choose friends for particular reasons or to employ some particular selection procedure. Just because, in the absence of prejudice and bigotry, someone qualifies as a potential friend, it doesn't follow that she is an appealing candidate for friendship or that, even if she is, we have any reason to pick her over someone else.

It is certainly reasonable that we would not ordinarily want to think of ourselves as required to pick friendships on the basis of factors other than whatever it is about the friend that makes connecting with her appealing. (*i*) We hope to share enjoyable times with friends, so we want to increase our chances of doing so by selecting as friends people likely to engage with us enjoyably. We have

81. This notion is central to McFadyen.

no reason to want to devote our limited time to interactions with people with whom we do not feel comfortable and close, people with whom we don't enjoy interacting. (*ii*) In friendship, we are vulnerable, and we have no reason to want to entrust someone with the opportunity to take advantage of our vulnerability if we do not believe we are likely to be understood and liked.

The same reasons need not ground our choices of different friends. Neither we ourselves nor our friends can reasonably object if we select different people as friends for different reasons.[82] There certainly can be no reasonable expectation that we permit ourselves, when choosing friends, to respond only to characteristics likely to be shared with others.[83]

Seeking *friendly relations* is another thing entirely. This might well be obligatory in a wide range of cases. And no doubt there might be specific instances, as with parents or children with whom one finds it instinctively difficult to be close, in which at least attempting to craft something like close friendship might be required.

Whatever the original occasion for friendship, what distinguishes the friendship from a more casual relationship is that the *connection* one forges is with the *person* so that this connection is in some sense independent of the factors that originally brought one together with her. One may continue to appreciate that initially occasioning factor or set of factors, of course, but the friendship becomes in an important sense detached from its initial prompt or prompts.

It doesn't even matter if one was initially drawn to someone for an entirely unworthy reason—to gain the prestige associated with membership in a given social circle, say, or to benefit from a wealthy person's generosity—provided the friendship as it develops ceases to be dependent on the presence of the originally occasioning factors (so that one remains close even if one's friend is evicted from her social circle, and you along with her). One's initial concern to gain access to the wealth or prestige of someone who is now one's friend can be seen as shameful and manipulative in the first case and embarrassingly superficial in the latter case and so as cause for regret. But a relationship begun even on

82. Julius Moravcsik develops helpful arguments related to the tension between loyalty and a supposed consistency constraint on the selection of friends. See Moravcsik, "Perils of Friendship" 132–51; cp. Suttles, "Friendship" 100.

83. Moravcsik ("Perils of Friendship" 137) seems to have this sort of consistency constraint in mind.

thoroughly regrettable grounds may still become a genuine friendship marked by intimacy with and attachment and committed loyalty to a person.[84]

Reasons for Love and Loyalty

We love God as we love our friends, and one way in which this is so is through our appreciation for qualities that are dim reflections of God's own excellences.[85] But we are not, as friends, simply or primarily developing dispositions to appreciate those qualities. They are not present in our lives merely to provide opportunities for our discovery of God's unsurpassable excellences. Thus, while we should come to recognize God as the ground and perfect embodiment of those qualities, our friends and friendships continue to merit our loyalty even as their qualities change.

As a friendship continues to grow, the particularities of the other remain important in various ways (even as the friends' own preferences and characteristics shift over time). However, once the friendship has come into being, a unique feature of the friend identifies her as unique, differentiates her from all others, and connects one with her. This unique feature is not any combination of abstract qualities. Rather, it is the qualitative and numerical distinctness of one's relationship with this person: a bond with someone who has come to be a part of my identity because of, and who shares with me, an ongoing narrative that is not identical with the one I share or have shared with anyone else.[86] The friend is uniquely specified as by her participation in a history of interaction, and the changing, developing person in all her complexity—rather than the qualities she exemplifies—is thus the object of one's love and loyalty. And our shared history leads to the increasing incorporation of the friend and the friendship into the self.[87]

The most basic reason for ongoing engagement with and loyalty to a friend is one's commitment to the friendship. In addition, while one makes a commitment, as it were, on one's own, one's promises and one's explicit or implicit invitations to reliance provide further reasons for engagement, since they entitle

84. *Contra* Nehamas, *On Friendship* 105.

85. Robert Merrihew Adams, *Finite and Infinite Goods: A Framework for Ethics* (New York: Oxford University Press 1999) 187–98.

86. See Neera K. Badhwar, "Friends as Ends in Themselves," *Philosophy and Phenomenological Research* 48.1 (Sep. 1987): 14.

87. I discuss equivalent issues in connection with marriage and romantic love in Chartier, *Practice* 48–53.

a friend to claim one's loyalty and attention. A further important reason is to avoid shattering one's identity or one's self—since a close friendship helps to constitute one's identity and a close friend is part of who one is—or disrupting the shared story one is writing with a friend.

It is in virtue of factors like these that we find it so hard to explain our love for our friends. We can point to factors that attracted us to them or occasioned our initial connections, but we can fumble inarticulately when asked to account for our love after a relationship has developed. A way to explain the inarticulacy one can experience, I suggest, is that one has moved beyond initially attractive and occasioning factors by integrating the friend into the self. One loves the friend, not for any abstract feature, but as someone with whom one has bonded by making one's relationship with her an aspect of who one is.[88] If we look for qualities, then, we're looking in the wrong place. In addition, because a commitment to a friendship is open ended, because the development of a self that incorporates a friend or a friendship is ongoing, our attachment, our self-investment, is not to a static relationship or identity but to an ongoing project not only of mutual discovery but also, because we and our relationships are themselves developing, of mutual redefinition and mutual adventure.[89]

Friendship is a risk, a venture. One can certainly admire a friend's qualities, desire to experience them, and so forth. But to love a friend is to love someone whose qualities can change and so to love someone even as she grows and develops and alters. Becoming a friend may involve making the wager that one will find it easy or enjoyable to stay connected despite a friend's changes; but to choose to be a friend is to plan on staying loyal even if adjusting to a friend's continued development doesn't always prove simple or pleasant.

Though of course they may be, neither one's commitment to a friendship nor one's promises to a friend need be unconditional. One can perfectly well incorporate limitations of various sorts into them. And some limitations, if they're not explicitly excluded, may be implicit, presumed, or commonsensical.[90] If there are to be limitations, however, they should ensure that a friendship is stable and reliable, that it can't and won't be abandoned simply because attitudes change or disagreements occur. The good of friendship depends on

88. See Robert Nozick, "Love's Bond," *The Examined Life* (New York: Simon 1989) 69–86; and Nehamas, *On Friendship* 108–35.

89. See Nehamas, *On Friendship* 136–7 (I don't mean to suggest that Nehamas would endorse the way I've put the matter here).

90. Gary Chartier, *The Logic of Commitment* (New York: Routledge 2018) 95–9.

diving deep, on being open to learning and growing and discovering friendship's real potential. Friends need to know they can be safely vulnerable with each other. And, if we are to mirror and convey God's love, we need to be prepared to offer friends gracious acceptance. The more unqualified our loyalty, the more we and our friends will be able to receive friendship's rich rewards.

Qualities Aren't Enough

Loyalty in friendship is loyalty to a friend as the subject of a unique history and as someone who has helped in part to constitute one's own identity rather than attachment to a set of qualities. So we need not think that, even in principle, loving one identical twin should mean loving the other.[91]

History provides opportunity for the potential friend's qualities—the features that render her likableness evident and that individuate her—to be disclosed, and these qualities will likely prompt initial engagement with a friend. It is, further, only in the course of a common history that trust can develop between people, and it is only on the basis of trust that genuine self-disclosure is possible. Someone—even the twin of a close friend—who has not shared a history with me has not participated in forming a relationship of mutual knowing and mutual trust.

What matters even more, however, is that my friendship is a bond with a distinct and distinctive person who has shared her or his life with me in the course of a particular set of events, with whom I've connected in and through and as a result of a unique, and therefore unsubstitutable, irreplaceable common history. In addition, in the course of that history, the person who is my friend becomes a distinct part of *me*; she helps to constitute my identity in a way that another who has not shared our particular joint history cannot.

The attachment resulting from our shared history and shared identity can be a powerful motive for ongoing engagement with a friend. And avoiding destruction of that shared identity can be a good reason to nourish the friendship rather than abandoning it when things get tough.

Viewing a friend as attractive and a friendship as worthwhile solely or primarily in virtue of the friend's particular qualities can be a way of attempting to escape vulnerability, just like a more explicit resistance to intimacy.[92] If one is

91. See Neera K. Badhwar, "Why It Is Wrong to Be Always Guided by the Best: Consequentialism and Friendship," *Ethics* 101.3 (April 1991): 483; and Badhwar, "Ends" 7, 22–3.

92. Moravcsik, "Perils of Friendship" 134–5, 142.

attached solely to qualities rather than to persons, the loss of a friendship may matter less—provided the qualities of the lost friend can be experienced through interaction with someone else. (Of course, one may *think* one is attached simply to currently appealing qualities only to discover that one's heart is not so easily managed.) But to opt for safety on this basis is to let go of the concern for the other *as other* that is a key element of any real friendship.

Dealing with Changes

Loyalty to a friend need not be dependent on the friend's possessing any particular individuating qualities. But some dramatic transition—death or debilitating illness, for instance, or confinement incommunicado—could render a friendship dormant.[93] The Christian can look forward to a life beyond death in which a friendship thus suspended can be reawakened.[94] She need not, then, understand continued willingness to take the friend's projects and well-being into account as simply expressions of "love based on the memory of the person

93. Badhwar, "Ends," quite reasonably instances Alzheimer's disease.

94. See, *e.g.*, John B. Cobb Jr., "The Resurrection of the Soul," *Harvard Theological Review* 80.2 (1987): 213–27; John Hick, *Death and Eternal Life* (Louisville, KY: Westminster John Knox 1994); David Ray Griffin, *Parapsychology, Philosophy, and Spirituality: A Postmodern Exploration* (Albany: SUNY 1997) 41–268; David Ray Griffin, *Reenchantment without Supernaturalism: A Process Philosophy of Religion* (Ithaca, NY: Cornell University Press 2001) 236–46; Edward F. Kelly *et al.*, *Irreducible Mind: Toward a Psychology for the Twenty-First Century* (Lanham, MD: Rowman 2007) 367–421, 577–643 (esp. 595–9); Gary E. Schwartz with William L. Simon, *The Afterlife Experiments: Breakthrough Scientific Evidence of Life after Death* (New York: Atria 2002); Huw Parri Owen, *Christian Theism: A Study in Its Basic Principles* (Edinburgh: Clark 1984) 132–3; Immanuel Kant, "The Critique of Practical Reason," trans. Thomas Kingsmill Abbott, *Kant*, Great Books of the Western World 42 (Chicago: Encyclopædia Britannica 1952) 344; Jeffrey Long with Paul Perry, *Evidence of the Afterlife: The Science of Near-Death Experiences* (New York: HarperOne 2010); Chris Carter, *Science and the Afterlife Experience: Evidence for Immortality of Consciousness* (Rochester, VT: Inner Traditions 2012); John Hick, *Evil and the God of Love*, rev. ed. (San Francisco: Harper 1977) 338–40; Julia Assante, *The Last Frontier: Exploring the Afterlife and Transforming Our Fear of Death* (Novato, CA: New World 2013) 23–92; Pim van Lommel, *Consciousness beyond Life: The Science of the Near-Death Experience* (New York: HarperOne 2010); Richard Swinburne, *The Evolution of the Soul* (Oxford: Clarendon-Oxford University Press 1985) 298–312; Stephen R. L. Clark, *God's World and the Great Awakening*, Limits and Renewals 3 (Oxford: Clarendon-Oxford University Press 1991) 146–68; and Stephen R. L. Clark, *The Mysteries of Religion: An Introduction to Philosophy through Religion* (Oxford: Blackwell 1986) 210–2. Cp. Jay B. McDaniel, "Can Animal Suffering Be Reconciled with Belief in an All-Loving God?," *Animals on the Agenda*, ed. Andrew Linzey and Dorothy Yamamoto (London: SCM 1998) 169–70.

loved" or of "homage to that memory."[95] She can treat this attitude, rather, in something like the way she would her stance in relation to a friend who has gone on a journey and will in due time return.

In the absence of such a dramatic transition, when the friend continues to be a full-fledged, communicative self but with altered characteristics, there is surely no need for the friendship to end, even if its content may shift to some degree. Loyalty in friendship is loyalty to the person who subsists over time.[96] Such loyalty need not be as difficult as is sometimes imagined. Self-committal to a friendship can on its own help to render the relationship significantly more emotionally satisfying. And one can come to find new things interesting, new perspectives illuminating, simply because one enjoys them with one's friend. One can therefore change with the friend *intentionally*.[97] I suggest that this is in fact what one often ought to do in a close friendship. Even when change is unreasonable (as when a friend embraces dangerous habits or destructive beliefs), one can still engage with and care about the friend, recognizing that she is not defined, that her identity is not exhausted, by her questionable choices.

Character

Related to the ideas that friendship should have some external object and that friends should be attached to each other's qualities is the idea that *character* should be the focus of friendship. To treat character in this way might be a matter of (*i*) treating attachment to a friend as a matter of attachment to her moral character. Or it might be a matter of (*ii*) treating friendship as focused on the goal of moral improvement—understanding friendship as "essentially based on virtue and mutual quest for virtue."[98] A friendship might then be a project of earnest mutual betterment. Alternatively, a morally serious person might think that the potential to improve a friend's doubtful character justified

95. Badhwar, "Ends" 15.

96. Nor need this involve any unduly baroque metaphysics of selfhood. See, *e.g.*, Paul Ricoeur, *Oneself as Another*, trans. Kathleen Blamey (Chicago: University of Chicago Press 1992) 113–68; Alasdair MacIntyre, *After Virtue: A Study in Moral Theory*, 2d ed. (Notre Dame, IN: University of Notre Dame Press 1984) 215–25; and John Searle, *Rationality in Action* (Cambridge, MA: Bradford-MIT Press 2001) 79–96.

97. See Paul Gilbert, *Human Relationships* (Oxford: Blackwell 1991) 73.

98. Bernard Häring, *The Law of Christ: Moral Theology for Priests and Laity*, trans. Edwin G. Kaiser, 3 vols. (Cork, Ireland: Mercier 1961–5) 2: 373.

the choice to be friends with her, even if she herself had no particular interest in being improved.

Either of these approaches might prove attractive in view of the desire for a stable anchor for friendship. If my friends only desire some service from me, or if we only enjoy superficial pleasure in and through each other's company, our relationships may seem both trivial and unstable. We sense that friendship must be focused on and sustained by something deeper and more stable, on the whole person of the friend. Thus, the appeal of a friendship focused on attachment to a friend's moral character rather than to more superficial and variable features of her body or personality, as with (*i*), or of an ongoing, open-ended project that can persist whatever else changes, as with (*ii*).

While it's easy to see the potential appeal of an approach that treats character as in one way or another friendship's focus, I think we should resist this approach. It's problematic just like other attempts to treat friendship as essentially about something other than intimate connection between the friends. It's also questionable because adopting it might unnecessarily restrict our range of friendships or the kinds of interactions in which we engage with our friends.

Character and Attraction

Others' excellences often make them appealing as friends. So a potential friend's moral character can, of course, be among the features that make the possibility of friendship with her attractive.[99] But that's different from supposing that this feature *must* be what draws us to friendship or that, whatever the source of our initial connection, our ongoing attachment should be to this feature.

We like and value and delight in and care about our friends for all sorts of reasons quite unrelated to their capacity to enhance our moral improvement, and there's no reason to treat moral character as the only legitimate reason for loving our friends. Moral excellence isn't the only kind of excellence. We can appreciate the appeal of someone's courage or generosity, say, without supposing that it would be unreasonable to be drawn to her as a friend in virtue of her charm, charisma, or intellectual power. And we needn't be drawn to others only in virtue of excellences at all: circumstances may bring us together, and we may simply discover that we connect.

99. See Martha Nussbaum, *The Fragility of Goodness: Luck and Ethics in Greek Tragedy and Philosophy* (Cambridge: Cambridge University Press 1986) 355, ctd. Paul Wadell, *Friendship and the Moral Life* (Notre Dame, IN: University of Notre Dame Press 1989) 57.

Given the diversity of reasons for which we are drawn to our friends, there's no reason to suspect that we or the friends with whom we've already connected would necessarily exhibit this capacity (apart from the minimum moral development we and they have had to exhibit in order to be friends at all). We might thus suspect not only that treating friendship as about character development would rule us out as potential friends but also that doing so would deprive us of friends we value.

Moral character can change; and the same character traits (if viewed in appropriately abstract fashion) can be evident in the lives of people other than our friends. So ongoing attachment to a friend's character isn't necessarily a guarantor of stability in a friendship, either. Loyalty to a friend—rooted normatively in one's commitments, one's promises, one's invitations to reliance, and one's shared identity and psychically in one's attachment to someone with whom one shares a history of developing mutual connection—seems like the best source of reliability in friendship.

Friendship and Edification

Choosing well is an important aspect of living well. If I want to live well, I will want to learn how to choose well. And, if I want a friend to live well (as I surely should), I will want her to learn how to choose well. There's nothing fanatical or moralistic about seeking character development for oneself and one's friends.

In addition, it's obvious that friendship can and does help us to grow morally. A set of virtues equips one to function effectively as a friend.[100] As a result, investing oneself in a friendship is, in effect, an invitation to acquire these virtues (even if they're not equally evident in all relationships). Ongoing interaction with a friend will, in addition, tend to help one to acquire greater openness, as one learns to respond constructively to a friend's disagreements, and greater self-awareness, as one learns about oneself from one's friend. These traits are both valuable in and of themselves and liable to enable one to grow in other ways. Many of us will exemplify them more fitfully and imperfectly than not, but friendship is nonetheless an opportunity to develop our characters even if moral growth is not a central and explicit concern.

100. See John Casey, *Pagan Virtue: An Essay in Ethics* (Oxford: Clarendon-Oxford University Press 1990) 186–7; and James Wm. McClendon Jr., *Systematic Theology* 1: *Ethics* (Nashville: Abingdon 1986) 172–3.

At the same time, however, recognizing the value of choosing well and friendship's contributions to it is not the same thing as supposing that friends should treat character development as the definitive purpose of their relationship, even if they welcome it as a concomitant of their growth in connection.

That doesn't mean that it's valueless or pointless for friends to seek moral improvement together. It might sometimes be reasonable for a friend to seek (delicately, sensitively, undemandingly) to encourage a friend's moral growth. But friends lose sight of their friendship if the quest for moral improvement displaces the pursuit of connection and a shared life. Relatedly, friends shouldn't seek to make moral growth a significant shared concern unless they *both* want it to be—any more than they should seek to make cabinetmaking, attending baseball games, or participating in the activities of the Society for Creative Anachronism or the Green Party a significant shared concern unless they both want it to be.

Indeed, they should be more trepidatious about trying to make character growth a central concern than other sorts of activities or experiences. It's more comprehensive, touching more aspects of someone's life. It touches the most hidden parts of a person's soul, so someone's attention to a friend's developing character can make the friend very vulnerable to her. And making it a central concern of the friendship means giving each friend a lot of power over the other.

Two friends could decide to treat their relationship as focused on character growth while not regarding themselves as having developed very much morally at the time of their decision. But it would be easy to view an understanding of friendship as focused on character growth as suggesting that friendship can be a preserve only of good people, only of those who have already developed in ways that enable them to enrich the characters of others. And this, in turn, seems to render friendship out of reach for most us, since we may doubt that we are likely to serve as exemplars of virtue or as sources of enrichment to others in their quests for moral growth. So it is perhaps unsurprising that Aristotle, who does think of character as central to friendship, assumes that someone will and should abandon a friend if she comes to be much more virtuous than the friend.[101]

While friends might thus already be hesitant about making moral growth a mutual project, someone should be doubly hesitant about taking on a friend as

101. Aristotle, *Ethica Nicomachea* 1165b <https://www.sacred-texts.com/cla/ari/nico/nico098.htm>.

an object of moral education when the friend has no interest in being part of such a project. Treating a friend this way if the friend is aware of one's goal can seem insulting and paternalistic. And doing so if the friend is unaware of one's goal can also be manipulative. It's not consistent with the equality and mutual knowing that are essential to friendship.

Even if making a friend's moral improvement essential to a friendship weren't insulting, paternalistic, and manipulative, however, this kind of focus just doesn't jibe with an understanding of friendship as fundamentally a matter of mutual connection. It involves viewing and treating the friend at arm's length, as clay to be molded, rather than as someone to whom one is becoming close and wants to become closer.

The increasing closeness that is a continuing goal of a developing friendship helps to make us who we are. The role of our contacts—in society, with friends, with God—in shaping our identities will be my focus in chapter 2.

2

Interactions

Friendship is a key element in the constitution and construction of our identities and capacities. And our interactions, including the interactions of friends and God's interaction with created reality, help to shape our identities (and, in turn, our friendships).

I begin this chapter by elaborating a view of persons as formed in and by social relationships and of friendship as an important element in the interactive formation of selfhood. I develop an understanding of freedom in friendship before addressing the degree to which the circumstances and development of friendship are not subject to our wills and thus place our own well-being outside our control. I examine the contribution of a social view of selfhood to thinking about friendship dynamics. And I examine the sense in which we might understand interaction with God as at the root of our friendships.

Persons, Selves, Friends

Understanding personhood as social helps us to understand friendship.

A Range of Categories

We use similar but different terms—human being, individual, self, person—for several related concepts. *Human being* is a biological concept, employed on the basis of ancestry and physical characteristics. *Individual* can be either biological or sociological. An individual may simply be a human being viewed as a member of the human species. But the word *individual* often carries additional weight. To speak of a person as an individual is often to say that she has developed a distinct and distinctive identity of her own and that she can and should make important decisions about her own life.

Self is a philosophical, psychological, or sociological category; the self is what one understands as the bearer of one's particular identity. It "is what one identifies oneself with, what a person cares most about, the loss of which amounts, for him, to self-destruction, either partial or total."[1] It may include projects and commitments and relationships clearly distinguishable from one's reality as a biological organism but integral to one's life seen as an ongoing narrative or venture. Selfhood may be seen as the project whose coherence gives unity to one's life story.

As a first pass at a definition, one might say that a *person* is a life-form with moral standing in virtue of her (current or potential or previously exercised) capacity to experience, understand, choose, plan, and reason. The capacity for centered, self-conscious agency does seem to be necessary to any plausible account of personhood. A person deserves to be treated as an end and not merely a means.[2]

Theology and Personhood

Some theologians have argued that the Genesis 1 creation story, which portrays humanity as created in relation (male and female *together* are God's image in the world), provides a basis for an understanding of persons as necessarily related. However, it is not altogether clear to what extent the narrative is intended to make this point. And, even if it is, while the story suggests intriguing possibilities, it does not seem able to ground arguments that would allow us to bypass reflection on the concrete human situation.

Also influential on ideas of personhood has been the Christian understanding of God as Trinity. The classical description of God as "three persons in one substance" has served as an important impetus for later Christian thinking about human personhood.[3]

1. Raziel Abelson, *Persons: A Study in Philosophical Psychology* (London: Macmillan 1977) 91. Thanks to Ben Abelson for the chance to engage regarding his father, Raziel.
2. See, *e.g.*, James W. Walters, *What Is a Person? An Ethical Exploration* (Champaign: University of Illinois Press 1997).
3. On the potential significance of Trinitarian thinking for our understanding of personhood, see, *e.g.*, Colin Gunton, *The Promise of Trinitarian Theology* (Edinburgh: Clark 1991) 86–103; Wolfhart Pannenberg, *Anthropology in Theological Perspective*, trans. Matthew J. O'Connell (Philadelphia:

Where the nature of personhood is concerned, the theologian does not need to cite the creation story or to advert to tenuous analogies between divine and human personhood in order to discern humanity's essential relatedness. She can, however, note the ways in which images of personhood derived from Scripture and the Christian tradition illuminate the human condition. Certainly, the images of humanity as woman-and-man-in-relation, of God as personal-in-relation, and of Jesus as God's self-gift all serve to point toward the value of emphasizing the relatedness of persons.

The social analogy for understanding talk about God as Trinity views the language of "Father," "Son," and "Holy Spirit" as language about three centers of activity, knowledge, and experience.[4] It views this language, that is, as talk about three persons in the contemporary sense, and its proponents suggest not infrequently that God-as-relational should be seen as a model for finite-persons-as-relational.

Talk of "persons" in the Trinitarian formula—"three persons, one substance"—likely didn't have anything to do with persons in our contemporary sense. (*Persona* initially meant, roughly, "theatrical mask.") And the social analogy seems to me to assume far more knowledge of the divine life than is realistically possible for finite minds.[5] It also appears needlessly to complicate our picture of God and to introduce what looks suspiciously like a surd element into the divine life. (Why should the necessary being of God comprehend, as on the social analogy, precisely *three* centers of awareness and activity?[6]) Alternatives in accordance with which Trinitarian language parallels talk about aspects of the experience, activity, or being of the finite person seem simpler and more defensible. So do ones that treat Trinitarian language as highlighting indispensable elements in our *knowledge* of God.[7]

Westminster 1985) 236; Wolfhart Pannenberg, *Systematic Theology*, 3 vols., trans. Geoffrey W. Bromiley (Grand Rapids: Eerdmans 1991–7) 1: 286–7, 296–7; Jürgen Moltmann, *The Trinity and the Kingdom: The Doctrine of God*, trans. Margaret Kohl (London: SCM 1981); Leonardo Boff, *Trinity and Society*, trans. Paul Burns (Eugene, OR: Wipf 2005); and McFadyen, *Call to Personhood*.

4. The best defense of social Trinitarianism with which I'm acquainted is David Brown, *The Divine Trinity* (London: Duckworth 1985).

5. For apt criticisms of social Trinitarianism, together with a pointer in what seems likely to be a helpful direction, see Karen Kilby, *God, Evil and the Limits of Theology* (London: Clark-Bloomsbury 2020) 5–16.

6. There are, of course, responses to this kind of concern. See, *e.g.*, Richard Swinburne, *The Christian God* (Oxford: Clarendon-Oxford University Press 1994) 170–91 (building on the thought of Richard of Saint Victor).

7. See, *e.g.*, Keith Ward, *Christ and the Cosmos: A Reformulation of Trinitarian Doctrine* (Cambridge: Cambridge University Press 2015); and Nicholas Lash, *Believing Three Ways in One God: A Reading

Even if the social analogy ultimately proved defensible, however, it's not clear how much would follow. Creatures resemble their Creator in various ways. But there is no basis for claiming, a priori, that a particular kind of creature should be expected to exhibit a given feature of the divine life. Persons are like God, both because all creatures are like their Creator and because, in particular, we understand God as personal. And we have reason to see God as social-cum-relational insofar as God is interactive with and affected by creation.[8] But we can't assume that any feature of divine personhood *must* be a feature of human personhood (unless we have independent reason to think of that feature as essential to personhood just as such; but, in this case, reference to divine personhood wouldn't play a central role in identifying the feature).

It is ultimately to creation—to the actual dynamics of how we function, to the ways we are constituted in the world God has made and is making—that I suspect we should attend if we want to understand how selves are constituted. Attention to creation reveals reality at multiple levels as inherently social.[9] That reality is social is theologically significant. But recognizing the social character of reality isn't a matter of reading an understanding of human personhood off of a prior account of divine personhood.

What We Learn When We Look at Creation

Created selves, it's clear, have permeable boundaries. And social interactions shape selves in a variety of ways. We are thus not atomic but *molecular* individuals.[10]

Our families, societies, and communities provide the backdrop against which we develop, affording each of us with language, culture, and a sense of history. Personal relationships mediate to us much of what our societies offer.

---

of the Apostles' Creed (Notre Dame, IN: University of Notre Dame Press 1993). See H. Richard Niebuhr, "The Doctrine of the Trinity and the Unity of the Church," *Theology Today* 3.3 (Oct. 1946): 371–84.

8. See, *e.g.*, Thomas Jay Oord, *The Nature of Love: A Theology* (St. Louis, MO: Chalice 2010) 80–116; Thomas Jay Oord, *Defining Love: A Philosophical, Scientific, and Theological Engagement* (Grand Rapids: Brazos-Baker 2010) 189–200; and Keith Ward, *Sharing in the Divine Nature: A Personalist Metaphysics* (Eugene, OR: Cascade-Wipf 2020).

9. Charles Hartshorne, *Reality as Social Process: Studies in Metaphysics and Religion* (New York: Free 1953).

10. See Sheldon Richman, "Molecular Individualism," *The Freeman: Ideas on Liberty* (Foundation for Economic Education), March 1, 1998 <https://fee.org/articles/molecular-individualism/>.

Commitments to relationships with other persons, with groups, and with institutions impose constraints on our being and behaving. The particular features of a particular interpersonal relationship and of one's partner in it shape one's interests and habit patterns. Another can come to be part of oneself in an important sense. And our interactions with God shape our identities and our interpersonal relationships, including our friendships.

Our individual genetic profiles result from unions of different people. Families play crucial roles in influencing the way we act and what we think and feel, in contributing to our intellectual, moral, and spiritual formation.

In addition, usually at birth, each of us enters a framework of words, images, and practices that already exists. We learn to understand ourselves by means of metaphors and analytical descriptions that are already available in our environments when we arrive in the world.[11] We learn to place ourselves within shared narratives of varied kinds. Our attitudes, perspectives, convictions, and behaviors are shaped in significant ways by the informal but vitally important institution of language. Other informal institutions, like markets that link us with strangers around the world, extend our capacities to influence and be influenced.

Formal social institutions—workplaces, schools, clubs and other affinity groups, churches, and states and their subdivisions—provide many of the contexts within which we act and help to convey and reinforce norms about proper thought and feeling and choice. Cultural products and social practices also convey to us an understanding of selfhood that we can use to organize and interpret our experiences and activities. At the same time, we represent all of these experiences, relationships, and events to ourselves in particular ways (themselves influenced by our cultural backgrounds and histories of interaction). And we *respond* to them in particular ways, thus making our own contributions to the creation of habits and attitudes.[12] Engaging with others calls for a free response which contributes to defining who one is. Relationships help one to discover who one is; but what one discovers is, nonetheless, a distinct particular identity (albeit one formed relationally).[13]

11. See Charles Taylor, *Hegel and Modern Society* (Cambridge: Cambridge University Press 1979) 87.

12. See McFadyen, *Call to Personhood* 255–6.

13. See Ray S. Anderson, *On Being Human: Essays in Theological Anthropology* (Grand Rapids: Eerdmans 1982) 45–6.

Christians have good reason to maintain that persons are agents, that they exhibit a creativity and a moral freedom that evince an ability to transcend in some measure their histories and environments. So the Christian will wish to affirm that the influence exerted by a person's social environment is not an iron-clad determinism. Rather, each agent's character qualifies her agency—limiting and constraining it, rendering some options realistically available and others not. No one chooses in a vacuum, ever.

Our societies affect us in significant part by means of the print and electronic media (including traditional media outlets and social media platforms). Some media are largely impersonal, not targeted in any way. Some are individually targeted. And many other varieties of cultural impact occur in and through face-to-face and remote interactions with particular persons. We learn ways of being in and through the specific ways in which patterns of existence are embodied by people who teach us by precept and example and reaction.[14]

Friendships play multiple roles in relation to social ties that help to make us who we are. Friendships can lead to procreation. Friends help to teach us language and to encourage our adoption of relevant norms. Participation in formal and informal institutions provides us with opportunities to develop and deepen friendships.

As we spend time with our friends, our interests are expanded. The stories we tell to make sense of our identities grow richer and more varied. The interests of which we need to take account when making day-to-day decisions increase in number; some decisions are now possible that weren't, while others—once attractive—are now unthinkable because our friends are inextricable parts of our lives. When I relate to a friend, I open myself much more completely, much less instrumentally, than in almost any other sort of relationship. And thus the full process of individuation is furthered.

Friends Help to Constitute Our Identities

While many relationships contribute to making us *how* we are, close friendships help to make us *who* we are:[15] friendships are *identity constitutive*. This may be true in several related ways.

14. See, *e.g.*, McFadyen, *Call to Personhood* 256–7.

15. See A. I. Melden, *Rights in Moral Lives: A Historical-Philosophical Essay* (Berkeley: University of California Press 1988) 130–2.

(*i*) I may adopt a friend's good, her well-being, as an aspect or element of my own good.[16] (*ii*) My relationship with a friend may be a complex array of undertakings in which I am so deeply invested that it shapes my actions and my self-understanding. (*iii*) My friend's identity and my own may in some important sense overlap, forming a *we*. The most comprehensive sort of *we* is arguably the kind constituted by romantic partners. But close friends—each of whom understands herself at least in part precisely in relation to the other—can also form a *we*.[17] (*iv*) For some people, *friendship itself* as an identity-forming social role will be important as well: I may be known not only as Annette's friend, or Nabil's, or Jeff's, or Aena's, but as someone who self-identifies, and is recognized by others, as a friend (just as being a spouse or a parent may matter for how someone is viewed quite apart from the question of *whose* spouse or parent she is).

Presumably, this will involve conscious awareness of my identification of a friend's good with my own, of our relationship as a centrally important project that forms part of my identity, of my friend's identity as overlapping with mine. To talk about identity-constitution is ordinarily to say that the friend or my relationship with her may be part of my self-understanding, my identity as subjectively understood. I may see myself as *defined* in part by her or by my relationship with her. But we might still in principle distinguish between the *existence* of each of these states and my conscious recognition of it. If I'm not terribly reflective, a friend and I might form a *we* without my ever having thought about our doing so.

The limits of the characteristically modern distinction between egoism and altruism are particularly evident where friendship is concerned.[18] In an important respect, my own well-being is inseparable from that of my friend.[19] And of course the friends' identification with each other provides further reason—apart from the care that is a crucial aspect of friendship—for them to treat the vulnerability each offers the other with solicitude.[20] Identifying the friend's good with one's own is a crucial part of the love one chooses in friendship. At the same time, the history of interaction that friendship involves gives one greater

16. See John Finnis, *Natural Law and Natural Rights* (Oxford: Clarendon-Oxford University Press 1980) 88, 141–4.

17. See Solomon, *About Love*; and Nozick, "Love's Bond" 69–86. On a pair of friends as constituting a *we*, see, *e.g.*, Becker, "Phenomenological Explication" 207.

18. On this distinction, see, *e.g*, Gary Chartier, *Flourishing Lives: Exploring Natural Law Liberalism* (Cambridge: Cambridge University Press 2019) 9–11.

19. Thomas, "Friendship" 232.

20. Alpern, "Nature of Friendship" 212.

understanding of a friend's perspectives, circumstances, and needs and thus of what it means to value and further that good.[21]

That one's identity should be contingent and particular, incorporating the friend and reflecting the friend's actions, follows from an understanding of the self as formed in the process of social interaction. For each interaction is distinctive, and each history of interaction that forms a particular character is itself distinctive. Friendship thus fosters the differentiation of the self and emphasizes (and helps to generate) its particularity.

Friendship and Otherness

Because friends' identities are particular, it follows that, even as we seek and to some extent achieve union with a friend, the friend remains *other*. And part of being morally responsible in friendship is offering the friend the respect that comes with being acknowledged as having a life of her own to live and perspectives and needs that may be quite different from mine.

Commitment and Identity

Deliberate self-investment—commitment—is an important way in which friends may come partly to constitute our identities.

Commitment (which need not be formal or explicit) helps to pattern one's life, to provide it with structure and direction. A life without commitment would appear integrated only in the unlikely event that one's desires never changed and one's circumstances were always the same. And, even in this case, it would be not *deliberately* but only coincidentally unified.

We need to make commitments because we need to *focus*.[22] Without commitment, our lives will shift form and focus, varying with changing moods and circumstances and lacking anything like genuine integration.[23] Though in large measure it arises out of the interplay between circumstance and desire, a commitment to a friendship allows one at least in some measure to transcend the

21. Alpern 206–8.

22. See Chartier, *Logic of Commitment*; and Joseph Allen, *Love and Conflict: A Covenantal Model of Christian Ethics* (Nashville: Abingdon 1984) 135.

23. See O'Donovan, *Ethics as Theology* 3: 139; and Lewis B. Smedes, *Caring and Commitment: Learning to Live the Love We Promise* (San Francisco: Harper 1988) 44. Smedes's interest is in serious promises rather than with commitments of the sort with which I am concerned here—which may complement and augment promises but aren't themselves interpersonal in character.

influence of these factors, to form a self that continues over time in coherent and stable ways, and so proves recognizable to the self and to others alike.

Of course one makes commitments regarding relationships with people other than friends, as well as causes and institutions. However, because of the range and intensity of one's interactions with a close friend, a commitment to an intimate friendship is an especially significant way of shaping oneself.[24] So much of one's life is open to a close friend that one's commitment to loving and connecting with her has the capacity to affect the smallest details of one's existence. There are innumerable points at which one's life touches that of a friend. A commitment to a friendship is individualized, with distinct contours created in the relationship itself. It can thus potentially affect more of one's life than any other commitment.[25]

Because relationships with friends qua friends seem to stand outside other social roles, a commitment to a friendship can help to unify an otherwise fragmented self. If in large part there's no script for one to follow in friendship, if one's behavior is not necessitated by societal patterns and expectations, then the experience of being a friend can foster—in part because it seems to presuppose—a sense of self that endures in and through changing role definitions.

Close friends are likely to be concerned with one another in their totality, so one's identity in a close friendship will probably be a relatively comprehensive one, one with significance for one's self-understanding and action in a variety of situations. Awareness of one's identity as a friend despite changes in one's social roles may be linked with investment in the comprehensive identity acknowledged, reinforced, and to some extent reshaped in a particular friendship. The ongoing friendship, supported by commitment, may thus be a source of and support for an enduring, integrated self.

The Self as a Friend's Gift

Friends *give us* ourselves. They do so when they do the things other partners in social interaction do for us—when they teach us language and social norms. (They likely do these things more frequently and with greater impact than most other people.) And they do so when being in relation to them helps to make us

24. See McFadyen, *Call to Personhood* 256–7.

25. Allowing for the fact that a commitment to marriage can be, among other things, a commitment to friendship. See Chartier, *Public Practice, Private Law* 32.

who we are. This means that who I am is in an important sense contingent on what my friends do. I am therefore particularly vulnerable to them.

A friend can affect me quite substantially (*i*) by acting to encourage me to think and feel about myself in particular ways, to understand the world differently, to behave differently; (*ii*) by including me in her or his own story and ongoing projects; (*iii*) by willingly disengaging from me, abandoning me, or even just reducing without fully eliminating the intensity and intimacy of her connection with me; or (*iv*) by dying or becoming incapable of interacting with me because of disability or geographic separation. A friend's impact on my life, my self-conception, can prove to be, in short, profound.

The Self as God's Gift

That persons *are* in relationship—that they receive themselves from each other as gifts—highlights, in a roundabout way, a distinctive theological insight into the nature of personhood. We are constituted in and by our relationships with each other. But we are at the same time constituted in and by our relationships with God. This is so given God's identity as Creator, grounding our existence and the existence of every finite thing with which we engage, as well as God's liberating, healing, and empowering providential activity in our societies and our individual lives. In some cases, we may consciously *understand* ourselves as God's creatures. Understanding ourselves in this way may involve simply our self-understanding; or it may involve actual awareness of God's presence and activity.

Experience of God is not, somehow, another *sort* of experience in the world, as if one might have the experience of being loved by a friend at one time and have experience of God at another. We may be more or less *aware* of God at different times, just as we are more or less aware of our relationships with each other. But God is present to us universally, in and through all our experience. Whether we view ourselves this way or not, our identities are *objectively* constituted by God's action.

Friendship and Freedom

We do not choose our need for friendship, which is a basic aspect of human well-being. We do choose our friends, even if our choices are more constrained than we might suppose. However, ironically, our relatively free selection of our friends then renders important elements of our lives subject to forces outside our control.

Freedom and Social Creatureliness

Friendship is rooted in the character of humanness. Its value to us reflects the kinds of creatures we are, and our disposition to seek friendship seems to be a persistent feature of human nature.[26]

C. S. Lewis characterizes friendship as "the least instinctive, organic, biological, gregarious and necessary" of our loves.[27] However, friendship in fact seems to be both a means to and a constituent of our flourishing as persons. Friendship is both a significant mediator of the fruits of social life and a distinctive contributor to the business of humanization. We recognize friendship as itself inherently valuable, offering us a rich kind of intimacy and connection: superficial relationships won't be enough, at least for most of us.[28] And the prevalence of friendship across cultures is further evidence of its deep value.[29]

Freedom and Circumstance

Circumstances shaped by a broad range of person-to-person and person-to-environment interactions—our own and others'—determine in large measure who we will consider likely candidates for friendship.[30] Given the importance of propinquity to the process of friendship formation and maintenance, it is vital that we have regular opportunities to interact with actual and potential friends, and such opportunities are not entirely under our control. Our

26. See Lydia Denworth, *Friendship: The Evolution, Biology, and Extraordinary Power of Life's Fundamental Bond* (New York: Norton 2020).

27. Lewis, *Four Loves* 70.

28. See Michael Stocker, "Duty and Friendship: Toward a Synthesis of Gilligan's Contrastive Moral Concepts," *Women and Moral Theory*, ed. Eda Feder Kittay and Diana T. Myers (New York: Rowman 1987) 63. Of course someone might choose to focus on things other than friendship, opting to emphasize scholarship or aesthetic experience or some other kind of flourishing while ignoring friendship, and this wouldn't have to be unreasonable, as long as the person recognized the genuine loss involved and acted despite it. What *would* be unreasonable would be to pretend that friendship wasn't valuable.

29. See Brain, *Friends and Lovers*.

30. See Diogenes Allen, *Christian Belief in a Postmodern World: The Full Wealth of Conviction* (Louisville, KY: Westminster John Knox 1989) 30–48.

histories of past friendships, our other experiences, features of our environment, and so forth may significantly limit the reasons we will take to be appropriate justifications for welcoming or not welcoming someone as a friend.[31]

Choosing Friends

Friendship brings to the fore a tension between boundedness and freedom.[32] To think aptly about this tension, it's important to distinguish between the way in which friendship is *occasioned* and the means by which it is *established*. We establish friendship by choosing love and loyalty—after, often enough, simply choosing to interact with little sense of what might come next. But the interactions that lay the groundwork for the establishment of a friendship are characteristically occasioned by the disclosure of one or more personal characteristics we find (or recognize that we might find) appealing—characteristics to which we must then decide how to respond.[33]

If we are not simply creatures of our environments and our genes, then we *do* exercise freedom in our choice of friends as we do elsewhere.[34] There is the real possibility of novelty and innovation in friendship. Indeed, freedom to choose our friends is basic to friendship. Even if a friendship emerges from some other, entirely unfree, relationship (perhaps it arises between, say, two cellmates in a prison), people in such a relationship must *choose* if they are to transform it into a friendship.[35]

31. See Lewis, *Four Loves* 47.
32. See Bondi, "Fidelity and the Good Life" 15, 43.
33. Thomas, "Friendship" 220–1.
34. See, *e.g.*, Alfred R. Mele, *Free: Why Science Hasn't Disproved Free Will* (New York: Oxford University Press 2014); Austin Farrer, *The Freedom of the Will* (London: Black 1958); Carl Ginet, *On Action* (Cambridge: Cambridge University Press 1989); David Ray Griffin, *Unsnarling the World-Knot: Consciousness, Freedom, and the Mind-Body Problem* (Berkeley: University of California Press 1998); Searle, *Rationality in Action* 269–98; John Thorp, *Free Will: A Defense against Neurophysiological Determinism* (London: Routledge 1980); Joseph M. Boyle Jr., Germain Grisez, and Olaf Tollefsen, *Free Choice: A Self-Referential Argument* (Notre Dame, IN: University of Notre Dame Press 1976); Mark Balaguer, *Free Will* (Cambridge, MA: MIT Press 2014); Richard Swinburne, *Mind, Brain, and Free Will* (Oxford: Oxford University Press 2013); Robert Kane, *The Significance of Free Will* (New York: Oxford University Press 1998); and Thomas Pink, *Free Will: A Very Short Introduction* (Oxford: Oxford University Press 2004).
35. See O'Donovan, *Ethics as Theology* 3: 139.

That choice is important doesn't mean, of course, that I *must* constantly be choosing your friendship all over again without regard to the history we've shared—or even that I *can* or *should* do this. My commitment to our friendship, my promises, my invitations to reliance, and your contribution to my identity, to my selfhood—all give me continued reason to affirm our friendship. At the same time, our shared history helps to attach me to you emotionally. Perhaps ironically, my free choice to enter a friendship with you creates a history that bonds us emotionally, spiritually. So the interactions that make up our shared history weave our lives together in ways that limit my freedom both emotionally and morally. My own past choices are thus part of the background from which my present experience of friendship emerges.

This isn't the only way in which friendship constrains freedom. Friendship requires a self-investment that will render one vulnerable to a friend; and one's vulnerability may sometimes lead to inhibitions of one sort or another rooted in the fear of angering, alienating, or disappointing a friend and thus risking the relationship in which one has invested oneself.

At the same time, friendship can expand freedom. As a friend, one is liberated from expectations connected with other social roles. One is thus freed to explore and shape the self that in some measure transcends those roles.

Contingency and Vulnerability

I lack a certain kind of freedom in friendship because I lack control over background events and over my friend's behavior.

Things rarely work out as we expect them to—especially when, as in friendship, we're dealing with free human persons who can be frustratingly unpredictable. Friendships are *contingent.* They come into existence and continue to grow in unstructured, unplanned, seemingly unmanageable ways. And these contingently formed, uncontrollable relationships structure and shape and corral our lives.

The freedom of friends and the contingency of the world's history both render us vulnerable.

> Friendship . . . does not keep us warm, and doesn't protect us; on the contrary, it exposes us to the most extreme of risks: that of losing, along with our individuality, the borders that guarantee its inviolability with respect to others. The exposure that friendship entails . . . cannot be experienced without pain. Exposure is a serious threat, both for the one

> who gives, but also for the one who receives. It is precisely this risk-taking that disturbs individual closure and immunity.[36]

To accept a friend as part of oneself is to put one's identity at risk. The end of the friendship, the absence or death of the friend, can constitute the end of the self to which the friendship is integral.

Vulnerability can be frightening. And knowledge that a friend is committed to being loyal—to remaining a friend, to not using friendship as an occasion for manipulation or judgment, and to developing and exhibiting the judgment needed to avoid causing injury inadvertently—can offer only qualified reassurance. After all, even people with the best intentions make mistakes and violate moral requirements. Good friends may injure us seriously. And the very qualities that make them prone to behaving unwisely or otherwise badly may, ironically, be among the qualities responsible for making them attractive as friends in the first place.

Even when a friend behaves well, of course, we may lose her—on the battlefield, on the highway, in the hospital, in an easy chair. What will happen to a friend, and so to a friendship, lies outside our control.

As a result, friendship is a threat. And one sort of self-protective moralism might therefore regard it not only as safer but, indeed, as obligatory to resist opening oneself in friendship. The wisest course can seem to be to emulate the narrator in "I Am a Rock":

> I've built walls—
> a fortress deep and mighty
> that none may penetrate.
> I have no need of friendship; friendship causes pain.
> Its laughter and its loving I disdain.
> I am a rock.
> I am an island.
> . . .
> And a rock feels no pain;
> and an island never cries.[37]

36. Mentinis, "Friendship" 75.

37. Paul Simon, "I Am a Rock," track 11 on Paul Simon and Art Garfunkel, *Sounds of Silence*, Columbia 1966.

It is perfectly reasonable, of course—in line with one's promises, one's own self-commitments, and so forth—to choose some goods over others. We can't do everything, we can't focus everywhere, and we thus have no choice but to dive deep, to opt to seek flourishing in one way rather than another. Deciding to become a lawyer means, at least for a typical person, deciding *not* to become a concert pianist. Deciding to become a criminal lawyer means, at least for a typical person, deciding *not* to become a patent lawyer. And so forth.

There is no requirement that one assign a particular priority to any one good or kind of good in advance of the commitments and attachments that shape one's life. So one might well choose self-investment in art or scholarship, say, in a way that rules out self-investment in friendship. But, in relation to many people's goals and preferences and commitments, the good that is friendship will present itself as very valuable indeed.

To be known and loved and nourished and amused by another, to be drawn out of oneself so that one discovers one's own capacity to love a friend, can be immensely powerful—indeed, transformative. Each person's tolerance for risk is different—there is no objective fact of the matter (apart from one's own promises and commitments) about how much risk one should be willing to tolerate in a particular case. But this means that it cannot, as a general matter, be foolish or wrong to take the risks attendant on friendship. One might experience an instinctive emotional aversion to those risks, but it doesn't somehow follow that they are not worth taking. It is at any rate worth carefully considering the capacity of friendship to liberate, move, empower, and nourish rather than passing up the gift of friendship out of thoughtless fear.

Social Selfhood and Conflicts among Friends

If friendships and friends are part of who I am, then, in one sense, conflicts with friends are especially threatening. It can be easy to begin from a stance of alienation, as if detachment were the norm and connection an always difficult achievement. If selfhood is social, however, we can avoid presupposing isolation and begin from within the context of relationship.[38] In this case, because I view my friend as in a sense part of me rather than as some sort of alien creature, restoring a damaged connection with a friend will seem less like trying

38. Moravcsik, "Perils of Friendship" 148–9.

to cross a seemingly unbridgeable gap and more like returning to health after an illness.[39]

As a result, we need not feel threatened by the challenge to change, if that's what we need to do, in order to repair a relationship. After all, we may wish to change various aspects of ourselves—perhaps to cultivate and extend them. We don't always, perhaps even ordinarily, find it frightening to do this. Further, we recognize that we may not always succeed in our efforts to change—without finding the prospect of failure here paralyzing. If we view friends and friendships as in some ways aspects of ourselves, we can perfectly well understand making changes in ourselves in order to repair friendships as no less reasonable than making changes in ourselves in order to grow and expand in other ways. And we can similarly recognize that it's worth risking self-extension and self-transformation to rebuild a shattered relationship or to strengthen a weakened one even though it's possible we might not succeed.[40] Seeing ourselves as relational helps us overcome barriers to making our friendships work.

Friendship and Providence

A friendship is always a gift. We do not compel the presence of our friends in our lives, and we would not wish to do so if we could. The friend enters my life unbidden. We know, of course, that various personal and situational factors *occasion* friendship, and yet we still believe that it is not simply an ineluctable product of the convergence of these factors. But can we say more than this? Can we say that a friendship is a gift given not simply by my friend, or by random circumstances, but by God?

Have We Chosen Our Friends?

Austin Farrer tells the story of a "close acquaintance" named Phillip, who ultimately killed himself. Farrer asserts of Phillip, "I should say as a Christian that God had given him to me for a friend."[41] Lewis gives particularly forceful expression to the notion that people we love and who love us are God's gifts. In friendship, he says,

39. Moravcsik 148.
40. Moravcsik 149.
41. Austin Farrer, *The Brink of Mystery*, ed. Charles Conti (London: SPCK 1976) 58.

> we think we have chosen our peers. In reality . . . any [number] of . . . [seeming] chances might have kept us apart. But, for a Christian, there are, strictly speaking, no chances. A secret Master of Ceremonies has been at work. Christ . . . can truly say to every group of Christian friends "You have not chosen one another but I have chosen you for one another." . . . At this feast it is He who has spread the board and it is He who has chosen the guests.[42]

What are we to make of such claims? It is not clear that we can say as confidently as Lewis does that from a Christian perspective, or in the life of a Christian, "there are, strictly speaking, no chances." To deny the reality of the chance and the contingent is to say that the world isn't really *creation* at all, because it exhibits no genuine freedom of its own. It is to paint a picture of the world such that there would be, for God, no difference between creating it and just imagining it, for it would have no capacity to be a source of genuine novelty.

Chance need not, in this context, mean utter randomness; we do not know whether any event is completely unaffected by its antecedents as it would need to be in order to qualify as utterly random. Chance here is simply the confluence of two relatively uncoordinated streams of activity—the stories of two friends who discover each other, surprised and delighted by an outcome they could not have predicted. Are there chances—instances of genuine indeterminacy—in this sense, or is an overruling providence able to guide and direct our social interactions so successfully that God can ensure that particular friendships are formed and thus that we are graced with the love of particular friends?

Thinking about Divine Action

To make sense of God's role in the formation of friendships, we need to think about the character of divine action in the world more generally. It's important to emphasize that (*i*) we speak of God as personal as a way of stressing divine freedom and love. And to predicate freedom and love of God is to emphasize that God is responsive to particular events in the world. A free God can respond creatively to what occurs in the world, and a loving God will attend to the features of each creaturely situation because every constituent of the creation is loved by God for its own sake. Thus, in short, divine action is particular.

42. Lewis, *Four Loves* 104–5.

(*ii*) Divine action is constrained. It occurs in and through ordinary natural processes and creaturely actions. A creation without freedom isn't *real*; it's a divine puppet show. God's action in relation to a genuinely real, and so genuinely free, creation is necessarily constrained. God's action takes place within the limits set by the regularities of the physical world and the freedom of creatures.[43]

It is only if we understand divine action as constrained that we can offer a remotely plausible account of the loss and wrongdoing in our world. If God were to be expected capriciously to rearrange the furniture of the world, we might expect that criminals' handguns would dissolve into thin air, cancerous tumors would never come into being, no one would ever have heard of earthquakes, and hateful thoughts would never enter anyone's consciousness. But it's clear that we live in a world in which loss and destruction aren't, in fact, prevented.

(*iii*) Divine action is characteristically indiscernible as such. God will be at work in every event in the creaturely world, but it doesn't follow that we can be

43. See John B. Cobb Jr., "Natural Causality and Divine Action," *God's Activity in the World: The Contemporary Problem*, ed. Owen C. Thomas, AAR Studies in Religion 31 (Chico, CA: Scholars 1983) 101–16; Arthur Peacocke, "God's Interaction with the World," *All That Is: A Naturalistic Faith for the Twenty-First Century*, ed. Philip Clayton (Minneapolis: Fortress 2007) 45–7; Arthur Peacocke, *Theology for a Scientific Age: Being and Becoming, Natural and Divine* (Oxford: Blackwell 1990) 159–63; Austin Farrer, *Faith and Speculation: An Essay in Philosophical Theology* (Edinburgh: Clark 1967) 60–7; Austin Farrer, *Saving Belief: A Discussion of Essentials* (London: Hodder 1964) 37–83; Brian Hebblethwaite and Edward Henderson, eds., *Divine Action: Studies Inspired by the Philosophical Theology of Austin Farrer* (Edinburgh: Clark 1990); Brian Hebblethwaite, "Providence and Divine Action," *Religious Studies* 14 (1978): 223–36; Brian Hebblethwaite, *Evil, Suffering and Religion* (London: SPCK 2000); David Ray Griffin, *A Process Christology* (Lanham, MD: University Press of America 1990) 206–16; Diogenes Allen, *Christian Belief in a Postmodern World: The Full Wealth of Conviction* (Louisville, KY: Westminster John Knox 1989) 165–81; John R. Lucas, *Freedom and Grace* (London: SPCK 1976); Keith Ward, *Divine Action* (London: Collins 1989) 119–69; Langdon Gilkey, *Reaping the Whirlwind: A Christian Interpretation of History* (New York: Crossroad-Seabury 1976) 303–6; Philip Clayton, *God and Contemporary Science* (Edinburgh: Edinburgh University Press 1997) 188–269; Thomas F. Tracy, ed., *The God Who Acts: Philosophical and Theological Explorations* (University Park: Pennsylvania State University Press 1994); Thomas Jay Oord, *God Can't: How to Believe in God and Love after Tragedy, Abuse, and Other Evils* (Grasmere, ID: SacraSage 2019); Timothy Gorringe, *God's Theatre: A Theology of Providence* (London: SCM 1991); Vincent Brümmer, "Farrer, Wiles and the Causal Joint," *Modern Theology* 8.1 (Jan. 1992): 1–14; and Vincent Brümmer, *What Are We Doing When We Pray? A Philosophical Inquiry* (London: SCM 1984) 60–73.

sure what goals God is pursuing or what means God is using to pursue them: "The hand of God is perfectly hidden."[44]

The Christian must affirm "that the world has meaning and purpose." But she must—if she "takes with full seriousness the implication of the claim . . . that the paradigm of divine action in the world is the passion of the Lord's anointed"—be skeptical of the notion "that this meaning and purpose may—whether in respect of particular events or of large-scale patterns in human history—be straightforwardly . . . 'read off' our individual or group experience."[45]

We may be able to talk at a general level about the nature of God's purposes in the world and to discern provisionally how given sequences of events might contribute to or reflect the achievement of those purposes. (We might think of the abolition of the transatlantic slave trade, for instance, as an outworking of providence because of the conviction that God is love and seeks to liberate creatures from oppression.) But we cannot presume to know what God is doing in a particular situation with anything like serene confidence. We postulate divine action as a result of our understanding of God; we will not, at least ordinarily, be able to treat providence as a necessary a posteriori explanation for individual occurrences in nature and history.

How Friendship Can Be a Gift of Grace

Given this picture of divine action, there are several things we can say about friendships as divine gifts.

(*i*) Friendship as a structure or pattern of relation is a divine gift. Our capacity, fitness, and desire for friendship result from our biological, social, and psychological characteristics.[46] And these characteristics are themselves reflections of God's general creative activity.[47] Insofar as divine activity is loving, it seeks the good, the flourishing, the fulfillment, of creatures. Thus, God may be understood as inspiring us to respond to and seek relationships, activities, and experiences that make for flourishing and fulfillment. Even, therefore, if God

44. Austin Farrer, *Love Almighty and Ills Unlimited* (London: Collins 1956) 95.

45. Nicholas Lash, "These Things Were Here, and but the Beholder Wanting," *Theology on Dover Beach* (London: Darton 1979) 182.

46. See Denworth, *Friendship*.

47. See Karl Rahner, *Foundations of Christian Faith: An Introduction to the Idea of Christianity*, trans. William V. Dych (New York: Crossroad 1978) 88–9.

has not specifically intended and fostered the formation of a specific friendship, God will have intended and fostered the disposition that inclines one to appreciate and experience this particular good.

(*ii*) Anything which occurs in the created order that is in accordance with God's purposes can be ascribed to God. Divine creative agency is a necessary condition of every event. But, when some action by a person is a necessary condition for an event's occurrence, we typically view her as responsible for the event, provided she intended the event to occur rather than simply viewing it as an unintended by-product of her action. Any divine decision will make some events more likely while rendering others less likely. God is aware of the possible consequences of every divine decision. In turn, God intends the occurrence of the good consequences facilitated by each decision. We can thus be thankful to God for any event we have reason to believe is a good one—and thus, in particular, for the formation of a friendship.[48]

(*iii*) Creaturely freedom and the integrity of the natural world significantly constrain what God can do in history. Nonetheless, God can challenge us by, in effect, prompting us to acknowledge all those possibilities of flourishing and fulfillment it would be reasonable for us to choose in a given situation if we had access to all of the relevant information. These might in some cases include potential friendships, even if also quite different goods, incapable of being pursued at the same time as friendships, that might be on offer simultaneously. There may be times when God's attracting, inspiring presence draws us beyond our current horizons and enables us to discern the potential value of a new relationship or gain a deepened appreciation for the significance of a seemingly commonplace one in which one is already a participant. And God's noncoercive influence may lead to confluences of circumstances such that one discovers or rediscovers friends.

We do not, I think, want any more than this to be true. We do not want God to stage-manage the universe in such a way that our friendships come into being as necessary consequences of divine choice. For if our friendships are divine gifts in the sense that God has somehow predestined them, then they cease to be gifts on the human level. What seems like the free self-offering of a friend would be, in fact, the outcome of an intricate divine plan that has overridden her freedom and mine. And thus the very evocative power of a putative self-gift, the surprise and delight that come with the realization that the other has chosen *me*, evaporates.

48. Brümmer, "Joint" 9–11.

Whatever the value of metaphorical language about friendship as a miracle, no authentic friendship could be brought about by miracle, could be created de novo. A history of interactions and desires and choices is crucial to the integrity of a friendship, and a friendship could not be brought into being by divine fiat, minus this history, without falsifying it irreparably. Miraculously creating feelings and commitments would rob those feelings and commitments of authenticity, and so of significance. By contrast, by altering the biochemistry of a person's brain, by making her see illusions, by making her hear nonexistent sounds, by altering her priorities or sensitivities, God would be bypassing the historical processes intrinsic to the formation of an authentic friendship. A necessitated love is no love at all.

On the basis of a general confidence in friendship's value and God's love—as well as our awareness of the possibility of particular, if constrained, divine action in the world—we can thank God for our friends as gifts of grace. Treasuring our friends in this way, we are loyal to them—for their sakes and for our own. But people sometimes see fidelity in friendship as an alien imposition on an essentially unstructured, free-form relationship. I will argue in chapter 3, however, that it makes sense to talk about obligations to our friends.

3
Obligations

We often instinctively assume that we have obligations to our friends even as we also feel, perhaps, that talk of obligation is out of place in the context of friendship—that we shouldn't allow our relationships with our friends to be structured by obligations or that talk of obligation in friendship makes no sense. In fact, however, friendship is rooted in and sustained by obligation.

I begin this chapter by suggesting that a moral dimension is integral to friendship. I emphasize the importance of obligation in friendship. Then, I challenge the contention that there could in principle be no special obligations to friends along with the notion that concern with obligation is inconsistent with the inherent spontaneity of friendship. I go on to explain why accepting obligations to friends need not involve or lead to undue restraints on our autonomy. Recognizing obligations to friends is, I suggest, a valuable way of acknowledging, expressing, and reinforcing our loyalty to them and safeguarding our connections with them.

A Presumption of Obligation

It seems to most of us that we have obligations to our friends and with respect to our friendships. Obligation helps to enable our friends to trust us. We can, in fact, identify generally assumed obligations to friends. And there are responses to the idea that we don't have obligations at all.

The Importance of Obligation

For most of us, how we behave in friendship is not simply a matter of our impulses and desires. We regard our friends as obligated to treat us in particular ways. And we take ourselves to have obligations to our friends and with respect to our friendships. Loving them, we want them to be able to count on us; we want to give them the gift of reliability, a gift we want them to give us.

If reliability is to be about more than how we or they happen to feel, it must be embodied in *obligations*—including obligations derived from commitments and ones created by promises and by trust-inviting patterns of behavior. We might even think of obligations as essential to making friendship what it is, with the result that a relationship not safeguarded by and incorporating obligations wouldn't really be recognizable as a friendship at all.[1]

Expected Obligations

Individual friends' expectations of each other emerge in the course of histories of interaction in which assumptions are modified and reinforced.[2] However, people do seem to treat at least some general obligations related to friendship as applying relatively consistently.[3] In relationships with friends of all sorts, you should

- avoid being jealous or critical of their other relationships,
- avoid pestering them,
- be tolerant of their other friends,
- decline to criticize them in public,
- keep safe the confidences they've entrusted to you,
- repay debts and favors, and
- respect their privacy.

In relationships with closer friends, you should

1. See Annis, "Meaning, Value, and Duties" 352 (arguing that our obligations to our friends are constitutive of our friendships).
2. Jacqueline Wiseman, "Friendship: Bonds and Binds in a Voluntary Relationship," *Journal of Personal and Social Relationships* 3.2 (June 1986): 196.
3. These rules are identified by Argyle and Henderson, "Rules of Friendship" 211–37.

- attempt to make them happy while in their company;
- care for them when they're ill;
- embrace intimate connection by engaging in self-disclosure, discussing such topics as sexuality and death, expressing anger, and sharing personal news;
- provide emotional support;
- share news of your successes;
- stand up for them in their absence;
- trust and confide in them; and
- volunteer to help them in times of need.[4]

What about Nihilism?

Maybe we're mistaken in thinking that these rules matter. Perhaps there are no obligations to friends or with respect to our friendships because there are no obligations at all. Maybe what we think of as correct or incorrect moral judgments are just ultimately capricious choices, reflections of our emotional attitudes, or delusions foisted on us by our cultures or our genes. The view that this is the case, moral nihilism, poses powerful challenges to morality in general. There is no knockdown refutation of moral nihilism, but there are certainly reasons not to embrace it.

(*i*) Moral nihilism doesn't fit especially well with our own experience of confronting moral problems that seem to have correct answers (including our experience of confronting issues arising in connection with what we take to be obligations to our friends). We experience obligations as real and as *mattering*.

(*ii*) We *can* demonstrably assess and act on *reasons*, including moral reasons, that don't present themselves as expressions of attitudes or as arbitrary posits.[5]

4. Argyle and Henderson 230–5.

5. See, *e.g*, Alasdair MacIntyre, *Ethics in the Conflicts of Modernity* (Cambridge: Cambridge University Press 2016); Annette Bryson, "Non-inflationary Realism about Morality: Language, Metaphysics, and Truth" (PhD diss., University of Michigan 2017); David Ray Griffin, *Process Theology: On Postmodernism, Morality, Pluralism, Eschatology, and Demonic Evil* (Anoka, MN: Process Century 2017) 41–67; Griffin, *Reenchantment without Supernaturalism* 285–319; David Wiggins, *Ethics: Twelve Lectures on the Philosophy of Morality* (Cambridge, MA: Harvard University Press 2006) 317–81; Hilary Putnam, *The Collapse of the Fact-Value Dichotomy and Other Essays* (Cambridge, MA: Harvard University Press 2002); Hilary Putnam, "Pragmatism and Moral Objectivity," *Words and Life*, ed. James Conant (Cambridge, MA: Harvard University Press 1994) 151–81; John Finnis, *Fundamentals of Ethics* (Oxford: Clarendon-Oxford University Press 1983) 56–79; Keith Ward, *Ethics and*

(*iii*) Versions of moral nihilism often seem dependent on epistemological and metaphysical assumptions we don't need to endorse. These include such suppositions as that theism isn't correct and that moral propositions could be true only if they were *made* true by Platonic universals or the like—and that there are no such things.

(*iv*) Moral nihilism seems to imply that, since moral norms are indefensible, epistemic norms—norms about truth, judgment, probability, even logic itself—must be indefensible, too. And, at least for many people, that seems like a very high price to pay for moral nihilism, not least because it raises questions about our ability to evaluate arguments for moral nihilism itself.[6]

Promises, Institutions, Intuitions, and Obligations

Even if there are obligations, there might be no obligations to friends qua friends. In the contemporary West, friendship is not a clearly structured institution, being a friend is not a defined institutional role, and relationships between friends aren't ordinarily shaped by explicit agreements. As a result, someone might wonder whether we're right to think that friends have obligations to each other.

Rejecting Obligation

Dan Passell, for instance, seeks to explain away our perceived obligations to friends.[7] He contends that friendship is "non-institutional" and that there are consequently "no rules or practices implied in friendship."[8] He argues that a

Christianity (London: Allen 1970); Keith Ward, *Morality, Autonomy, and God* (London: Oneworld 2013); Nathan Nobis, "Truth in Ethics and Epistemology: A Defense of Normative Realism" (PhD diss., University of Rochester 2004); Philippa Foot, *Natural Goodness* (Oxford: Clarendon-Oxford University Press 2001); Ralph Wedgwood, *The Nature of Normativity* (Oxford: Clarendon-Oxford University Press 2007); Renford Bambrough, *Moral Scepticism and Moral Knowledge* (Atlantic Highlands, NJ: Humanities 1979); Russ Shafer-Landau, *Moral Realism: A Defence* (Oxford: Clarendon-Oxford University Press 2003); T. M. Scanlon, *Being Realistic about Reasons* (New York: Oxford University Press 2014); and Terence Cuneo, *The Normative Web: An Argument for Moral Realism* (New York: Oxford University Press 2007).

6. See Nobis, "Truth in Ethics"; and Cuneo, *Normative Web*.

7. Dan Passell, "Friends," *Journal of Value Inquiry* 14.1 (1980): 1–6. Passell returned to this issue in "Duties to Friends," *Journal of Value Inquiry* 25.5 (April 1991): 161-5. I did not become aware of his later article until after submitting the manuscript of *Understanding Friendship* to Fortress, and I have not addressed its arguments here.

8. Passell 4.

sense of obligation to friends arises "from *feelings* of obligation which are not necessarily connected to real obligations." And he attempts to explain the felt need to live up to a friend's expectations (by, *e.g.*, taking a bridge game seriously) in completely nonmoral terms by calling attention to feelings of sympathy and prudence:

> You know . . . what a disappointment it is when your partner lets you down. You find it natural to project your own feelings onto him. . . . As you don't want him to spoil your fun, you feel . . . that he wouldn't want you to spoil his. More than this, you might wonder if the incident wouldn't cause him to draw back from you; to find it more difficult to devote himself wholeheartedly to activities with you, much as you might be, should the situation be reversed, with him.[9]

Thus, he maintains, we suppose that we have obligations to friends because "of sympathetic feelings we have for our friends." And such feelings could not serve as the bases of obligation, since it is not feelings but, rather, objective "circumstances [which] determine obligations."[10]

Intuitions and Special Duties

Passell offers three examples which he believes "are conclusive" in establishing the thesis that there "are no special duties to friends."[11]

Consider the case of a onetime friend who appears on one's doorstep asking for help. Passell sharpens the example by proposing that one only discovers at the moment of encounter that one no longer regards the other as one's friend. Because friendship is not institutional, because it lacks "essential rules or procedures," the relationship with the ex-friend must be governed by "noninstitutional duties," all of which are "wider in scope than friendship." Of course, if there is a noninstitutional duty to offer assistance in circumstances like those in which one finds oneself when confronting one's friend, one has a duty to assist anyone similarly situated, and not merely a friend.[12]

9. Passell 4–5.
10. Passell 5.
11. Passell 1.
12. Passell 5–6.

The second case involves a similar doorstep encounter, this time one in which an apparent stranger asks for one's aid, is refused it, and then removes a disguise, which reveals him as a friend. Passell asks, "Has he in the process also revealed to you an obligation to meet his need? Hardly."[13]

Finally, he suggests a further example: one wonders whether to tell a friend about a medical report that indicates that one has a serious heart condition. Fear and anguish about revealing this calamity compete with the recognition that one's friend would desire and expect to be informed. According to Passell, "The question is, do you have an obligation to tell him anyhow?" He replies, "I think that the answer is simply, no. You are free to tell him or not."[14]

Friendship as Noninstitutional?

Basic to Passell's case is the notion that friendship is noninstitutional. But it's not obvious that we should agree that friendship has no institutional character.

Our tendency to avoid giving formal recognition to friendship is in striking contrast to practices in other societies. Much more structure is evident in friendship in many other cultures.[15] For many people, friendship's importance requires that it be ceremonialized and publicly acknowledged,[16] as it may be among children even when not among adults.[17] That friendship isn't a *formal* role or institution doesn't mean it has no distinguishable character. Its character is *tacit*, "a kind of institutionalized non-institution," an "interstitial institution."[18] And the existence of widely shared standards of behavior for friends helps to give friendship an institutional character.[19]

That friendship is a *tacit* institution can be a source of complication, of course, since friends may not agree regarding the nature, extent, or significance of their obligations to each other—even while failing to realize that they aren't

13. Passell 6.
14. Passell 6.
15. Horst Hutter, *Politics as Friendship: The Origins of Classical Notions of Politics in the Theory and Practice of Friendship* (Waterloo, ON: Wilfrid Laurier University Press 1978) 8.
16. Brain, *Friends and Lovers* 18–19, 38.
17. Brain 22–4.
18. Paine, "Exploratory Analysis" 128; Suttles, "Friendship" 98.
19. See Dorothy Emmet, *Rules, Roles and Relations* (London: Macmillan 1966) 169–70.

on the same page.[20] But careful attention to patterns of behavior and explicit conversation can reduce ambiguity and align friends' expectations.

Provided friendship has sufficient structure to qualify as a tacit institution, to shape people's expectations of themselves and others and to invite particular kinds of reliance, Passell's argument, which assumes that duties are either institutional or general,[21] would be blunted from the start. There is, indeed, arguably enough definition to friendship for duties to friends to qualify as institutional.

Even if friendship in general isn't a socially acknowledged institution, however, a particular set of friends could structure their relationship using explicit promises. They could also generate morally claimable obligations by interacting with each other in consistent, predictable ways that invited each one to rely on the other.

Passell could argue that the only institutional duties were ones embodied in explicit, formally structured institutions. He suggests that such institutions are typically contractual (he offers no alternative examples). Of course, the obligations we typically care about most in marriage aren't contractually specified. The same is true of parents' obligations to children and children's obligations to parents.

Most people are even more confident that there are special obligations to spouses, parents, and children than they are that there are obligations to friends. If Passell's argument implies that there are not, a reductio ad absurdum might be waiting in the wings.

If there are, however, then, since duties to spouses, parents, and children aren't defined by contracts or explicit institutional roles, they must—if Passell is right that there are only institutional and general moral requirements—be derivable from general moral requirements. And if obligations to parents, spouses, and children can be derived from general moral requirements, it's unclear why obligations to friends couldn't be as well.

Alternatively, we might think that institutional norms need not be formal and explicit. Such norms could be sufficiently stable and definite for participants to adhere to them in much the way people who have never studied grammar, and might even be unable to read, can follow grammatical rules.

20. See Haapanen, "Close Friendship" 6, 97; Wiseman, "Friendship" 203–4; and Becker, "Phenomenological Explication" 140, 207.

21. Passell, "Friends" 5–6.

Passell's Intuitions

What about Passell's three examples?

I think his conclusion in the first case—that a general duty of benevolence requires help to the former friend—is probably correct. However, granting that this is the case doesn't tell us whether there might be specific duties to people who are current rather than former friends.

The next case involves the disguised friend who asks for assistance, is refused it, and then reveals himself to be a friend. In the process of revealing his identity, has this friend "also revealed to you an obligation"? Passell peremptorily answers, "Hardly." But I doubt many friends would share his intuition. And they would surely be able to support their own intuition by maintaining that friendship was a tacit institution with sufficient definition to yield obligations or that special duties to friends could be derived from more general obligations. (Since Passell hasn't shown that there aren't special duties independent of general ones—he's only mapped out an account of duties designed to render special ones superfluous—they could also appeal to underived special duties. Perhaps they might argue that such duties explained our intuitions in this case better than alternatives.)

Passell judges that no moral claim arises apart from a duty of general beneficence. But why should we think this? It's easy to imagine multiple schemes of general moral requirements from which robust special duties could be seen to flow. It's not enough to *assert* that the only duty to others is a duty of general beneficence.

In addition, if no moral force attaches to our relations with our friends, then trust, which Passell grants is integral to friendship, seems out of place. If I can only trust my friend when she happens to feel trustworthy, if I'm not entitled to rely on her *consistently*, then I can't really trust her at all.

Are we morally obligated to involve our friends in our private lives when doing so might be challenging, embarrassing, or likely to expose us to thoughts and feelings we might like to avoid? In connection with his third example, Passell writes, "I think that the answer is simply, no." But, if the answer is "No," it is not *simply* so. Again, many friends will have intuitions that are, at minimum, more complex than Passell's. We might well think that at least some friends in some situations *were* entitled to some details regarding our otherwise private lives. And, again, we might provide justifications rooted in some combination of general moral requirements and institutional requirements of one sort or another—or, again, for all Passell has shown us, in independent special moral requirements.

Passell has provided no warrant for the view that it would make no moral difference whether one informed one's friend of one's illness. He can't simply appeal to the conclusion he reached after developing his first example—that the only duties to friends are the same as the duties one has to everyone else. After all, that's precisely what is at issue. His first examples don't establish that conclusion, and his later examples don't render it any more intuitively plausible.

In short, Passell hasn't established that there are no obligations to friends qua friends. Many friends won't share his intuitions regarding his thought experiments. And he's given us no good reason to accept his intuitions, in any case. Special obligations to friends should have the same kinds of roots as obligations to spouses, parents, and children: they might flow from general or institution-specific requirements. Or they might depend on independent requirements particular to friendship.

Obligation and Spontaneity

Perhaps, then, there *are* obligations to friends. But perhaps acting on these obligations as obligations is inconsistent with the inner demands of friendship itself. In this case, obligations to friends can't do the work I've suggested it's crucial they do.

Trust is an important aspect of friendship, and trustworthiness must be a matter of obligation. It can't be a function of my feelings, desires, or goals, since these can change. If I want my friends to be able to trust me, they must be able to trust me even when I might prefer not to be trustworthy. But perhaps acting out of obligation is incompatible with acting out of friendship.

We might think that, as a friend, I need not only to behave well but also to behave well in the right way, for the right reasons.[22] To act out of friendship, I need to act out of immediate, direct concern for my friend and for our relationship, not simply in order to meet an obligation.[23] And to act like this, we might suppose, is to act in a way marked by "an essential element of spontaneity, itself

22. Gabriel Marcel, *Creative Fidelity*, trans. Robert Rosthal (New York: Crossroad 1982) 152. I refer in the text to a generic objector rather than to Marcel; I don't want to saddle Marcel with my objector's contentions or to mischaracterize Marcel's own interpretation of or attempted solution to the problem.

23. Marcel 154–5.

radically independent of the will."[24] But of course I cannot *promise* to behave spontaneously; and, when I acknowledge and adhere to an obligation as such, I am certainly not behaving spontaneously. So perhaps there could not, in principle, be an obligation to be faithful to a friend.[25]

Suppose you've been hospitalized. I've told you of my plan to visit you on a certain day. And suppose that, on the only day I am able to visit, I am confronted by an unexpected opportunity to spend my free time with an intensely desirable stranger. I want to be with this stranger. However, knowing what it means to be your friend, reaffirming my commitment to our friendship, I go to the hospital instead.

On the objection I've envisioned, my visit is not really an act of friendship at all but an act of duty, and the two are incompatible. My action fails to have the key characteristic of an action "out of friendship," on the assumption that such an act must be rooted in spontaneous feeling.

We don't need to accept this requirement. Spontaneous feeling is not essential for fidelity. If I go to see you while you're hospitalized simply because I fear divine judgment, then I'm not, indeed, being a genuine friend. But if I go because I am committed to our friendship, because connecting with and caring for you is a priority I have embraced, even though I feel wistful about the need to postpone my romantic getaway, I am still, certainly, acting as a friend. My fidelity is genuine. I am doing what friends do as a matter of course. I may feel ambivalent, but I'm acting freely out of an underlying orientation that I've chosen to make more definitive of who I am than my feelings of desire or regret.

Given that people really do think that friends should adhere to rules, they cannot reasonably assume that adherence to these rules can or should always be a matter of spontaneity. Any thoughtful person will recognize that there's no necessary coincidence between what a rule dictates and what I feel like doing. To affirm the existence of the rules, therefore, is to acknowledge that I may sometimes need to act for a friend, out of friendship, in a way that's not spontaneous.

Suppose roles were reversed. I would want you, as my friend, to act out of such a basic orientation toward me and toward our friendship. I would likely feel deprived if you instead acted out of generically moral or narrowly self-interested reasons. But acting out of a genuine commitment to our friendship, or out of a genuine focus on me rooted in a promise or in invited reliance, is

24. Marcel 155.
25. Marcel 157.

sufficient to render your behavior authentic. I wouldn't assume that it had to be prompted or accompanied by any particular feeling.

The fact that an action aims at the good of a friend qua friend or at the nourishment of the friendship itself is sufficient to render the action intelligible and, at least in many cases, justified. Related factors—projects shared with the friend, common attitudes and convictions—can also serve to warrant the choices someone makes by a friend qua friend.[26] And all of these factors can quite satisfactorily *explain* those choices as well; particular feelings, spontaneous or otherwise, aren't essential.

Valuing the particularity of the other—in this case, perhaps, indeed, quite spontaneously—provides a reason for *entering* into a relationship with a friend. The shape taken by that relationship in this particular case is a function to some extent by the inner demands of interpersonal love, to some extent of the friends' acceptance of social expectations regarding friendship, and to some extent of the friends' own commitments and promises. Once I am immersed in that relationship, the relationship itself provides me with reasons for action, and, in virtue of taking up these reasons, I act out of friendship. Accepting those reasons is enough to make my action authentic, however I happen to feel.[27]

My friend herself and my friendship with her are valuable to me precisely in virtue of my commitment regarding our friendship. My friend and our friendship are *also* valuable to me because of my promises to her, because of my implicit or explicit invitations to her to rely on me, because of my participation in the history of interaction that connects me with her, and because of the role of my friend, our friendship, or both in constituting my identity. I have *established* the place of my friend and our friendship in my life, making it a priority, in these ways.

Commitments, promises, and attachments can help shape affective responses. Thus, if I commit to a friendship, and if my psyche is in good working order, recognizing the value of my friend and of our friendship will be accompanied by feelings, impulses, attitudes that will signal the importance I've given to this relationship. But I can still be a loyal, faithful friend even if my feelings have been blocked or suppressed or redirected for one reason or another. I can still act out of my chosen valuation of you and of our friendship when I

26. Michael Stocker, "Values and Purposes: The Limits of Teleology and the Ends of Friendship," *Journal of Philosophy* 78.12 (Dec. 1981): 763; cp. Daly, "Morality of Human Nature" 76.
27. For a discussion of similar issues in the context of romantic love and marriage, see Chartier, *Public Practice, Private Law* 33–41, 149–52.

choose to visit you in the hospital rather than to lose myself in a romantic idyll. In so doing, I act out of friendship.[28]

Obligation and Autonomy

It may be reasonable to affirm the reality of obligation, the reality of obligation *in friendship*, and the consistency between our understanding of friendship on the one hand and appealing to and acting out of obligation in friendship on the other. However, we may still wonder whether it is *wise* to shoulder obligations in friendship.

We may enjoy imagining that friendship is a relationship whose contours we create, at our own discretion, on an ongoing basis.[29] We may be tempted to build total freedom into our account of friendship. We may believe that friendship allows us to experience *both* community *and* autonomy at the same time.[30]

As a result, we may worry that accepting obligations to friends and with respect to our friendships will constrain our freedom and self-expression.[31] If we think obligations aren't essential to friendship, we may wonder whether the kind of friendship that does incorporate obligations is worth entering. If we think that obligations help to constitute friendship, we may wonder whether becoming a friend is worthwhile, given the need to accept such obligations. And we may worry that friends themselves will take advantage of our loyalty. But choosing limits on our autonomy is perfectly reasonable, and being a friend doesn't have to mean being bullied or manipulated.

How Much Freedom Do We Want in Friendship?

A conception of friendship as free of obligation seems difficult to square with the loyalty we also want to give and receive.

28. Emotions are not feelings. They are judgments, evaluative recognitions—recognitions of meaning or value. Ordinarily, they are accompanied and signaled by sensations. But they "can be *defined* in terms of these evaluative recognitions alone." Martha C. Nussbaum, *Upheavals of Thought: The Intelligence of Emotions* (Cambridge: Cambridge University Press 2001) 64 (my italics). Another way to think about this might be to say that an emotion presupposes or prompts or embodies an evaluation, but it's the evaluation that's ultimately decisive, not the signal provided by the emotion.

29. See Haapanen, "Close Friendship" 2, 5–6.

30. See Haapanen xii, 2, 36.

31. See Haapanen 178.

In friendship, we need reliability embodied in obligation precisely because friendship matters, because it offers us so much, because it invites so much vulnerability.[32] We often give friendship the importance we do in our lives in and through the acceptance of such obligations. And we allow ourselves to be vulnerable to our friends precisely because of the shelter provided by these obligations.

If we are always free, then we are always free to abandon our friends or to treat our relationships with them as relatively unimportant. We might try to resolve the tension by assuming that we will, in fact, always happen to feel inclined to be loyal, so that loyalty will always be an expression of our freedom. We might always choose to stay connected with our friends because we always happen to want to do so. It's not clear, though, why we should expect our feelings and desires to be constant (or why, even if something happened to cause them to be, that should be decisive for our choices). And assuming that they will be constant seems unrealistic.

We understand, however, that we will experience varying desires, that we will confront different possible goods in different situations, including goods incompatible with loyalty to our friends. If friendship *is* to involve loyalty, if we are to be trustworthy friends, then we will need to act in accordance with obligations that may run counter to our impulses, our desires, or our other priorities. There is an important sense in which we cannot "gain the benefits of a close-knit family-like community and still retain a maximum of personal freedom and autonomy."[33] Contrary to what we might hope, we can't experience the "personal satisfaction [that friendship promises] without having to work very hard for it, indeed, having to 'think' about it."[34] We need obligations to make friendship work.

Chosen Limits on Freedom

Obligations to friends and with respect to friendships narrow the options we may reasonably select. But friendship's implications for autonomy aren't different in kind from the implications for autonomy of choosing life paths and acknowledging circumstances more generally. Anything we do, any choice we

32. See Wiseman, "Friendship" 193.

33. Haapanen, "Close Friendship" 36–7.

34. Haapanen 39.

make, affects the range of possibilities we confront and the array of considerations favoring or disfavoring particular actions.

We obviously have obligations, in particular, to all sorts of people who are not friends, with respect to all sorts of relationships that are not friendships.[35] We do not suddenly assume obligations when we enter the world of friendship after previously having had none. And we have *self-assumed* obligations quite apart from those that accompany, sustain, or help to constitute friendship—obligations assumed through promises, by means of commitments, in connection with invited or created vulnerability,[36] through the acceptance of professional roles, and so forth. So the special subclass of *chosen* obligations is not unique to friendship either. There is no reason to be concerned *especially* about autonomy where friendship is concerned.

Perhaps one might think, however, that, with so many other obligations constraining one's freedom, it made sense to avoid accepting *further* obligations by becoming a friend. If one *is* concerned in this way, surely it should make a difference that one accepts friendship's constraints as freely as, probably more freely than, one does in the case of any other relationship. More than that, however, it should matter that accepting obligations to friends and with respect to friendships is part and parcel of friendship, which depends on these obligations.

By choosing to be someone's friend, you've ruled out pursuing or realizing certain goods that might otherwise be options for you, at least in certain ways (whether you know it or not). But committing to friendship makes possible your participation in a range of goods otherwise not available to you. The relevant goods are qualitatively different, so there's no basis for pretending that the ones you could realize absent the constraints flowing from a given friendship somehow outweigh the ones you can realize by becoming a particular person's friend. The goods are simply distinct, and it's up to you to choose—not to choose from moment to moment, in a vacuum, but to commit to one or another configuration of priorities and affections and to realize the goods made possible by the path you've chosen.

35. I realize that some people use the word *obligation* only in connection with promises and the like, just as some people refer to *duties* only in connection with institutional roles. But I think standard usage treats these terms as semantically capacious.

36. See Robert E. Goodin, *Protecting the Vulnerable: A Reanalysis of Our Social Responsibilities* (Chicago: University of Chicago Press 1985).

Power Struggles with Friends

Choosing loyalty to friends makes us vulnerable to them. We might worry not only that our obligations to our friends might limit our options but also that our friends themselves might try to do so, that choosing to become and remain friends with people inclined to do this could pose ongoing risks to our freedom.

Friends can, indeed, actively seek to limit each other's autonomy. They may seek to do so on paternalistic grounds—because they find it easier to bully and manipulate than to persuade. They may do so out of personal insecurities of various sorts, perhaps seeking validation for their own choices by pushing their friends to make similar decisions. Or they may do so on the basis of unfair preferences for their own plans and projects, their own well-being—or even out of (presumably unacknowledged) jealousy or hostility.

Friends are emotionally and cognitively imperfect. They often do not see themselves or manage their own emotions skillfully. They sometimes choose unreasonably, perhaps very unreasonably. This is part of what it is to be a finite, fallible, sinful human being. Sometimes, a friend's moral limitations manifest themselves in betrayal, neglect, or mean-spiritedness. But someone's limitations can sometimes come to expression in attempts to control a friend, attempts that can, indeed, threaten the friend's autonomy.

Power struggles can result in constraints on our autonomy. However, (*i*) such power struggles are not unique to friendship—they occur in relationships with family members and colleagues at work and fellow members of affinity groups (and one suspects they are more common among family members than among friends). The need to confront them is not a problem unique to friendship. In addition, (*ii*) they are not endemic to friendship, and they certainly aren't necessary features of friendship. Friends can be thoroughly respectful of each other's autonomy. Further, (*iii*) the challenges friends pose to each other's autonomy need not be successful: they can quite reasonably be rejected and resisted. (*iv*) We can actively push back at bullying and manipulative behavior, emphasizing its inappropriateness.

Finally, (*v*) someone might quite reasonably decide to live with the challenges and, indeed, with the recognition that she might sometimes give in to them in order to participate in the good of friendship in general or in the good that is some particular friendship. The only objective way of ordering or weighting the goods in question (those affected by her friend's behavior, those in which she's unable to participate because of that behavior, those her friendship makes possible, and so forth) is for her to make commitments establishing her priorities.

In virtue of those commitments, she might well (explicitly or implicitly) rank a life that includes a friendship with a given person, a friendship that happens to involve power struggles, ahead of a life that doesn't include power struggles with that friend but that also doesn't include her relationship with the friend. She *needn't* commit in this way; but she might well choose to do so. And, if she does, then she's made the risks worth taking; she's established the values the relevant goods have *for her*. It's not that she's used some independent, objective metric to identify them as worth taking; rather, her commitment has established the metric that she's using—so that, in virtue of the commitment, they *are* worth taking.[37]

Friends are imperfect—finite, fallible, sinful. We know this because *we* are friends and we are imperfect. The failings and wrongs of friends can be met with love, acceptance, forgiveness. And these include the wrongs involved in attempts to compromise our autonomy. People have no good reason to try to subject their friends' wills to their own. But the possibility that friends might behave in this way is not only no justification for rejecting particular friends but, even more, no reason to shun friendship more generally.

There are doubtless other challenges to acknowledging or accepting obligations specific to friendship than the ones I consider here. But I hope I've addressed a sufficiently wide range and representative sample that it makes sense to consider whether plausible accounts of friendship's moral status are available.

37. See Finnis, *Fundamentals of Ethics* 91–2:

> If we have decided to build a highway through the desert, . . . we can use cost-benefit computations to select among materials and methods of leveling and road-building. But it was not, and could not rationally have been, cost-benefit computations which guided our prior commitment to the level of economic activity (trade) and personal mobility which calls for highways of this sort. We know that the building and use of highways of this sort involves the death of tens of thousands of persons, and the horrible injury of hundreds of thousands more, each year. But we have not made any computation which shows that the goods participated in and attained by that level of trade and mobility exceed, outweigh, are proportionately greater, than the goods destroyed and damaged by that level, or any level, of deaths and injuries. Nor, on the other hand, could any computation yield the conclusion that the deaths and injuries are an evil which objectively outweighs, exceeds, etc., the good of mobility, etc. . . . The justification, and equally the critique, of any basic commitment [in light of which a choice like this might be assessed] must be in terms of the requirements of practical reasonableness, which give positive direction even though they do not include any principle of optimizing . . . , and even though they permit indefinitely many different commitments (as well as, also, excluding indefinitely many other possible commitments!).

Friendship is an ethical relationship.[38] To help to explain why it makes sense to understand friendship this way, I've focused in this chapter on philosophical objections to talk about obligation in friendship, responding to them in philosophical terms. While I will continue to draw on philosophical resources in chapter 4, I will also examine a variety of explicitly theological approaches and affirmations. I will explore ways in which friends' moral claims on each other might be understood to flow from Christian love and in which, even when we and our friends are morally flawed, our self-investment in friendship can be a morally important exercise of our freedom in love.

38. See Søren Kierkegaard, *Either/Or* 2, trans. Walter Lowrie, ed. Howard A. Johnson (Garden City, NY: Anchor-Doubleday 1959) 324–7.

4

Loves

Friendship is a paradigmatic instance of love. And love is central to Christian ethics. Impartialist construals of Christian love don't seem very hospitable to friendship. However, friendship can be recognized as a fitting expression of love from multiple perspectives. The love of friends can be given and received despite differences and defects. And friendship can find its place within an attractive model of Christian love.

In this chapter, I seek to clarify the relationship of friendship to Christian love and, as a result, to understand love more clearly. I begin by examining accounts of love as essentially impartial—as responding in the moment to whomever one encounters or as bringing about what are thought to be "the best overall consequences." I emphasize a range of difficulties confronted by impartialist views, including the fact that love understood along impartialist lines is unlikely to be able adequately to take account of friendship.

I go on to explore several different ways in which we might understand love in order to make sense of friendship as a distinct and important element of love: love as directed by divine commands, love as piety, love as shaped by vocation (understood as an important independent element of a variety of moral views), love as ordered by covenant, love as structured by virtue rooted in biblical narrative, and love as shaped by the creation-rooted goal of flourishing—for ourselves and others. I propose a brief evaluation of these alternative possibilities. Then, after reflecting on the question whether the love that is friendship might be limited by a requirement that friends be virtuous, I briefly elaborate a model of Christian love's dimensions that I hope is at least relatively true to the complexity of our experience and the diversity of ways in which our lives can go well.

Christian Love as Inconsistent with Friendship?

We assume that friendships exert moral claims and that self-investment in friendship is morally appropriate, even admirable. But it is difficult to make sense of our assumptions from the standpoint of some interpretations of the Christian moral life. One, for instance, urges us to love by focusing our attention and care on whomever we happen to encounter in the moment. This approach rules out anything like long-term reliability in or self-committal to friendship. Another encourages us to love by attempting to take everyone's interests into account impartially; on this kind of approach, obligations to friends and self-investment in friendships can be, at best, derivative and insecure.

Because both of these approaches are inhospitable to obligation in friendship, I could have engaged with them in chapter 3. However, I think it makes sense to consider them here too. They are significant not only because they challenge obligation in friendship, the topic of the previous chapter, but also because they make it hard to understand the reasonableness of self-investment in friendship. They are construals of Christian love both in friendship and more generally and thus deserve to be considered in connection with my attempt in this chapter to clarify the nature of Christian love. And they merit criticism rooted not just in philosophy but also in theology, a key focus of this chapter.

Love in the Moment

On one construal, Christian love can be understood as heedless attention to any other one happens to encounter.[1] Love viewed this way is responsive in the same essential way to each person with whom I interact. Someone becomes a priority for me precisely because I chance upon her. This seems to have been, for instance, the view of Leo Tolstoy. Søren Kierkegaard seems to have adopted a similar position (even if not in all of his moods).

Understood in this way, love seems inconsistent with the development of friendships and other personal relationships, as also with long-term projects of all sorts and, indeed, of anything like a robust personal identity. I will tend, if I seek to love this way, to proceed through my life reactively, refocused by each

1. See Gillian Clark and Stephen R. L. Clark, "Friendship in the Christian Tradition," *The Dialectics of Friendship*, ed. Roy Porter and Sylvana Tomaselli (London: Routledge 1989) 41.

new encounter. It will be hard not to ask questions like this one: "Shall I . . . marry the first woman I find who will have me and whom I can make happy?"[2]

The call to engage in moment-by-moment love seems to flounder given an obvious question. On this idea of love, I am to seek the good of the other I encounter in the moment. But in what does that good consist? If the call to love in the moment is a general moral prescription and not an individual moral task, then shouldn't the other I am seeking to benefit be concerned with the good of the others whom *she* encounters in the moment? And shouldn't they, in turn, be concerned with the good of those *they* encounter moment by moment? On the other hand, if they should be concerned with their own substantive goods, if these goods are worthwhile objects of pursuit for them (so that they aren't acting wrongly by focusing on and investing in those goods), why is it unreasonable for me to behave in the same way?

Relatedly, one might wonder what I'm *doing* just before or even as I encounter someone to whom I must, in love, respond. Why am I in a particular place at a particular time? Where do I go and what do I do once I've responded to a particular other? Should I undertake some plan or project? If so, why? How am I to distinguish among alternative undertakings? It is hard to see how I can decide what to do in between encounters without reference to some actual commitments and preferences of my own. Suppose it's reasonable to attend to these. A commitment isn't a commitment if I abandon it in response to whatever alternative presents itself. So I can't take my commitments seriously if I treat whomever I happen to encounter as a priority.

It will be difficult, at minimum, for the idea of love in the moment to take anyone's well-being, the value of anyone's projects, into account. Even if the idea of love in the moment might be thought to be implicit in some biblical teachings or narratives, it does not seem to find much support in the Bible generally or in the remembered practice of Jesus. And in both of its biblical versions—"You shall love your neighbor as yourself"[3] and "Do to others as you would have them do to you"[4]—THE GOLDEN RULE presupposes that an agent's own flourishing matters, that she will reasonably be concerned with her own well-being and will be pursuing her own projects. Love in the moment seems to rule out recognizing the independent worth of anyone's well-being and anyone's projects. Even if it is construed in a way that does leave room for doing so, however, it is

2. Gene Outka, *Agape: An Ethical Analysis* (New Haven, CT: Yale University Press 1972) 269.

3. Lev 19:18.

4. Luke 6:31.

thoroughly inhospitable to a whole range of human goods—those (including, but not limited to, friendship) that involve long-term, focused self-committal. Among these goods is, as Tolstoy himself came to conclude, the production of novels, since writing a novel requires the kind of focused attention that is effectively ruled out by love in the moment and since no one is likely to have time to read a novel, in any case, while lurching from unpredictable encounter to unpredictable encounter.

A Consequentialist Interpretation of Christian Love

On another view, Christian love involves not responding to whoever I'm personally encountering but, rather, promoting what is taken to be the overall good.[5] Joseph Fletcher offers a particularly clear statement of this sort of position.

Fletcher characterizes Christian love as "giving love—nonreciprocal, neighbor-regarding."[6] This kind of love is, he says, "the one and only universal law."[7] Such love is the expression of "a good will"[8]—or, more precisely, of "*goodwill in partnership with reason.*"[9] It "is what is due to all others, to our various and many neighbors whether we 'know' them or not."[10] And it seeks to produce what Fletcher calls "the greatest amount of neighbor welfare for the largest number of neighbors possible."[11] (We are to live for our neighbors; but—even apart from the alienating quality of this approach—we might reasonably wonder, then, what the neighbors themselves are for.) Fletcher's approach interprets Christian love as a kind of consequentialism,[12] the idea that what makes an act

5. For reasons I note below, I doubt that expressions like "overall good," "aggregate welfare," and "greatest amount of neighbor welfare" are meaningful. To avoid awkward and tedious phrasing, I won't remind the reader of this when they appear in the text.

6. Joseph Fletcher, *Situation Ethics: The New Morality* (London: SCM 1966) 79.

7. Fletcher 27.

8. Fletcher 64.

9. Fletcher 69.

10. Fletcher 95.

11. Fletcher 95.

12. Fletcher is not alone. See also, *e.g.*, James Keller, "Christianity and Consequentialism: A Reply to Meilaender," *Faith and Philosophy* 6.2 (1989): 198–206; and William Frankena, "Love and Principle in Christian Ethics," *Faith and Philosophy: Philosophical Studies in Religion and Ethics*, ed. Alvin Plantinga (Grand Rapids: Eerdmans 1964) 206, 208–9.

right in a given situation is that, of those available to the agent, it's the one that can be expected to bring about the greatest aggregate good.[13]

When he considers the reported dispute regarding the anointing of Jesus at Bethany, Fletcher anachronistically attributes to the disciples the view "that love must work in coalition with utilitarian distribution, spreading the benefits as much as possible. Jesus is cast into the role of defending Leo Tolstoy's doctrine that love wears blinders, sees only the neighbor *there*. If we take the story as it stands, Jesus was wrong and the disciples were right."[14] Along similar lines, Fletcher relates a version of a famous thought experiment offered by William Godwin, suggesting that you should choose to carry a medical genius rather than your father out of a burning building if you're aware of the meaning and implications of Christian love.[15]

Henry Sidgwick saw ethics as concerned with "the point of view of the universe."[16] An approach like Fletcher's seems to suggest that being moral means taking up God's own point of view. Loving as Fletcher urges us to love means loving in a way that embodies and expresses the comprehensiveness and universality of God's love, rather than its particularity and intensity, despite our own finitude.

13. There are, of course, other varieties of consequentialism—ones that focus on, for instance, rules ("Follow the rules that, if followed by everyone, would bring about the most good") or practices ("Sustain the practices that bring about the most good"). It can plausibly be argued that if performing a particular action will bring about the most good, the consequentialist will have good reason *not* to perform some alternative to that action, an alternative that will bring about less good, even if that alternative is required or permitted by a rule or practice the consequentialist might endorse. Rule and practice consequentialism thus reduce to act consequentialism. The case for this sort of view has been made most famously by David Lyons, *Forms and Limits of Utilitarianism* (Oxford: Clarendon-Oxford University Press 1965). Lyons is a critic of consequentialism, but the unabashed utilitarian Jack Smart has endorsed (and, indeed, radicalized) Lyons's view; see J. J. C. Smart, "An Outline of a System of Utilitarian Ethics," *Utilitarianism: For and Against*, by J. J. C. Smart and Bernard Williams (Cambridge: Cambridge University Press 1973) 10–2.

14. Fletcher, *Situation Ethics* 97. It hardly seems as if much imagination would be required to interpret Jesus's stance in a way that didn't treat him as committed to Tolstoy's view.

15. Fletcher 115. See William Godwin, *An Enquiry concerning Political Justice and Its Influence on General Virtue and Happiness*, 2 vols. (London: Robinson 1793) 1: 82–3 (bk. 2, ch. 2).

16. See Bernard Williams, "The Point of View of the Universe: Sidgwick and the Ambitions of Ethics," *Making Sense of Humanity and Other Philosophical Papers 1982–1993* (Cambridge: Cambridge University Press 1995) 153–71.

Love and Self-Investment

There appears to be no room for preference and particularity in Christian love understood in this way.[17] It is realistically incompatible with the long-term consistency required to sustain particular commitments, promises, relationships, and projects and make them successful and meaningful.[18]

Suppose that, with each choice, I attempt to bring about what Fletcher would characterize as the greatest amount of neighbor welfare possible. In this case, there will at least very frequently be undertakings that, by claiming my attention, will prevent me from focusing on my relationships and projects.

The practical effect of trying to love in consequentialist fashion will often be very much like that of trying to love in the moment. My attention will be jerked from cause to cause, activity to activity, because, in each situation, there will be new opportunities to bring about putatively great goods quite unrelated to my projects and relationships.

It is hard to see how, loving as Fletcher proposes, I would ever be justified in *initiating* deep personal ties or long-term, resource-demanding projects in the first place. At each moment when I might otherwise be able to begin a relationship or activity, I will probably confront some option more likely to maximize aggregate welfare.

Loving like a consequentialist seems likely to prove alienating. That's true not only because it probably won't leave room for personal relationships and projects but also because, even if I do retain such relationships and projects, they will need to be *justified* in instrumental terms. I will need to convince myself that they are conducive to the overall good. That's not, of course, the way we ordinarily think about our relationships and projects; we typically treat them as intrinsically worthwhile and generally not in need of further justification.[19] Viewing them as in need of instrumental justification means that I will find it easier to *think* of them and *treat* them instrumentally, too.

17. Outka, *Agape* 269.

18. See Fred R. Berger, "Love, Friendship, and Utility: On Practical Reason and Reductionism," *Human Nature and Natural Knowledge: Essays Presented to Marjorie Grene on the Occasion of Her Seventh-Fifth Birthday*, ed. Alan Donagan, Anthony N. Perovich Jr., and Michael V. Wedin (Dordrecht, Netherlands: Reidel 1986) 12.

19. See Badhwar, "Guided by the Best" 483–504.

Fidelity

Seeking to model God's faithful love,[20] remembering Jesus's affirmation of marital permanence,[21] recalling examples of constancy like those of Jacob and Hosea and the injunction to "be faithful until death,"[22] Christians have recognized the importance of a norm of fidelity and trustworthiness that is difficult to sustain on consequentialist grounds.

> If a person genuinely means to attach an exception-making criterion to his promises or to his marriage vow, if he means to live by a rule of practice which states that the marriage covenant holds, that promises should be kept except when by a direct appeal to what Christian love requires it would be better *not* to keep them, he had better say so, since the one he promises or his marriage partner (unless they are Fletcherites who have been briefed) will not understand it that way.[23]

We need to be loyal, reliable people in a way that rules out appeals to what are taken to be the overall consequences of our acts to overrule our promises and commitments and invitations to reliance. To recognize genuine fidelity as a central aspect of Christian love is to decline to treat a consequentialist account like Fletcher's as an adequate interpretation of such love.

Rooting Attachment in Impartiality

Someone who understands Christian love in something like the way Fletcher does might try to argue for an indirect approach to the maximization of neighbor welfare.[24] Such an approach could still identify the action it was right to perform in a given situation as the one that produced the most aggregate neighbor welfare. However, on this kind of approach, we wouldn't typically decide what to do by reasoning *directly* about consequences on a case-by-case basis. Instead, we would cultivate *characters* marked by stable regard for and investment in particular relationships and projects. Our characters might lead

20. See, *e.g.*, 2 Tim 2:13.
21. See, *e.g.*, Matt 19:6–8.
22. Rev 2:10; see also Gen 29:18–30; Hosea.
23. Paul Ramsey, "The Biblical Norm of Righteousness," *Interpretation* 24.4 (Oct. 1970): 426.
24. See Outka, *Agape* 273–4.

us to perform actions in particular cases that didn't maximize neighbor welfare. But it still might be right, still the choice likely to be productive of the most neighbor welfare, to cultivate just those characters. This might be because we were most likely to bring about good consequences on a long-term basis if we had stable characters and because other sorts of characters—ones that might lead us to produce more neighbor welfare—weren't realistic options for us.[25]

I don't believe this approach can make an account of Christian love like Fletcher's consistent with deep self-investment in personal relationships and projects. The kind of focused character needed to sustain those relationships and projects will probably dispose me quite consistently to act wrongly from a consequentialist perspective. So someone who wants me to love the way Fletcher thinks I should love probably should not want me to cultivate this kind of character.[26]

In addition, to cultivate and act on this kind of character seems likely to lead to cognitive dissonance, detachment, and, quite possibly rejection of the character one has developed in favor of one even less appealing from a consequentialist perspective. And a model that calls for the cultivation of a character at odds with one's deepest beliefs, and disregard for the evident implications of those beliefs, seems likely to be problematic as a model of Christian love because of its inherent dependence on self-deception.

The Idea of the Overall Good

Consequentialism is implausible on multiple grounds.[27] Even if the indirect approach could be made to work, a consequentialist understanding of Christian

25. See Peter Railton, "Alienation, Consequentialism, and the Demands of Morality," *Philosophy and Public Affairs* 13.2 (Spring 1984): 134–71, esp. 157–9.

26. See William H. Wilcox, "Egoists, Consequentialists, and Their Friends," *Philosophy and Public Affairs* 16.1 (Win. 1987): 75–9.

27. In addition to the works by Grisez, Shaw, Finnis, and Boyle I cite below, see, *e.g.*, Gilbert Meilaender, *Faith and Faithfulness: Basic Themes in Christian Ethics* (Notre Dame, IN: University of Notre Dame Press 1991) 89–113; Oliver O'Donovan, *Ethics as Theology* 2: *Finding and Seeking* (Grand Rapids: Eerdmans 2014) 201–5, 208–10; MacIntyre, *After Virtue* 61–3, 67–8, 185; David S. Oderberg, *Moral Theory: A Non-consequentialist Approach* (Oxford: Blackwell 2000) 65–76, 97–101, 132–3; Paul Hurley, *Beyond Consequentialism* (New York: Oxford University Press 2009); Alan Donagan, *The Theory of Morality* (Chicago: University of Chicago Press 1977) 172–209; and Bernard Williams, "A Critique of Utilitarianism," Smart and Williams, *Utilitarianism* 77–150.

love would still be untenable. Such an understanding relies on the idea of bringing about the greatest overall good in a given situation.

Recall Fletcher's injunction: seek "the greatest amount of neighbor welfare for the largest number of neighbors possible."[28] Fletcher is simply talking the way consequentialists usually talk. The consequentialist injunction is to maximize welfare, or the good, or something similar. But there's a serious problem with the idea of "the greatest amount of neighbor welfare" and equivalent notions.[29] For talk about the greatest amount of welfare seems to assume that all the various particular goods, all the constituents of welfare (or well-being, or flourishing, or fulfillment), that obtain in a given situation can be combined to form something we might think of as "overall neighbor welfare." Essential to this approach is "the thought of a homogenizing measure that will serve to make every different value quantifiable and computable."[30] Our language can sometimes lead us to think and talk this way. But it ultimately doesn't make sense.

The various aspects of welfare that obtain in particular situations differ qualitatively.[31] None of them can be reduced to any of the others, nor are all of them expressions of or means to something else, like pleasure or happiness or the satisfaction of preferences. *Sensory* pleasure—experienced, for instance,

28. Fletcher, *Situation Ethics* 95.

29. I happily acknowledge my dependence in the remainder of this section on the works of Germain Grisez, John Finnis, and their collaborators. For their criticisms of consequentialism, see, *e.g.*, Germain Grisez, "Against Consequentialism," *American Journal of Jurisprudence* 23 (1978): 21–72; Finnis, *Natural Law and Natural Rights* 111–9; Finnis, *Fundamentals of Ethics* 80–108; John Finnis, Joseph M. Boyle Jr., and Germain G. Grisez, *Nuclear Deterrence, Morality, and Realism* (Oxford: Clarendon-Oxford University Press 1987) 177–296; and Germain G. Grisez and Russell Shaw, *Beyond the New Morality: The Responsibilities of Freedom*, 3d ed. (Notre Dame, IN: University of Notre Dame Press 1988) 111–4, 131–3.

30. O'Donovan, *Finding* 203.

31. See, *e.g.*, Owen J. Flanagan, "Ethics Naturalized: Ethics as Human Ecology," *Mind and Morals: Essays in Cognitive Science and Ethics*, ed. Larry May, Marilyn Friedman, and Andy Clark (Cambridge, MA: Bradford-MIT Press 1996) 22; MacIntyre, *Virtue* 198–9; Hilary Putnam, "Dewey's Central Insight," *Pragmatism as a Way of Life: The Lasting Legacy of William James and John Dewey*, by Hilary Putnam and Ruth Anna Putnam (Cambridge, MA: Harvard University Press 2017) 286–8; Williams, "Critique" 80, 144–5; Gary Chartier and Jere L. Fox, "Incommensurable Goods," *Edward Elgar Research Handbook on Natural Law Theory*, ed. Jonathan Crowe and Constance Lee (Cheltenham, UK: Elgar 2019) 252–65. Cp. John Dewey, "The Conception of Happiness," *Ethics*, by John Dewey and James Tufts (New York: Holt 1908) 275–7; John Dewey, *Human Nature and Conduct: An Introduction to Social Psychology* (New York: Modern Library-Random 1922) 216–22.

in chocolate consumption and orgasm—is only one of many different kinds of goods. And *emotional* pleasure signals, when our psyches are in order, our awareness of value. We take particular pleasures in particular friendships, particular instances of knowledge or play, and so forth. The pleasures aren't what we're seeking: they're pointers to the worth of what we're seeking. And they're qualitatively different from each other in any case. Similarly, the satisfaction of preferences is valuable just insofar as the things we prefer are valuable.

Since there's no underlying or target variety of welfare, there's no way of collapsing all the aspects of welfare in a given situation together in the way that's needed to form a unitary quantity that can be maximized so that something like "the greatest amount of neighbor welfare" possible can be calculated. There's no objective way of combining or ranking goods apart from (*i*) the qualitative superiority conferred by reasoning well and (*ii*) choices. Some features of potential decisions can rank them decisively ahead of others—notably, when one decision involves reasoning well (reasoning fairly, for instance) and another doesn't. And particular persons can rank-order aspects of welfare by means of their commitments, as can persons deliberately cooperating on some project. But this is a matter of *choice*.

This doesn't mean that there aren't *shared* aspects of welfare. Friendship is essentially such an aspect of well-being. The common good—the social and legal framework designed to secure the flourishing of the moral subjects in a given community—is another.[32] But these are still *particular* intrinsic (as in the case of friendship) or instrumental (as in the case of the common good) dimensions of welfare. They aren't replacements for or aggregates of other aspects of well-being. So there's no such thing as the overall welfare of the members of any given population. There are only the various particular aspects of the well-being of each of the population's various members. And because there's no such thing as the overall good, as a meaningful aggregation of everyone's welfare, consequentialism is untenable. There's no unitary quantity to maximize. So it makes no sense to interpret Christian love as a version of consequentialism.

Better Ways of Thinking about Love

Love is absolutely central to the biblical witness. God is repeatedly described as loving. The development of the idea of God *as* love, an outgrowth of

32. See Gary Chartier and Jere L. Fox, "Natural Law, the Common Good[,] and the State," Crowe and Lee, *Edward Elgar Research Handbook* 347–68.

prophetic ethical monotheism reinforced by the words and actions of Jesus, is central and essential to a satisfactory conception of God. And the notion that love is at the heart of ethics is profoundly important and, when properly understood, clearly right.

It's important to understand Christian love in a richly nuanced way that acknowledges the diverse constituents of well-being and recognizes and affirms the varieties of love's forms, expressions, and objects. There are more attractive ways of thinking about Christian love than love in the moment and love as a kind of consequentialism. I want in what follows to consider several alternate ways of construing Christian love:

- as directed by generic and particular divine commands
- as shaped by creational structures
- as targeted by vocation
- as ordered by covenants
- as characterized in and particularized by narratives
- as aptly attentive to human flourishing

Viewing each of these accounts of love on its own terms, I will seek to understand how it might make sense of the love that is friendship.

Divine Commands

Many Christians have located the source of ethical obligation in commands issued by God.[33] Obviously, committing oneself to a divine command *metaethic* need have no substantive consequences for one's understanding of normative ethics; God could presumably command one to live a Kantian, consequentialist, Tolstoyan, or egoistic life. But a divine command ethic need not depend on or involve any austerely unified account of the right or the good as reducible to a single, simple injunction. Such an ethic can thus take account of the "pluriformity of the moral field,"[34] permitting us to recognize and affirm a plurality of goods and moral claims.

33. The best elaboration and defense of divine command theory: Adams, *Finite and Infinite Goods*.

34. For this phrase, see Oliver O'Donovan, *Resurrection and Moral Order: An Outline for Evangelical Ethics*, 2d ed. (Grand Rapids: Eerdmans 1994), *e.g.*, 183, 195, 202.

A divine command view might be concerned with situational commands issued to particular individuals, generic commands issued to all individuals, or generic commands seen as intended to govern societies. And it might understand divine commands as delivered by means of special revelation in the Bible or the individual conscience or by means of general revelation in nature and familiar social patterns.

Friendship and Alternative Divine Command Models

Because a divine command theory can conceive of friendship as a direct or indirect divine institution, such a theory can take a more satisfactory account of the exclusiveness and limitation characteristic of friendship than could moral schemes that attempt to ground friendship's moral status in universal love or respect. We might envision a divine command as mandating or proposing various particular friendships or as establishing friendship as a kind of social relationship while inviting us to choose our friends.[35]

A divine command view might make sense of friendship's moral claim and of our self-investments in friendship in multiple ways.

(*i*) It might focus on the Decalogue as containing a variety of largely negative prohibitions. These prohibitions would not require anyone to form friendships, and they would not, of course, yield any special friendship-related obligations. They would, however, create an open space, free of obligation, within which one could pursue and develop friendships. Proceeding this way would respond effectively to the moral imperialism characteristic of impartialist understandings of Christian love by refusing to moralize large swaths of life. On the other hand, however, it would not take adequate account of what we ordinarily take to be obligations to friends and the positive moral significance of self-investment in friendship.

(*ii*) It might adopt a broader but still Bible-focused account of divine commands and seek to discern positive commands related to friendship in various biblical passages—in Proverbs, for instance.[36] Doing this would substantially enrich moral thinking about friendship, in particular by focusing on obligations with respect to friends and on friendship's role in constituting the self.

35. Emil Brunner, *The Divine Imperative: A Study in Christian Ethics*, trans. Olive Wyon (Philadelphia: Westminster 1947) 518.

36. See, *e.g.*, John E. Johnson, "The Contribution of Proverbs to Ethics" (ThD diss., Dallas Theological Seminary 1984) 180–210.

(*iii*) It might seek to find friendship's moral weight in commands issued to individual people. Focusing such commands could certainly, in principle, make possible recognition of both obligations to individual friends and the positive value of investing time and resources in friendship.[37]

(*iv*) It might see divine commands as revealed and reflected in (though not constituted by) a range of biological impulses and patterns of social life. This sort of approach might involve commands to participate in friendship understood as an order of creation or to welcome friendship as an element of a sphere of freedom outside the formal orders.

Orders or Mandates

This last approach, the idea that human society is rightly structured by divine "mandates" or "orders," is a characteristic feature of much classic Protestant work in social and political ethics. Talk about orders or mandates is typically rooted in an understanding of ethics as a matter of divine commands; however, while such commands might often be thought of, as in (*i*)–(*iii*) above, as concerned with individual conduct ("Thou shalt not commit adultery") and even as addressed to individuals in very particular circumstances, the mandates or orders can be seen as commands concerned with patterns of social life. Sometimes, mandates are seen primarily as needed because of human sinfulness;[38] by contrast, in others, they appear, rather, as responses to the structure of creation.

An approach focused on orders or mandates is nominally different from one concerned with natural law. So, for instance, Ray Anderson suggests that, while there *is* a reliable structure to the family, there can be no "natural theology of friendship."[39] For Anderson, the structure of the family "is not located within the natural order," nor is it grounded "in the freedom of the individual." Instead, it "is rooted in the creative Word of God and its purpose, which expresses itself through the order of creation."[40] Presumably, a similar judgment underlies his conviction regarding friendship.

37. Karl Barth, *Ethics*, ed. Dietrich Braun, trans. Geoffrey W. Bromiley (Edinburgh: Clark 1981) 191.

38. Cp. Paul Ramsey, *Nine Modern Moralists* (Englewood Cliffs, NJ: Prentice-Hall 1962) 202.

39. Ray S. Anderson, personal comm., sum. 1989.

40. Ray S. Anderson and Dennis Guernsey, *On Being Family: A Socio-theology of the Family* (Grand Rapids: Eerdmans 1986) 17.

At a metaethical level, an orders-or-mandates view differs from a natural law account of social life because the divine *will* is at the root of the obligation we encounter in a given social structure rather than the inherent features of human persons. But it seems at first blush to be quite similar in practical terms. There are arguably differences, however.

(*i*) In contrast with the epistemology characteristic of some natural law views (and, to be sure, some less sophisticated divine command views), the existence and shape of a divine order cannot be read off existing social circumstances or biological conditions. Consider, for instance, how common it is for friendship patterns to be based on collective exclusion. Are friendships that cross lines of class, ethnicity, race, religion, sex, or gender consistent with relevant divine mandates, for instance? On an orders-or-mandates view, any attempt to understand God's purposes by examining extant conditions would presumably need to be checked and qualified and interpreted in light of revelation. For instance, we might qualify judgments about ideal institutions drawn from observing existing social or biological realities in light of the divine love revealed in Jesus, along with the recognition that the shapes of those institutions are distorted by sin.[41] The divine order cannot simply be equated with what *is*, even though an orders-or-mandates view rightly treats God's creation as worthy of love.[42]

(*ii*) A divine order or mandate, while it is concerned with and undergirds creational structures, might *change* in response to altered circumstances. Divine freedom provides proponents of an orders-or-mandates view with a further reason to distinguish an appeal to mandates from a ratification of the status quo and to be open and attentive to evidence that God is, in fact, *changing* a given order.

Recognizing freedom with respect to our choice of friends and with respect to our expression of friendship is compatible with supposing that, given the value of freedom and individuality, the phenomenon of friendship *as such* is not optional.[43] (Introverts beware!) An adherent of an orders-or-mandates view might thus maintain that there was a divine order or mandate for the institution of friendship in addition to ones for social phenomena such as the family.[44]

41. Brunner, *Divine Imperative* 214–5. See Adams, *Goods* 306–9.

42. See Dietrich Bonhoeffer, *Ethics* (London: SCM 1955) 87, 101–3.

43. Barth, *Ethics* 190.

44. James Olthuis, *I Pledge You My Troth: A Christian View of Marriage, Family, and Friendship* (New York: Harper 1975) 21, 110, 114, 119–20.

Friendship could be seen as an element of a social framework resulting from divine providence and thus mandated by God.[45]

Alternatively, instead of seeking, or finding, a divine order or mandate for friendship, one might posit a "sphere of freedom," *distinct* from the realms of activity with which the divine mandates are putatively concerned. We might see friendship as located within this sphere of freedom. Dietrich Bonhoeffer, for instance, seems to suppose that, while the family, work, the state, and the church are all *necessary* realms of Christian being and acting, these are "encompassed" by a "free expanse of liberty" within which culture finds its place. In this scheme, friendship is an aspect of culture.[46] The Christian is free to enjoy friendship as—not something ordained or mandated as such but, rather—a relationship we are invited to welcome within the sphere of freedom.[47]

This sphere of freedom is not, however, merely the realm of the *permissible*. Entering it and enjoying it are themselves activities in which God commands us to engage.[48] The command offers a positive justification for the exercise of freedom.[49] We can see participation in the free sphere of culture just as such as enjoined by a divine command.[50] So activity in this sphere is not merely permissible but a positive good.

Can anyone "in our time," Bonhoeffer asks, "still with an easy mind cultivate music or friendship, play games and enjoy himself? Certainly not the 'ethical' man," he suggests, "but only the Christian."[51] So affirming a divine command at the root of culture can ground a protest against the equation of Christian ethics with a narrow moralism.[52]

Theocentric Ethics

James Gustafson's distinctive proposal for a theocentric ethic bears an obvious resemblance to the approach to social phenomena by way of divine mandates,

45. See Adams, *Goods* 252–70.
46. Bonhoeffer, *Ethics* 243.
47. Bonhoeffer 253.
48. Bonhoeffer 141, 251–3.
49. Bonhoeffer 249.
50. See Brunner, *Divine Imperative* 484.
51. Bonhoeffer, *Ethics* 253.
52. Bonhoeffer 233, 235, 251.

differing primarily in that Gustafson's approach lacks the personalist, voluntarist quality of traditional talk about orders or mandates.

Gustafson doubts that much recent work in theological ethics has been sufficiently theological. He therefore attempts to articulate an approach that *is* clearly theological—but, perhaps surprisingly, without any appeal to metaphysics. One way of thinking about Gustafson's approach is as attempting to capture the phenomenology of the moral life in a traditionally theistic context without the attempt to provide a robustly realist *grounding* for that phenomenology. He isn't so much actively defending nonrealism or antirealism but, perhaps, trying to capture the essence of a genuinely theological ethic while bypassing the metaphysical challenges associated with traditional theism.

Central to his approach is recognition of the importance of reverence, or piety, for the sources of the constraints human agents confront, of the influences to which they are subject, of the given structures within which they function. Special relationships, including friendship, can be valued precisely as gifts given in and through the natural order and the social order resultant from it. Our need and appreciation for them is a function of our natures and of circumstances quite beyond our control, and the presence of particular friends in our lives is, again, a matter of activities and processes not, for the most part, under our direction.[53] Friendships are significant "biosocial structures."[54] In different ways, they extend and reduce our contingency.[55] Gratitude and responsibility appropriately flow from their importance to us and from our interdependence and vulnerability.[56]

Biological drives and tendencies can be rightly responded to as products of God's structuring of our world and as pointers to our (creaturely) contingency.[57] Ethics must build on and recognize the actual features of humans as biological and social creatures.[58]

The basic principle informing Gustafson's reflection is the judgment that we "are to relate ourselves and all things in a manner appropriate to our and their

53. James Gustafson, *Ethics from a Theocentric Perspective* 2: *Ethics and Theology* (Chicago: University of Chicago Press 1984) 164.

54. Philosopher Mary Daly's phrase nicely captures a feature of friendship in virtue of which its ethical significance can be addressed using the resources Gustafson provides. See Daly, "Morality of Human Nature."

55. Gustafson, *Ethics* 2: 164.

56. Gustafson 2: 164–5.

57. Gustafson 2: 160.

58. Gustafson 2: 161.

relations to God."[59] We can discern divine action, meriting our reverence, "in and through orders in human society."[60] And these orders could be understood to include friendship.[61]

Gustafson's piety treats the glory of God as of greater significance than the glory of humanity and distinguishes God's purposes in the world from ours. The resulting sense of dependence coheres with our experience of structures that lie outside our dominion. However, we can understand these structures sufficiently to gauge at least provisionally what it might mean for us to respond aright to a reality greater than ourselves.[62] This kind of response is not simply a matter of observation and rational reflection, however, since ethical inquiry treats as givens "our natural impulses and desires,"[63] even if we have reason to assess them critically as well.

Gustafson sees the human being as a participant in a variety of patterns of interaction, larger ones inclusive of smaller ones.[64] His talk about special relations is almost exclusively about the family, and there are differences between friendships and family relationships that prevent a wholesale application to friendship of moral analysis focused on the family. But his understanding of the crucial value of relationships and communities for individuals is certainly relevant to friendship as well as to family life.[65]

The friendship group is a relevant whole just as the family is.[66] Friendship groups can be seen as transpersonal entities with distinct dynamics and characteristics. Within the limits imposed by the more inclusive wholes of which it is a part, a friendship can be seen to have a distinct moral status from the standpoint of theocentric ethics—though not one that should encourage us to ignore responsibilities to other groups to which we are connected, to strangers, and for the nonhuman world.[67]

59. Gustafson 2: 153.

60. James Gustafson, *Ethics from a Theocentric Perspective* 1: *Theology and Ethics* (Chicago: University of Chicago Press 1981) 221–2.

61. See Gustafson, *Ethics* 2: 6–7; and Gustafson, *Theology* 1: 31–62.

62. Gustafson, *Ethics* 2: 8.

63. Gustafson 2: 8; cp. Gustafson, *Theology* 1: 284–7.

64. See Gustafson, *Ethics* 2: 11.

65. See Gustafson 2: 16.

66. See Haapanen, "Close Friendship" 110.

67. Gustafson, *Ethics* 2: 223–4, 241.

Vocation

A vocation is a call—whether mandatory or invitational—to a particular task or cluster of tasks.[68] One might have a vocation to be a friend.

Understanding the Concept of Vocation

The idea of vocation is naturally at home in the context of a divine command ethic. It might also take the form of an addition to another sort of moral theory, an addition in virtue of which divine commands were issued to individuals who generally confronted moral obligations without voluntaristic roots. It might even be understood as entirely nonvoluntaristic, as an expression of the idea that "each person has a unique personal purpose, arising from . . . historical and social conditions . . . and temperaments and abilities."[69]

Someone takes herself to have a vocation (however she names her experience) if she judges that a particular action is appropriate in a given context without attempting to subsume it under some generic type, if she concludes that *she* must do something without assuming that anyone else must do so. A theist who believes in vocations might see this as an instance of vocation, recognizing that it's perfectly possible for someone to receive a vocation—in any number of mediated ways—without conceptualizing it *as* a vocation.[70]

68. For simplicity's sake, I speak here, at least most of the time, on the assumption that there *are* vocations, despite the qualifications I will note later. For the best available accounts of vocation, see Adams, *Goods* 252–317; Ward, *Ethics and Christianity* 141–54; O'Donovan, *Finding* 222–30; Lawrence A. Blum, *Moral Perception and Particularity* (New York: Cambridge University Press 1994) 104–23, 167–9; Germain Grisez and Russell Shaw, *Personal Vocation: God Calls Everyone by Name* (Huntington, IN: Our Sunday Visitor 2003); and David L. Norton, "Education for Self-Knowledge and Worthy Living," *Ethical Issues in Contemporary Society*, ed. John Howie and George Schedler (Carbondale: Southern Illinois University Press 1995) 155–76. See also Chartier, *Logic of Commitment* 56–66; David Norton, *Personal Destinies: A Philosophy of Ethical Individualism* (Princeton, NJ: Princeton University Press 1977); Gail Sheehy, *Passages: Predictable Crises of Adult Life* (New York: Bantam 1977); and Gail Sheehy, *New Passages: Mapping Your Life across Time* (New York: Ballantine 2011).

69. Keith Ward, *The Christian Idea of God: A Philosophical Foundation for Faith* (Cambridge: Cambridge University Press 2017) 171.

70. See Adams, *Goods* 262–70.

Vocation and Love

A vocation can be understood as God's allocation of abilities, opportunities, and duties to love.[71] While God loves the whole creation, on this view, a vocation assigns to a given person a specific *element* of creation to love.[72] The function of a vocation, then, is to focus one's love.

The Attractiveness of the Idea of Vocation

The prospect of a vocation can be appealing because a vocation might be thought to help someone to focus, to take responsibility for goods that are distinctively her own. A vocation could help her to resist the fragmentation of her identity. It could meet her need for a distinct moral center in the midst of conflicting claims by keeping her from being torn apart, crushed, or immobilized by the diverse demands she confronts. It could help her manage the demands of conflicting goods by identifying those for which she was and wasn't responsible. By offering her a personal mission, it could give her a sense of her life's moral importance. And it could offer her a measure of security in virtue of the knowledge that the tasks in which she was engaged were ones that *fit* with who she really was.[73]

Vocations to Friendship

The idea of vocation provides an important means of understanding friendship's moral status. One can think of a vocation as encompassing friendship in general. The thought here might be that one is suited to be a friend, called to open oneself to others in friendship. Alternatively, a vocation might be a call to a particular friendship. On this view, the friend is among those neighbors God calls us actively to love. Another possibility is that someone's vocation might leave space open for friendship by not mandating responsibilities inconsistent with being a friend. If this is the right way to understand vocation, then, one

71. Gilbert C. Meilaender, *Friendship: A Study in Theological Ethics* (Notre Dame, IN: University of Notre Dame Press 1981) 89–95.

72. Meilaender, *Friendship* 91; cp. 32, 100.

73. See Adams, *Goods* 300–4, 309–14; and Barth, *Dogmatics* 3.4: 567–88.

might say that, in the segment of life unclaimed by one's social vocation, one can answer the call of friendship.[74]

A moral requirement to be this person's friend or to welcome friendship into one's life is not needed to render friendship ethically or spiritually important. On the other hand, it seems clear that the life of friendship *is* one of the diverse means by which we love our neighbors and ourselves.[75] So it's easy to see why friendship, or a particular friendship, could be seen as among one's vocational responsibilities.

Discerning Vocations

While God could offer a vocation in more dramatic ways, it will often be the case, for those who take there to be vocations, that a vocation can be recognized through reflective attention to the way things *are*—to one's heart's desires, one's abilities, and one's circumstances and the ways in which they fit together.[76] One might seek to identify a vocation by attending not only to its fit with the story of one's life (while aware that a vocation might serve as a liberating *disruption* of one's story) but also to a deep sense of emotional attachment to it—together, perhaps, with a related sense of its inescapability.[77] Particular relationships and opportunities can be seen as having been given to us by God and to be morally weighty as a result.[78] And this surely includes the responsibilities we believe we have to our friends.

Vocations and Other Responsibilities

A vocation as ordinarily understood doesn't happen in a moral vacuum. It is not the only source of moral obligation, it is not a divine validation of the status quo, and it does not license someone to act unjustly. If there are vocations, a vocation will connect one with things that are genuinely valuable, and so worth loving. And it will offer further focus to responsibilities already constrained by

74. Meilaender, *Friendship* 102; Bonhoeffer, *Ethics* 225.

75. There's no reason to think of a vocation as concerned solely with work or public responsibility. Barth suggests that the idea that "a man's vocation is exhausted in his profession is no more true than that God's calling . . . is simply an impulsion to work." Barth, *Dogmatics* 3.4: 599.

76. See Adams, *Goods* 304–9.

77. See Adams 313–4.

78. See Adams 304–9.

any existing—presumably more general—moral requirements that are relevantly applicable.[79] It will not purport to trump these requirements.

Even if a potential vocation exhibits a discernible fit, involves the attempt to realize a genuine good, and can be pursued realistically in ways consistent with appropriate moral constraints, it doesn't follow that the vocation should automatically trump other responsibilities.[80] Individual discernment is still necessary as one seeks to determine how a vocation one judges oneself to have can be related to one's other responsibilities, including other vocational ones. If there are vocations, they can ground our ties with our friends, prompting us to pursue friendships, invest in them, and care for our friends. But an appeal to vocation is insufficient to tell us just what we can or should do when obligations seem to conflict.

Covenant

God's covenantal love to us can be seen as a model for and ground of our own fidelity to the various covenants in which we find ourselves.[81] These covenants can channel our love in particular directions.

The emphasis on covenant is a powerful response to the equation of Christian love with consequentialism. Special relationships are obviously important, and an account of Christian love that can't take proper account of them is for that reason implausible. A better alternative is needed, and a focus on covenant provides one such model.[82]

Covenants might be modeled on promises. Indeed, it's not entirely clear how covenants should be understood to *differ* from promises. The word *covenant* suggests a weighty seriousness that one might associate, in particular, with especially robust promises, though a great deal presumably depends on the details of a specific covenantal relationship. And some sorts of covenantal bonds might well be rooted in the dynamics of developing relationship rather than in explicitly promissory language.[83]

79. See Adams 308–9.

80. So Robert Merrihew Adams, "Vocation," *Faith and Philosophy* 4.4 (Oct. 1987): 461.

81. See Ramsey, "Norm" 419; and Bruce Mervyn Hucker, "Who Is My Neighbor? A Study in the Ethics of Love and Preference" (PhD diss., Princeton Theological Seminary 1975) 230–2, 257. See Allen, *Love and Conflict.*

82. See Paul Ramsey, *Deeds and Rules in Christian Ethics* (New York: Scribner 1968) 212, critiquing Fletcher, *Situation Ethics* 113, 115.

83. See Allen, *Love and Conflict* 41.

Even though the deep ground of covenantal obligation might be universal love, the covenantal approach recognizes that love requires reliability in particular cases. It won't do to appeal to impartial love to undermine covenantal obligations on a case-by-case basis.[84] Summary rules, simply guides to our moral behavior which reflect judgments of probability and which are always subject to revision in light of some more fundamental moral principle or principles, are not enough. Love requires constancy. It requires something like rules of *practice*, which obtain within the confines of ordered forms of life. To admit exceptions to such rules is simply to opt out of those forms of life altogether (except insofar as the forms of life are so constituted that some flexibility is possible).[85] Thus, no one may reasonably and "without restriction" focus on what might yield "the greatest amount of neighbor welfare" when

> deciding whether to keep *his* promise. Whoever says that he is entitled to break his promise because that was . . . the most loving thing to do . . . may be suspected of not understanding what it means to say "I promise" and of not understanding the defenses the practice, which defines the promise, allows to him. He remains *obliged* so long as . . . considerations of Christian love are sufficient to establish this as the most love-embodying practice.[86]

We need to recognize ourselves as finite creatures choosing within the contexts provided by our covenants.

Whether we ought to have a certain practice at all is one question. How we are to relate to the existing practices in which we participate is another. "*The practice* itself is to be justified by a direct application of Christian love. One asks *which practice* most embodies or fulfills love."[87] But practices can and should be structured so that we can trust and rely on each other. Forms "of steadfastness in responsibility and accountability one to another would seem to be the most likely inference from Christian love, if that has any relevance at all" to human affairs.[88]

84. See Ramsey, "Norm" 426.

85. See Ramsey, *Deeds* 163–4, 428.

86. Ramsey 138; cp. John Rawls, "Two Concepts of Rules," *Philosophical Review* 64.1 (Jan. 1955): 3–32. Ramsey uses the expression "without restriction" himself; the other quoted phrase is, of course, from Fletcher. See Ramsey, *Deeds* 164; and Allen, *Love and Conflict* 134–5.

87. Ramsey, *Deeds* 134.

88. Ramsey 164.

Particular covenants reflect the historical particularity that is unavoidable for finite creatures with specific locations in time and space. And acceptance of one's covenants is a source of identity and integrity.[89] Covenants safeguard relationships with specific persons who are precious to God and should therefore be precious to us.[90]

The covenantal approach can acknowledge the moral force of a special relationship derived from the history that links two persons and that thus helps to structure the context within which each acts and to redefine the expectations of each. These expectations need not be formalized. Ongoing interactions can create expectations and dependencies that can serve as sources of obligation.[91]

A covenantal view of love can therefore account for one's covenant-based obligations to a friend qua friend with reference to several factors: one's explicit promises, the general demands of reciprocity, the expectations one has created over time by interacting with one's friend, and background social norms that shape one's own and one's friend's expectations regarding behavior in friendship. A covenantal model of Christian ethics provides a meaningful account of obligation and self-investment in friendship, and so of how friendship can form a part of the Christian life of faithful love.

Virtue and Narrative

We can understand Christian love as channeled in light of our place in God's story and shaped in light of God's action as narrated in that story.

Narrative, Community, Ethics

The primary point of ethical reflection, according to advocates of this position, should be the formation of selves. Individual moments of ethical decision-making acquire their significance in the context of larger personal and communal stories. And only by learning those stories, only by making one's own story a part of the right story, will one be able truly to display the kind of ethical discernment reflected in them, and so to become a person genuinely

89. Allen, *Love and Conflict* 47–8.

90. Allen 136.

91. Christina Hoff Sommers, "Filial Morality," *Journal of Philosophy* 83.8 (Aug. 1986): 446; cp. Allen, *Love and Conflict* 135–6.

sensitive to the right moral considerations. One may be able to parrot behavioral or theoretical responses to particular problems. But to parrot is not to have acquired the skill necessary if one is to respond appropriately to new situations. We learn general principles by attending to examples, proponents of this view suggest, rather than determining how to respond in specific cases by recalling broader rules.

Ethics "investigates, analyzes, criticizes a way of life, a morality, that is itself story-formed."[92] So Christian ethical discourse cannot be reduced to concern with moral propositions; for the purpose of the gospels is not to teach abstract principles. Rather, the gospels are morally significant because they identify

> characters (Jesus and the disciples) and a realm or setting (the coming kingdom). These are united by a plot—the Gospel story. This story becomes moral demand, moral guidance, moral *telos* for readers just to the extent that we get the point of the story, recognize the one there called Christ as our Lord, and thus confess ourselves to be among the disciples in the kingdom. So to recognize, confess, be born into the kingdom is to take up the way of life called Christian; it *is* Christian morality.[93]

Theology is an exercise in abstraction. It attempts to discern and disclose the realities brought narratively to light. Ethical claims acquire texture in and through narratives. Treating them as abstract propositions evacuates them of their texture. A speech act always takes place against a narrative backdrop—the act of stating a proposition just as much as the act of telling a story.[94] Thus, individual actions acquire meaning in the context of the Christian story as a whole. Assertions about what I or we should do (including what I should do as a friend, what we should do as friends[95]) become significant only when understood in relation to this narrative. Stories make up traditions, and traditions shape communities.[96] Communities, in turn, relate stories and thus contribute to the development of traditions. And they encourage engagement in

92. McClendon, *Systematic Theology* 1: 332. In what follows, I treat McClendon and Stanley Hauerwas as representatives of an approach to theology and ethics emphasizing virtue and narrative without seeking clearly to distinguish their positions. This section is an exposition of what I take to be their views; I don't stop to remind the reader of this at every turn.

93. McClendon, *Systematic Theology* 1: 346.

94. McClendon 1: 343.

95. McClendon 1: 348.

96. Stanley Hauerwas, *The Peaceable Kingdom: A Primer in Christian Ethics* (London: SCM 1983) 24.

practices—crucially, for Christians, liturgy, baptism, and Eucharist—that help to shape behavior and self-understanding.[97]

God's identity is narratively disclosed, and our own identities are story-dependent. In getting to know other people, we often relate our stories. This reflects our sense that an understanding of who we are requires an understanding of the trajectories that give direction to the current moment, the assumptions and experiences that ground present action. But if we are to let God be God, then we must allow our individual stories to find their place within the biblical identity narrative that vouchsafes to us the character of God.[98] And if we are to display integrity, then we will have to be true to who we are—and thus, above all, to our identities as disclosed by the biblical narrative.

Why Narrative Matters

To affirm the centrality of narrative for Christian theology and ethics is to affirm at least three things.

(*i*) We must conceive of ourselves, our identities, our world as contingent. While a narrative depends on the existence of continuity, it ceases to be a narrative at all if its elements follow out of necessity. That a narrative account of our existence is required reminds us of the fact that things could be other than they are.[99] God's including us in a larger story gives meaning and hope to our lives without eliminating their contingency. We can see this as a paradigmatic instance of grace.[100]

(*ii*) Because narrative is communally recorded and understood, to make it the center of Christian existence requires identification with a community that relates—and has related—the Christian story. And because communities are historically extended, one's identity within the community of faith is an unavoidably historical one.[101]

(*iii*) Christian convictions take narrative shape because Christians find the center of God's revelation in the story of Israel and of the Incarnation.[102]

97. Hauerwas 26, 108.
98. Hauerwas 27.
99. Hauerwas 28.
100. Hauerwas 27.
101. Hauerwas 28.
102. Hauerwas 28–9.

Character is shaped by self-understanding, which in turn is formed by identification with a communal narrative.[103] What the Christian narrative must do to be effective is to shape a particular kind of community. It is only within such a community that individual moral characters can find meaning. We can understand virtues as habits and dispositions required by the practices that sustain a particular kind of community life. For there to be Christian virtues, then, there must be a particular kind of Christian community life within which they are integrated.[104]

The virtues characteristic of the Christian community are those "necessary for remembering and telling the story of a crucified savior."[105] The theological virtues of faith, hope, and love derive their specifically Christian meanings from the story of Jesus and the church's response to it.[106] And ethics more broadly is in significant part about acquiring habits, perspectives, and dispositions by locating ourselves within the Christian story.[107] Moral judgments thus reflect not simply basic principles but communal identity, which is narratively shaped. Practice comes first, with principles derived from it.[108] We engage in casuistry in order to bring behavior, narrative, and theory into something like reflective equilibrium.[109]

Narrative and Particularity

A narratively formed ethic grounds a sharp response to impartialist accounts of Christian love. Rather than opting for an abstract ethic of universal benevolence, we should look to the narratives recited by the church to make sense of Christian love.[110]

We may be uncomfortable with particularity in a way that encourages us to embrace abstraction and impartialism. We sense that everyone is loveable, but we are quite unable to love everyone as a unique person, so instead, we opt to

103. Hauerwas 30.
104. See Hauerwas 29–34; cp. 45.
105. Hauerwas 103.
106. Hauerwas 103.
107. Hauerwas 117.
108. Hauerwas 119.
109. Hauerwas 120.
110. Stanley Hauerwas, "The August Partiality of God's Love—a Sermon," *Reformed Journal* 39.5 (May 1989): 11; Stanley Hauerwas, "Athens May Be a Long Way from Jerusalem but Prussia Is Even Further," *Asbury Theological Journal* 45.1 (1990): 63.

treat everyone in accordance with generic standards.[111] This kind of impartiality ignores the reality of those we love.[112] Instead, however, we should—the Christian story suggests—love people with passionate particularity as Jesus did, on the assumption that our varied loves will all contribute to the growth of God's realm.[113]

To abstract the meaning of Christian love from its context in the history of Israel and the church is to miss its point. Because God loves us in our particularity, because our particular choices and identities make a difference as regards what God does and experiences, because God *elects* Israel and the church[114]—for all these reasons, we cannot endorse an interpretation of Christian love as impersonal, impartial.[115]

It is often maintained that, because God's love is universal and impartial, ours should be as well. But what if we turned this idea on its head? Perhaps we ought to love as God loves; but, if so, it matters that God's love is particular. We can love another in her particularity because that is how God loves each of us. God's love, revealed in Jesus, is a model for our own; we join God in loving, and God's love is mediated through our own.[116]

God is concerned with the irreplaceable identity and value of every sentient.[117] In attending to us, God takes into account the unique features of our situations and characters; God loves us not merely as instances of human nature but as distinct individuals.[118] We are called to imitate such divine love.

The divine infinity makes it possible for God to love every creature with full, unswerving attention, just as it is.[119] None of us is God. None of us is infinite. So none of us can love all creatures in this way. Indeed, none of us can love any *single* creature as God can.

111. Hauerwas, "Partiality" 11–2.

112. Hauerwas, "Athens" 63.

113. Hauerwas, "Partiality" 12.

114. Hauerwas 11.

115. Hauerwas 11–2.

116. Stanley Hauerwas, "Companions on the Way: The Necessity of Friendship," *Asbury Theological Journal* 45.1 (1990): 45.

117. Hauerwas 45 (Hauerwas has "creature"). Hauerwas draws on Helen Oppenheimer, *The Hope of Happiness: A Sketch for a Christian Humanism* (London: SCM 1983) 131–9. Oppenheimer's emphasis on the irreplaceability of persons as crucial to their value is reflected in my own approach.

118. See Hans Urs von Balthasar, *A Theological Anthropology* (New York: Sheed 1967) 187–8. Thanks to Hauerwas for this reference.

119. Hauerwas, "Companions" 44.

A Tolstoyan, swerving randomly hither and thither to meet the needs of each person she encountered, could recognize that a generic account of human needs and human nature would not suffice to guide her actions, that she would need to consider the distinctive characteristics of each beneficiary of her love. Such consideration would obviously not suffice to shape a character fit for friendship, for she would lack the constancy and the *sustained* attentiveness required to be a friend.

However, God exhibits just such constancy and attentiveness. To be sure, divine fidelity is as elusive as divine universality; our own fidelity participates in, while only faintly imitating, God's. The idea of election is illuminating here. God elects Israel and elects to become incarnate precisely in the stream of history that is Israel's. And God does this while still loving all people,[120] embracing each of us as a unique, irreplaceable individual.[121] We make a difference to God. And we understand love much more adequately when we recognize that God can be *affected* by what we do and undergo.[122] A recovery of this element of mutuality in our relationship with God might help to shape our relations with other people. We need to recognize the degree to which we are not self-sufficient, the degree to which other people matter to us, to our happiness, to our characters. And the life of friendship is in part an attempt to live out of this realization.

Narratives of Friendship

Certainly, a community which repeats the story of Ruth and Naomi—with their focused and faithful love for each other—and which is drawn into that story can hardly do so without questioning the validity of models of love that exclude particular loyalties and attachments.[123] And of course other narratives of particular love dot the canonical biblical landscape. The passionate particularity of David's love for Jonathan (and Saul) is probably the most noteworthy,[124] but it isn't unique. For instance, hot-tempered enough to lose a companion and probable friend, Saint Paul nonetheless demonstrates an intense loyalty

120. Hauerwas, "Partiality" 11.

121. Hauerwas, "Companions" 44.

122. Stephen G. Post, *A Theory of Agape: On the Meaning of Christian Love* (Lewisburg, PA: Bucknell University Press 1990) 66.

123. Hauerwas, "Partiality" 11.

124. George W. Beiswanger, *The Character Value of the Old Testament Stories*, University of Iowa Studies in Character 3.3, ed. Edwin D. Starbuck (Iowa City: University of Iowa Press 1930) 20, 23, 30.

to and dependence on his friends; the distinctly personal references one finds throughout his letters highlight the importance of friendship to the apostle.

Stories of Jesus, Stories of Friendship

Jesus seeks the support of his friends in Gethsemane and clearly finds personal friendship significant elsewhere. Mary, Martha, and Lazarus are the recipients of Jesus's special attention. Jesus accepts Mary's very particular and lavish love-gift of ointment[125]—without, to Fletcher's dismay, invoking a utilitarian moralism to condemn it—in the context of what seems to have been an enjoyable and quite nonutilitarian social event.[126]

Another Bethany story—that concerning Jesus's affirmation of Mary's desire to converse with him while Martha bustles about in preparation for a meal[127]—may have circulated in the early church as a guide to those entertaining guests.[128] The story will doubtless carry a variety of other overtones when repeated today; but to relate it now will surely be, among other things, to reinforce an image of Jesus as convivial, as sensitive to the importance of friendship.

Despite the persistent suspicion of "particular friendships" within monasticism,[129] Jesus's friendship with the beloved disciple of the Fourth Gospel served for some monks as a model for intense friendship; and there is no reason to suppose that only monks and nuns should find it compelling. Again, the multiple associations and symbolic complexity of events in the Johannine narrative must be taken into account in the course of any thorough reading of the relevant passages; but the references to "the disciple whom Jesus loved"[130] remain on the surface of the text. The stories in the gospels which suggest that Peter, James, and John formed an inner circle around Jesus substantiate a similar picture of Jesus as depending on and offering focused affection.

Jesus's apparent prior knowledge of the forgiven woman who anoints him in Luke 7 is perhaps evidence of a relationship in which Jesus figures as her

125. Matt 26:6–13; Mark 14:3–9; John 12:1–8.

126. Robert K. Johnston, *The Christian at Play* (Grand Rapids: Eerdmans 1983) 121.

127. See Luke 10.

128. See the discussion of Luke 10 in I. Howard Marshall, *The Gospel according to Luke: A Commentary on the Greek Text* (Grand Rapids: Eerdmans 1978).

129. Thanks to Liz Carmichael for reminding me to emphasize this feature of monastic life.

130. John 21:20.

friend.[131] And while accusations of friendship with "tax collectors and sinners"[132] need not all imply the kind of intimate conviviality we see in some of Jesus's personal relations, they suggest it as a possibility. At the very least, the Jesus whose identity is disclosed in these narratives is one who is open to others in the way that friendship requires.

Further, of course, the lifestyle tauntingly ascribed to Jesus by the Pharisees in the gospel narratives is that of one who could, when he chose, be the life of the party. There is in the life of the Jesus of the gospels the kind of *space* required to make friendship happen—as there is also attention to particular loving relationships within that space.

What about the story of Jesus's enjoining his hearers to throw dinner parties, not for friends and relatives and neighbors, but for the poor, the lame, and the blind? Jesus's purpose here seems to be to undercut the prevailing system of reciprocal obligations that kept the needy in positions of subservience. By limiting socioeconomic exchange to their peers, members of the social elite "created a situation of imbalance and competition" and acted to "strengthen their authority as leaders and the existing social order."[133]

In consequence, Jesus's teaching "should not be understood as a general prohibition of inviting relatives and friends." Friends and neighbors celebrate with those who have found the lost sheep and the lost coin in Jesus's parables. And Luke includes in his Cornelius narrative a reference to the fact that the Roman centurion convoked "his kinsmen and close friends" to await Peter's arrival.[134] Luke seems not to have seen a conflict between Jesus's injunction and the behavior of Cornelius or that of the figures in the parables. And the narrative context for the injunction—the narrative of Jesus's own behavior and the communal narrative of social relations within which Jesus's action found some of its meaning—must surely play a part in rendering the two compatible.

Narratives of Connection

Other biblical narratives, not directly concerned with friendship, underscore the significance of special relationships more generally. Consider, for instance,

131. Johnston, *Christian at Play* 120.

132. Luke 5:30.

133. Halvor Moxnes, *The Economy of the Kingdom: Social Conflict and Economic Relations in Luke's Gospel* (Philadelphia: Fortress 1988) 131.

134. Moxnes 131.

that of Joseph, whose fidelity to his particular history contributes in a circuitous way to the grand narrative of the people of Israel, which God is seen in the Old Testament to be constructing. While the gospels make clear that Jesus rejects his relatives' attempts to constrain his fidelity to his vocation, they also describe him as "obedient"[135] to his parents for a long period prior to his public ministry. In canonical perspective, at least, the same Jesus who identifies anyone who "does the will of God" as "my brother and sister and mother"[136] is the one who from the cross takes care to entrust his mother into the hands of the Beloved Disciple. Such stories form in us the disposition to a loyalty that is likely to enrich friendships as well as family relationships.

Practicing Particularity

Not only biblical narratives but also Christian practices shape character and virtue and help to orient our love toward the particular. Consider the practice of foot washing in conjunction with eucharistic celebration, embraced by various free churches. Here, though we celebrate and form universal community as we partake of the one body, the expression of love which precedes the reception of Christ's body and blood takes the form of individual ministry to a particular other: in such a ritual, believers are all one body, but each washes someone else's feet.

Sabbath observance is also a practice of foundational importance to many Christians. For Sabbath rest means freedom from the demand to produce, to secure our value through work, and to separate ourselves from others in and through hierarchies. Helping to define the rhythm of Christian life is a festival that is constituted by liberation from work and from the associated need for achievement.[137]

135. Luke 2:51.

136. Mark 3:35.

137. On the meaning of Sabbath time, see, *e.g.*, Lynne M. Baab, *Sabbath Keeping: Finding Freedom in the Rhythms of Rest* (Downers Grove, IL: IVP 2005); Donna Schaper, *Sabbath Keeping* (Cambridge, MA: Cowley 1999); Wayne Muller, *Sabbath: Restoring the Sacred Rhythm of Rest* (New York: Bantam 1999); Marva J. Dawn, *Keeping the Sabbath Wholly: Ceasing, Resting, Embracing, Feasting* (Grand Rapids: Eerdmans 1988); Tilden Edwards, *Sabbath Time: Understanding and Practice for Contemporary Christians* (New York: Seabury 1982); Charles Scriven, *Jubilee of the World: The Sabbath as a Day of Gladness* (Nashville: Southern 1978); Kenneth L. Strand, ed., *The Sabbath in Scripture and History* (Washington, DC: Review 1982); Sakae Kubo, *God Meets Man: A Theology of the Sabbath and Second Advent* (Nashville: Southern 1978); Roy Branson, ed., *Festival of the Sabbath* (Washington, DC: Association of

Moral judgment, for advocates of narrative- and virtue-centered ethics, involves testing the coherence of our various convictions and practices as contributors to an ongoing pattern of life formed by a commitment to discipleship. It will be ethically significant, on such a model, to ask whether the ongoing celebration of the Sabbath is not inconsistent with consequentialism. Does not the Sabbath provide free time—for the worshipping community, for those in need, but also for friends?[138] If the Sabbath is understood as a weekly protest against self-deification, as a denial of the human ability to be responsible for the universe, then is not an appreciation of particular loves more appropriate for a community that practices this celebration than an impartialist universalism? Is not the Sabbath a celebration and reenactment of liberation (rooted in our status as parts of God's good creation) and thus, in particular, of liberation from the need to be *doing*, to be producing good consequences? And does not the availability of this kind of liberation call consequentialism profoundly into question? For an account of Christian love centered on virtue and narrative, the Sabbath—along with a range of other narrative, practical, and theological resources—can help to ground an understanding of Christian love that strongly affirms particularity.

Flourishing

We can understand Christian love as rightly directed at various aspects of flourishing and fulfillment as these are realized in our own lives and the lives of other creatures.[139] We can thus understand love as a matter of regard for moral subjects,

---

Adventist Forums 1985); Barth, *Dogmatics* 3.1: 98–9, 313–38; 3.4: 47–72; Niels-Erik A. Andreasen, *The Christian Use of Time* (Nashville: Abingdon 1978); Niels-Erik A. Andreasen, *The Old Testament Sabbath: A Tradition-Historical Investigation*, SBL Dissertation Series 7 (Missoula, MT: Scholars 1972); Niels-Erik A. Andreasen, *Rest and Redemption*, Andrews University Monographs (Berrien Springs, MI: Andrews University Press 1978); John Brunt, *A Day for Healing: The Meaning of Jesus' Sabbath Miracles* (Washington, DC: Review 1981); Herbert W. Richardson, *Toward an American Theology* (New York: Harper 1967) 108–60; Samuele Bacchiocchi, *Divine Rest for Human Restlessness: A Theological Study of the Good News of the Sabbath for Today*, Biblical Perspectives 2 (Berrien Springs, MI: Bacchiocchi 1980); and Abraham J. Heschel, *The Sabbath: Its Meaning for Modern Man* (New York: Farrar 1951). Thanks to Roy Branson, Fritz Guy, Sakae Kubo, and Charles Sandefur for bibliographic work alerting me to most of these sources.

138. Barth, *Dogmatics* 3.4: 66.

139. This Aristotelian-Thomist view has found expression in many forms. I have drawn here (and elsewhere) with great appreciation on the variant articulated and defended especially by Germain

expressed in and through regard for their flourishing—the development of the created potential of each—and so as *focused* or *directed* in light of what flourishing looks like, including what it is to reason and choose well with respect to flourishing.

On this view, friendship is a fundamental constituent of flourishing or fulfillment, what we can call a *basic* good. Particular friendships are established through our promises and commitments and others' invited reliance on our actions. Taking seriously these promises and commitments and avoiding the unfairness of ignoring invited reliance are the sources of friendship's moral weight; and these are ways of choosing well and thus of flourishing.

As I have already suggested, morality is the domain of objective constraints on conduct and character. But of course that highly formal definition leaves open the *nature* and *point* of constraints worth affirming. Constraints of that kind are, I suggest, ones that can't be ignored or dismissed without undermining one's ability to live a genuinely good life.

By using the word *good* here, I don't mean to import preexisting notions of moral goodness, so that a good life is one that happens to exhibit what are already taken to be moral qualities. Instead, I'm concerned with goodness in the broadest sense, so that a good life can just as easily be referred to as a flourishing life, a fulfilled life, a life marked by well-being or welfare or self-realization.

There are, of course, multiple ways in which a life can go well. And there are various ways of identifying them. We might start by thinking about the basic reasons for which we do things:

Grisez and John Finnis. The explicitly theological version can be found in, *e.g.*, Germain Grisez, *The Way of the Lord Jesus* 1: *Christian Moral Principles* (Chicago: Franciscan Herald 1983); and Germain Grisez and Russell Shaw, *Fulfillment in Christ: A Summary of Christian Moral Principles* (Notre Dame, IN: University of Notre Dame Press 1991). The position is articulated in philosophical terms in, *e.g.*, Grisez and Shaw, *Morality*; Finnis, *Law*; Finnis, *Ethics*; John Finnis, *Aquinas: Moral, Political, and Legal Theory* (Oxford: Clarendon-Oxford University Press 1998); and Finnis, Boyle, and Grisez, *Nuclear Deterrence*. I have also drawn on other, related, contemporary work, including Mark C. Murphy, *Natural Law and Practical Rationality* (New York: Cambridge University Press 1999); and Timothy Chappell, *Understanding Human Goods: A Theory of Ethics* (Edinburgh: Edinburgh University Press 1998). I explain my own variant in several places, among them *Flourishing Lives*; *A Good Life in the Market: An Introduction to Business Ethics* (Great Barrington, MA: AIER 2019); *Public Practice, Private Law*; and *Anarchy and Legal Order: Law and Politics for a Stateless Society* (Cambridge: Cambridge University Press 2013).

- Why are you heading to lunch at Don Santiago's? *To meet Chris.*
- Why are you meeting Chris there? *Because it seems like a good place to have a relaxed conversation.*
- Why do you want to have a relaxed conversation with Chris? *So we can connect, catch up, become closer.*
- Why do you want that? *In order to nourish our friendship.*

An interlocutor might, of course, ask more questions at this point. But my action would be quite intelligible without answers to any of them. Friendship provides a perfectly good reason for action without any further elaboration or explanation. And that's a sign that it's a basic element of flourishing. Similarly, emphasizing my desire for the flavorful food on offer at Don Santiago's explains my decision to eat there in a fully comprehensible way; and this suggests that seeking the pleasure associated with eating is a perfectly good reason to do something without the need for any additional justification or clarification.

Another way of identifying basic aspects of well-being might be to reflect on what's involved when we think about *injuries*. Being the target of malevolent gossip might make me sad, anxious, or angry; and I might experience these emotional reactions, in turn, because of my fear that the gossip will (perhaps among other things) disrupt one or more friendships.[140] There wouldn't be any further need to make sense of my reaction: concern about my friendships would be sufficient.

I might attend to cross-cultural evidence, noting the evident appeal of friendship in multiple cultures and the widespread recognition of its value (a recognition that might even involve treating it as a formal institution).[141] Or I might ask, simply, whether friendship was something I would *recognize* as part of a flourishing life, rather as I might ask whether a shiny coat or the ability and desire to play should be seen as an aspect of a dog's flourishing. Or I might ask whether friendship was a way of exercising an array of capacities—for communication,

140. I'm using friendship-specific examples here, but of course I might also worry that the gossip might disrupt business relationships, that the disruption of these relationships might lead to a loss of income, and that the loss of income might impede my ability to buy a painting, and so to participate in the good of *aesthetic experience*. Or perhaps the loss of income might limit my capacity to make a significant donation to my alma mater, and so to contribute to others' participation in the good of *knowledge*.

141. See, *e.g.*, Brain, *Friends and Lovers*; and DuBois, "Gratuitous Act" 15–32. Again, I might recognize a range of human (and nonhuman) goods in this way.

coordination, identification, affection, loyalty, and so forth—characteristic of creatures like myself. And so forth.

On multiple grounds, then, I might reasonably come to see friendship as a basic aspect of my well-being, an aspect that didn't need explaining or justifying with reference to any deeper or more general variety of well-being. And of course I might identify various additional general categories of fulfillment in similar or other ways. These might include, say, aesthetic experience, bodily well-being, harmony with reality, imaginative immersion, knowledge, life, meaning in life, mental capacity, peace of mind, play, practical reasonableness, self-integration, sensory pleasure, and skillful performance.[142] Each of these dimensions of flourishing, fulfillment, or welfare can be seen as, among other things, a development or expression of an underlying created potential.[143]

These various ways in which a life might go well are qualitatively distinct. There's no sense in treating any of them as more basic than any of the others. None can be reduced to any of the others, nor is any one the *point* of any or all of the others. Nor is there some *other* substantive thing (*flourishing* and *well-being* are just generic labels for the condition of which all of these things are consistent), as I noted in discussing consequentialism, of which all of them are instances or that all of them promote. As I've emphasized, *choosing* well—exercising *practical reasonableness*—is a dimension of *living* well. And there are multiple ways of choosing well with respect to the various elements of well-being. Each of these is a way of loving or of supporting love.[144] I'll refer to them collectively as ways of loving well or as requirements of love in action.

(*i*) RECOGNITION. Choose in ways designed directly or indirectly to further or realize genuine aspects of well-being. Acting in accordance with this principle

142. This list is largely the same as the one advanced by Finnis, Grisez, and other recent natural law theorists. See, *e.g.*, Chappell, *Understanding Human Goods* 37–45; Murphy, *Natural Law* 96–138; Alfonso Gómez-Lobo, *Morality and the Human Goods: An Introduction to Natural Law Ethics* (Washington, DC: Georgetown University Press 2002) 6–25; Grisez and Shaw, *Morality* 77–88; Grisez, *Principles* 121–5; and Finnis, *Law* 59–99. One notable difference from the approach favored by Finnis and Grisez in particular is the identification of sensory pleasure as a basic good (an issue regarding which I agree with Chappell). For my defense of the claim that it is, see Chartier, *Public Practice, Private Law* 115–9.

143. On the general nature of these goods, see, *e.g.*, Henry Veatch, *For an Ontology of Morals* (Evanston, IL: Northwestern University Press 1971) 99–124; Richard Kraut, *What Is Good and Why: The Ethics of Well-Being* (Cambridge, MA: Harvard University Press 2007); and Dewey, "Conception of Happiness" 280.

144. Grisez and Shaw (*Morality* 117) speak appealingly in this connection of "guidelines for love." I think it's also useful to see the relevant requirements as ways *in which* we love.

is an important aspect of love because it involves concern for someone's actual welfare; love isn't about nourishing anyone's fantasies.

(*ii*) THE PAULINE PRINCIPLE. Don't choose in a way designed purposefully or instrumentally to injure any basic aspect of well-being—in one's own life or another's. Acting on this principle is an important aspect of love because loving yourself and others means recognizing and treating every dimension of everyone's well-being as genuinely valuable, whether or not it's your primary focus.[145]

(*iii*) COMMITMENT. Use commitments to organize (at least some of) your efforts to further or realize various aspects of well-being; make commitments and keep them except when it's reasonable not to do so. Embracing this principle is an important aspect of love because realizing some dimensions of welfare requires deep, focused self-investment: to love superficially means that you and others will miss out on various basic goods.[146]

(*iv*) EFFICIENCY. Seek your goals in ways that don't unnecessarily reduce the time, energy, money, and the like available for the pursuit of other goals. Adhering to this principle is an important aspect of love because we can love more effectively when we don't get distracted and waste resources as we pursue our objectives.

(*v*) THE GOLDEN RULE. Don't treat those affected by your actions *arbitrarily*. When you treat some people differently than you treat others, do so in order to (directly or indirectly) further or realize some basic aspect of well-being. (It's reasonable to, say, pick good athletes for your soccer team instead of choosing the members at random.) And do so in a way that's consistent with a standard you'd be willing to accept if it were applied consistently to you and those you cared about. Following this principle is an important aspect of love because

145. This principle qualifies as "Pauline" because of Saint Paul's resoundingly negative response in Rom 3:8 to the question, "And why not say . . . , 'Let us do evil so that good may come'?" Paul's words concern doing evil to bring about some good end; for the sake of convenience, I've combined what could be treated as two principles, choosing to include under the same heading not only the prohibition on instrumental injury but also the prohibition of injury perpetrated for its own sake (as, for instance, out of hostility). For the label "the Pauline Principle," see Finnis, *Ethics* 109; and Donagan, *Theory of Morality* 149. For elaborations and defenses of the principle, see, *e.g.*, Murphy, *Natural Law* 204–7; Finnis, *Ethics* 109–27; Grisez and Shaw, *Morality* 129–39; Finnis, Boyle, and Grisez, *Nuclear Deterrence* 286–7; and Finnis, *Law* 118–25.

146. See Chartier, *Logic*.

everyone is uniquely valuable, irreplaceable, and thus lovable, and to recognize everyone's unique value is to avoid arbitrarily dismissing anyone.[147]

We can identify friendship as a basic aspect of well-being, so acting in order to initiate or develop a friendship will be consistent with RECOGNITION. In turn, THE GOLDEN RULE will generate a number of obligations to friends. It will do so in virtue of explicit promises to friends, implicit invitations to reliance issued by one's conduct (and perhaps by one's words) when one is a friend, and, more generally, the norms of the tacit institution of friendship to the extent that these norms are assumed by and shape the contexts of friends' interactions.

Obligations with respect to friends and friendship will also be established in virtue of COMMITMENT. Commitments establish one's friends as priorities, so that nurturing and otherwise benefiting one's friends, engaging with them, and investing oneself in and enriching one's relationships with them will rightly claim one's attention on an ongoing basis. Commitments will also ground the creation and sustenance of projects *shared* with friends—whether in virtue of mutual benefit, mutual interest, or the expectation that such projects will deepen friends' connections with each other.

Obligations to or with respect to friends qua friends will also follow from THE PAULINE PRINCIPLE, which will preclude deliberate attacks on one's own or others' friendships as well as injuring such relationships deliberately in order to reach particular goals. (It may, of course, be consistent with THE PAULINE PRINCIPLE to cause foreseen but unintended injury to a friendship, as when one reveals to one friend that another friend is embezzling money from a shared enterprise and has ignored appeals and opportunities to repay it. The revelation may lead to a relational rupture, but the rupture is neither the intended outcome of the revelation nor a means to some other goal. It is a regrettable side effect.)

Christian love lies at the heart of flourishing, and flourishing is the rightful object of Christian love. An understanding of love rooted in flourishing can explain, justify, and encourage our interactions with our friends and our long-term relationships with them.

147. For biblical expressions of this principle, see, *e.g.*, Lev 19:18 and Luke 6:31. For elaborations and defenses, see, *e.g.*, Finnis, *Law* 106–9, 304–5; Finnis, *Aquinas* 140; Finnis, *Ethics* 75; Finnis, Boyle, and Grisez, *Nuclear Deterrence* 284; John Finnis, "Commensuration and Practical Reason," *Incommensurability, Incomparability, and Practical Reason*, ed. Ruth Chang (Cambridge, MA: Harvard University Press 1997) 227; Grisez and Shaw, *Morality* 119–20; and Grisez, *Principles* 220. See R. M. Hare, *Freedom and Reason* (Oxford: Clarendon-Oxford University Press 1963).

Friendship and Love

If Christian love is abstract, universal, impartial—whether it's Tolstoyan or consequentialist—it can't make sense of obligations to friends or of self-investment in friendship or other special relationships. That ought to make us skeptical about understanding Christian love in this way. Skepticism seems particularly sensible given that there are so many better ways of understanding love. Thinking about these alternatives can help us to understand friendship, and love in general, more adequately.

While each of the positions I've discussed has merits, I suggest that the most satisfactory is the one that understands Christian love as oriented on human flourishing and that sees friendship as a variety of love understood in this way.

A divine command ethic can explain friendship as a divinely directed facet of human culture, or as an element within some more inclusive divine institution—or, indeed, as a response to situation-specific divine commands to individuals. Divine command views can thus effectively capture the diversity of human moral experience and action, the variety of goods that we confront and seek to realize, the full range of Christian love's appropriate foci.

We might wish to think of divine commands as directing Christian love by means of creational structures—mandates or orders of creation. The fact that the divine command approach focuses on the choices of a personal God means that an account of love that makes divinely commanded orders central can perhaps look more critically at individual institutions or behavior patterns than Gustafson's approach. A given creational structure can be seen as embodying God's purpose. However, when there is uncertainty, that purpose can (for the Reformed and Lutheran thinkers who often make appeals to orders or mandates) be interpreted with reference to other things we take ourselves to know regarding divine purposes. These include, most notably, the things we discern in and through the life, ministry, death, and life beyond death of Jesus. But various biblical passages outside the gospels may be treated as relevant, too. Orders or mandates can sometimes seem—and doubtless they sometimes are—unduly rigid, functioning to, in effect, place a divine imprimatur on the status quo. But their broader theological context features the potential for a degree of flexibility and a potential for criticism of social institutions.

An approach that focuses on flourishing and fulfillment can exhibit features like those that make divine command views attractive. It can build in a recognition of multiple goods from the ground up. At the same time, such an approach doesn't feature the same liabilities as a divine command view. It doesn't run the risk of seeming to depict God as a capricious tyrant or to endorse a voluntaristic, arbitrary view of the good and the right, one that risks evacuating talk of divine love of any content.[148]

An emphasis on flourishing can also incorporate even more flexibility, at least in some ways, than an orders-or-mandates divine command theory. A flourishing-oriented approach can begin with our created characteristics just as the approach stressing orders and mandates can. But instead of identifying developed complex structures—family, workplace, state—as reflective of the divine will, this approach can see our created natures as rightly expressed in a broad range of institutional environments, all perfectly acceptable as long as they treat goods as goods and are thus consistent with the requirements of love in action. The approach emphasizing flourishing also avoids the voluntaristic flavor of the stance emphasizing mandates or orders as the heart of social and political ethics, even if one of those mandates is a mandate to enter and enjoy the free space of culture: the mandates-or-orders view would, of course, encounter the familiar difficulties besetting divine command views. If there is no structure of friendship inherent in creation, why would it be loving for God to *impose* one? An emphasis on flourishing doesn't need to confront this sort of question, since it takes friendship's status as a genuine aspect of well-being to be a function of the way we've been created, not of a divine command independent of our natures.

Gustafson's proposal for theocentric ethics offers a way of channeling love that's somewhat similar to the orders-or-mandates approach. For theocentric ethics, love is rightly ordered in light of our status as creatures—our finitude, our contingency, our interdependence, and a range of biological drives and circumstances that constrain our choices and aspirations. On this sort of view, we might identify friendships as among the relationships that order our shared lives, with the patterning of our shared existence shaped by various biological and sociological constraints, and with friendship taking its place in relation to more inclusive wholes which determine its limits. Theocentric ethics highlights those aspects of our natures and circumstances which encourage the formation and maintenance of special relationships. At the same time, this recognition of the contexts within which individual relationships occur helps to keep us from absolutizing these relationships and prompts us to acknowledge their limitations.

148. See Chartier, *Analogy of Love* 189–204.

A flourishing-oriented approach can also take account of these features of human life. At the same time, it can provide a more critical, reflective perspective on the human situation, one that begins from but does not end with our status as ecologically embedded organic creatures. Such an approach can affirm various aspects of flourishing not only as objects of desire or reflections of biological constraint but also as surviving critical scrutiny on a variety of fronts. It can offer us tools for reflective scrutiny of proposals to treat our biological characteristics as grounds for action. And, because of its inherent focus on the welfare of sentients (nonhuman as well as human, on my preferred version),[149] it can avoid the kind of antihumanism, marked by a tendency to treat nonsentient reality as valuable apart from its role in the flourishing of sentients, to which a position that views natural constraints as appropriate occasions for piety may perhaps sometimes be prone.

The notion of vocation can be deployed to ground special obligations to friends and others by permitting special relationships to be understood as divine gifts entrusted to one's care. A vocation can also offer a moral agent robust personal integrity, with a distinct moral identity. And a vocational approach to understanding friendship's moral significance can recognize the importance of loving particular people and of calls to love that reflect an agent's particular identity.

An understanding of Christian love rooted in flourishing can do these things, too. It can emphasize the importance of self-committal that both shapes an agent's ongoing identity and reflects her preexisting characteristics and passions. This approach need not run the risks associated with a voluntaristic understanding of vocation, which must ultimately treat a vocation as a willful divine imposition (even if it is framed as an invitation rather than as a command). But it also need not encounter the difficulties associated with nonvoluntaristic understandings of vocation. These views seem committed to the idea that a given path is uniquely suited to or uniquely required of an agent (so that God simply, in effect, *reveals* to the agent what's required and what fits by conveying a vocation to her). However, human goods are diverse, the future is indeterminate, and our commitments can reshape our preferences and inclinations (so that these should not be treated as simply *given*). It's unclear, then, that in a typical case there will *be* any *single* path or set of nearby paths that fits with an agent's identity in a way which makes following this path or set of paths the agent's only reasonable moral option. An approach focused on flourishing can

149. See Chartier, *Anarchy* 93–108.

thus safeguard the moral agent's freedom, which a vocation has the potential to compromise.

A covenantal model of Christian love rightly understands that particular relationships have distinctive moral standing and recognizes the value of freedom in establishing these relationships. Friendship can be conceived of as one of those human covenants—imitative of, responsive to, and conveying God's covenant fidelity—to which Christian love gives rise and within which Christian love is channeled. The covenantal view can also, by stressing the historical development of relationships, take account of the growth of friendship outside the bounds of explicit institutionalization (though it need not resist the formalization and celebration of friendship when these things occur).

A model of love as oriented toward flourishing, while it will certainly appreciate the importance of mutual covenants, can also acknowledge the force of self-committing choices that needn't involve promises *to* anyone in focusing our loves. It can embrace the stress in the covenantal account on the historical character of personal identity. It can offer explicit recognition of the diversity of ways in which lives can go well, something that may be omitted by a covenantal approach. And it can thus enhance the intelligibility and appropriateness of covenants with friends by underscoring the character of friendship as an aspect of human flourishing. It allows, in short, for the affirmation of a key insight of the covenantal model while allowing for a thicker, richer account of the good and the right.

An approach to Christian love focused on virtue and narrative can ground friendship and other special relations in the particularity of God's love for individual creatures and communities and in the practices characteristic of the church's life, narratively discerned. Because of the nature of the biblical stories on which Christian narrative-cum-virtue ethics will likely draw, this approach will be less likely to embrace the sorts of rigoristic fantasies which abstract impartialism might find it easier to endorse. The stories and practices on which Christian ethicists attentive to narrative quite reasonably focus are ones that acknowledge the worth of particular divine and human love. An approach emphasizing virtue and narrative also rightly stresses the importance of flexibility and skill in making moral judgments and of stories in helping us to learn what making such judgments well actually looks like. It is not inimical to principles, but it resists treating principles as highly abstract and interpretable apart from context.[150]

150. Hauerwas, *Kingdom* 19–22; McClendon, *Systematic Theology* 1: 334–46.

An approach to Christian love that emphasizes flourishing can also stress the value of flexible judgment and the helpful role of narrative in moral learning. It can also, at the same time, emphasize that principles yield clearer and more reliable judgments while also proving independently defensible: there are reasons, for instance, to avoid purposeful attacks on noncombatants that don't need to be teased out of narratives. There really may, of course, be times in which abstraction is apropos: the generic features of an act (as, for instance, the characteristics in virtue of which the act amounts to a purposeful attack on noncombatants) may be entirely sufficient to rule it out. A stress on flourishing as an aspect of created being can acknowledge the limits on the value of theological filters and reinterpretations of creational insight and can allow creation, in turn, to inform theological formulations. And an approach to which flourishing is central can keep the focus of ethics where it belongs, on the well-being of actual moral subjects, thus avoiding the risk that a narrative approach can turn into a sophisticated defense of arbitrary voluntarism.

A flourishing-oriented understanding of love can agree with a narrative-focused approach that we flourish precisely as social creatures. Our sociality doesn't change the basic ways in which we flourish, but it provides alternative paths to flourishing and alternative capacities for flourishing. Our flourishing, rooted in our created natures and consisting of our reasonable participation in diverse aspects of well-being, takes multiple forms. Friendship is one. To affirm and safeguard friendship is part of what it means to live a flourishing life.

Christian love might be understood in a variety of ways. The best, I suggest here, sees love as shaped, expressed, and channeled by the requirements of love in action and thus as directed to and through the various aspects of flourishing. Friendship is not the only way we can love, of course: we love when we engage in play, when we create beauty, and so forth. But friendship is one fundamental way in which we can flourish and thus one fundamental expression and object of Christian love.

Moral Rectitude

The understanding of friendship as an aspect of Christian love I've tried to articulate can provide us with tools that help us think through an important set of worries related to friendship.

It might be tempting to suppose that one should only be friends with someone who possesses one or more virtues—that friendship depends on "similarity of life, morals, and pursuits among the just."[151] It might also be appealing to think that, character aside, serious wrongdoing rendered people ineligible for friendship. One might believe, then, that one should withhold love from actual or potential friends because of their character flaws or morally objectionable choices. One might do so because of the worry that (*i*) a friend who wasn't a good person wouldn't treat one well. One might have the sense that (*ii*) someone who wasn't morally worthy didn't *deserve* the great good of friendship. One might suppose that (*iii*) a person without a morally good character couldn't be attractive as a person, and so as a friend. One might suppose that (*iv*) a friend without a morally excellent character would be a source of *impurity* or that (*v*) such a friend might affect one's behavior in ways that led one unreasonably to injure one or more aspects of my own or another's well-being. One might be concerned that (*vi*) association with a morally flawed friend might be bad for one's reputation or self-image. One might also imagine that (*vii*) a friend who had acted wrongly should sometimes be rejected as a matter of loyalty or that (*viii*) rejection was an appropriate way of motivating improved behavior. But one should, I believe, be very hesitant before treating people's moral choices or characters as justifying or requiring one's rejection of them as friends.

Some Virtues Equip Us to Be Friends

While friends may exhibit very different character traits, certain virtues may be required to sustain any recognizable friendship. (I've already noted my preference for an ethical approach rooted in principles. Such an approach can recognize that there are virtues—settled dispositions to choose wisely in accordance with the relevant principles.) Even allowing for the varieties of friendship within and across cultures, the nature of friendship is such that one will not be able to function effectively as a friend if one does not exhibit a range of traits at least to some degree.[152] Perhaps these might include trustworthiness, fairness, truthfulness, loyalty, generosity, affection, candor, patience, sympathy, fidelity, respect,

151. Ælred of Rievaulx, *Spiritual Friendship*, trans. Mary Eugenia Laker (Kalamazoo, MI: Cistercian 1977) 1.38; cp. 2.43.

152. Perhaps this is what Cicero, for instance, has in mind when talking about the relationship between friendship and virtue: Marcus Tullius Cicero, *Lælius de amicitia*, trans. William Armistead Falconer (London: Heinemann 1915) 20 (§6) <https://penelope.uchicago.edu/Thayer/E/Roman/Texts/Cicero/Laelius_de_Amicitia/text*.html> (Oct. 16, 2020) ("Without virtue friendship cannot exist at all").

and benevolence.[153] There are obviously character traits, similarly, that are at least in tension with friendship; among them might be untrustworthiness, fickleness, infidelity, coldness, and stinginess.[154]

Whatever someone's *other* character traits, she will be unable to function successfully as a friend without embodying a range of specific features. She need not do so perfectly or in the same manner as someone else; and, of course, the *degree* to which she does so may not be tested throughout much of the life of a given friendship—perhaps not at all. And she may not necessarily exhibit them to the same extent in other relationships as in her friendships. But she must exhibit them to some degree for her to be recognizable as a friend at all. In *this* sense, then, virtue is a precondition for friendship.

Those unwilling to acquire or develop certain basic virtues cannot be friends, not because of moralistic exclusion by others, but because they simply are not currently capable of, or at least willing to participate in, friendship. The kind of person who can be a genuine friend is significantly limited as regards characteristics she can exhibit while remaining a friend.

This doesn't mean, of course, that friends will always behave well. A friend can treat one very poorly, and there's no reason to ignore it when a friend does so. One may of course quite reasonably take steps to protect oneself if a friend is behaving badly. But reasonable self-protection is very different from rejecting a current or potential friend on the basis of an abstract assessment of her character. There's no need to let fear or judgment deprive one of the opportunity to discover that person's unique gifts.

One should be able to distinguish between protecting oneself from being treated badly (perhaps there are some friends one should never involve in one's financial affairs, others to whom one should never tell secrets) and rejecting someone entirely as a possible or actual friend. And there will often be occasions for grace. Even people with good characters sometimes act wrongly. And forgiveness is a vital source of support for the continuing development of our friendships.

153. Casey, *Pagan Virtue* 186–7; McClendon, *Systematic Theology* 1: 172–3. I've added "respect" to the list, given the importance of recognizing a friend as *other*. See Badhwar, "Guided by the Best" 484, 499.

154. See Casey, *Pagan Virtue* 186–7. Casey instances "envy, wrath, incapacity for proper anger, vanity, lack of proper pride, cowardice, disloyalty, lack of affection," lack of generosity, and lack of self-respect.

As a friendship develops, each friend can reasonably insist that the other treat her in appropriate ways. The moral demands imposed on friends explicitly by each other but also by the inner logic of friendship can help friends to develop the virtues of friendship over time. And friends' acceptance of each other seems more likely to foster growth than the threat of rejection.[155]

Friendship Isn't Something You Deserve

Contrary to what an overly moralized view might suggest, friendship isn't a reward for good behavior. Being someone's friend isn't a matter of giving her an honor for which she has to qualify, of presenting her with a gold star in recognition of her virtue. Friendship is an outgrowth of resonance, connection, care, and delight—responses that lead to commitment and loyalty. I wouldn't want to be presented with friendship as an award; so THE GOLDEN RULE dictates that I not treat my offer of friendship to someone else that way either.

Moral Excellence Isn't the Only Thing That's Appealing

All of the various ways of flourishing can be attractive. That includes genuine moral goodness (a matter especially of practical reasonableness and self-integration). But this kind of goodness isn't the only kind of flourishing that's attractive. And its absence is hardly sufficient to make someone unappealing on all fronts. There are, for instance, excellences that a stereotypical rascal or scamp exhibits that can be sources of attraction even as they accompany traits we rightly regard with dismay.

Everyone we know is, of course, a mixture of appealing and unappealing qualities. Of course, no one is likely to exhibit all of the character traits we're likely to regard as desirable, though most people will possess *some* excellences. One might be attracted to these even if others, including specifically moral ones, are quite absent. And undoubted, even exceptional, virtues can coexist with

155. The nurturing, accepting family, whatever the explicit religious avowals of the parents, is far more likely to produce children with religiously healthy attitudes than is the family—whatever the parents' overt convictions—that instills fear, guilt, and repression or that declines to offer children structure. See Anderson and Guernsey, *On Being Family* 132–6. Similarly, the same sorts of primary group dynamics that predispose a person to favor fascism in one context can prepare her to be a committed communist in another.

unmistakable vices: people are complicated, and it's rarely possible or helpful to render truly global verdicts on their characters.[156]

People's various qualities are of incommensurable value, so there's no objective sense in which their flaws could in principle outweigh their excellences. How we weigh their qualities when we're deciding whether to become friends with them is up to us. And we're more than free, therefore, to emphasize the positive, to look for deal*makers* rather than deal*breakers*, an approach that is not only ethically appealing but also likely to increase our capacities to enjoy our friends and our lives. What it *doesn't* make any sense to do is to treat individual defects as if they automatically canceled or overwhelmed good qualities and thus ruled people out as potential friends.

We don't want to be tested for moral flawlessness before we're accepted as friends. We don't want to be limited to accepting as friends those who qualify in light of a moral review. We might thus well agree with Mary Elizabeth Hunt: "People I want to be around do not subject their relationships to a standard of political correctness."[157] So THE GOLDEN RULE gives us some reason to avoid testing friends' virtues.

No One Can Make You Impure

A morally flawed friend is not a source of impurity because no one is a source of impurity. There is moral responsibility, of course, but there is no such thing as a taint—the moral or spiritual equivalent of a noxious odor—that attaches to someone in a way that makes her worthy of being avoided just as such. Purity is not an aspect of flourishing.

Christians remember that Jesus was dismissed as "a glutton and a drunkard, a friend of tax collectors and sinners"[158] and that he challenged purity rules. His opposition to purity rules seems to have been among the most important reasons he evoked opposition.[159] Those who retell the story of Jesus and who

156. Gilbert Meilaender puzzles thoughtfully over the joint appearance of undoubted vice and unquestionable virtue in "Virtuous Evildoers: On the Paradoxes of Virtue," *First Things* (Institute on Religion and Public Life), Feb. 2018 <https://www.firstthings.com/article/2018/02/virtuous-evildoers>.

157. Mary Elizabeth Hunt, *Fierce Tenderness: A Feminist Theology of Friendship* (New York: Crossroad 1990) 170.

158. Matt 11:19.

159. See, *e.g.*, Marcus J. Borg, *Conflict, Holiness, and Politics in the Teachings of Jesus* (Harrisburg, PA: Trinity 1998) 8–10, 14, 17, 248.

understand their own stories as occurring within that story should find that they experience particularly strong motivation to resist the temptation to reject friends (or others) on the basis of concern with purity.

We are not defiled by our contact with flawed people any more than others are defiled by their contact with us (since we, too, are morally imperfect). The attempt to find some account of impurity consistent with a reasonable morality is an exercise in rationalization: one does not, for instance, in any way commit oneself to endorsing any particular choice by a given person or any particular character trait she exhibits because one loves *her*. If one did, then God's approval of our actions and dispositions could be inferred on the basis of God's love for us. My purpose in nourishing connection with someone need have nothing to do with encouraging that person's flaws or the injuries to others that might flow from them.

Fear of Influence Shouldn't Keep Us from Loving Friends

Out of love for third parties, for our friends, and for ourselves, we might hesitate to accept a friend's influence.

Both because friendship itself requires certain moral virtues and because among those is respect for a friend's otherness, there is some reason to assume that a friend won't *push* one to love inadequately—to engage unreasonably in actions likely to cause, constitute, or bring about injuries to oneself or others or to involve disregard for one's responsibilities to oneself or others. Of course, at the same time, friends are, like the rest of us, morally imperfect, and so may not exhibit the virtues of friendship consistently or flawlessly. And of course friends may simply differ sincerely and thoughtfully about moral matters: what seems like blatant immorality to me may strike you as a harmless violation of some pietistic restraint or a valuable means of self-assertion. So friends may confront various sorts of challenges and conflicts related to moral differences.

It's certainly reasonable to expect friends to avoid pressuring us to do things we believe are wrong. And perhaps one might want to step away from a conversation or disengage from an outing if one feels oneself drawn toward doing something one believes one will subsequently have reason to regret. But that's no reason to reject one's friends. And of course it makes even less sense to decline to open oneself in the first place to a friendship one would otherwise find appealing because one fears a state of affairs that hasn't even come into being.

In virtue of pressure or example, a friend might prompt one to behave badly in a way that exerted a negative effect on one's own flourishing or on someone else's. One certainly needs to take this possibility into account when deciding whether to initiate a friendship, whether to continue a friendship, or how to interact with a friend. Whether choosing to engage with the actual or potential friend in this case is reasonable depends on whether choosing to do so is consistent with the requirements of love in action.

(*i*) It would be consistent with RECOGNITION if one's purpose was to participate in the genuine good of *friendship*, an authentic aspect of flourishing (or some other genuine constituent of well-being).

(*ii*) It would be consistent with THE PAULINE PRINCIPLE provided the occurrence of any resulting injury wasn't the purpose of one's choice to begin or maintain the friendship or to engage with the friend in particular ways.

One might decide to accept or continue a friendship or to interact with a friend in a particular way precisely in the hope that the friend's influence will lead one to behave in ways one otherwise wouldn't. (Perhaps because one knows or takes oneself to be a coward, unwilling to choose on one's own to perform an action one finds appealing.) So, in particular, one might decide to embrace or persist in a friendship, or to welcome opportunities to share particular sorts of experiences with a friend, in order to become the kind of person who will injure someone else in a particular way—by betraying that person, stealing from that person, slandering that person . . . To choose in this way—to engage with someone, in general or in a particular manner, *for the purpose* of bringing oneself to the point at which one will unreasonably injure someone else—is, in effect, to accept causing the injury itself as a purpose. And this, in turn, is inconsistent with THE PAULINE PRINCIPLE. It is always wrong to choose to injure.

But of course one might be led in virtue of a friendship to cause injury to someone else even though one's choice to initiate or maintain the friendship, or to engage in a particular way with one's friend, was a reflection of some motive quite unrelated to the injury. In this case, the injury would be inadvertent: it would be an outcome of one's choices with respect to the friendship, an outcome one anticipated as certain, likely, or possible; however, causing it wouldn't be among one's *purposes* in choosing to commence or continue in the friendship or to behave in relation to one's friend in a particular way. The same is true of the unreasonable choice lying behind the injury. If causing injury, or making oneself the kind of person more likely to cause injury, is neither one's purpose nor a means to some other end but simply a by-product or side effect of, say, the decision to nourish a friendship, then that decision need not be inconsistent with THE PAULINE PRINCIPLE. (Remember that this doesn't mean it would necessarily be reasonable *all things considered*; the other requirements of love in action have to be satisfied, too.)

(*iii*) In principle, COMMITMENT might be relevant in more than one way. One might have committed to avoiding the formation of a friendship with the person in question. One might also, separately, have committed to not causing the relevant kind of injury. And one might have committed to taking special care not to cause any injury, purposeful or inadvertent, to those likely to be affected. In cases like these, forming or maintaining a friendship would be inconsistent with COMMITMENT. But such cases seem pretty improbable; we don't make commitments of the envisioned sorts very often. In their absence, there's no reason to think it would be.

(*iv*) It would be consistent with EFFICIENCY provided choosing to pursue or sustain a friendship or interact with a friend in relevant ways didn't impede progress toward a goal one had committed to seeking in a manner that didn't allow for these friendship-related activities.

(*v*) It would be consistent with THE GOLDEN RULE if one could reasonably accept the risk of causing the relevant sort of injury.

In this connection, it's important to think about (*a*) the likelihood that the actual or potential friend will exert influence by pressure or example with the potential to lead one to harm one's own or another's well-being, (*b*) the likelihood that the influence will actually lead one to harm one's own or another's well-being, and (*c*) the likelihood that the potential harm will be of a given quality and severity. In light of these considerations, one will need to think about whether one would be acting arbitrarily in acting in a way with the potential to lead to the kind of injury in question (one with the relevant magnitude, the given probability of occurrence, and so on). As one does so, it will be important to remember that our ability to predict the future is limited. We should not assume that we know what sort of impact a friendship will have on us. And we should not begin with the most catastrophic assumptions about its likely impact (any more, no doubt, than we should begin with naïve optimism). One might also want to take account of other factors, including good outcomes that might result from pursuing or continuing in the friendship or engaging with the friend in the relevant way—good outcomes *apart from* the flourishing of the friendship itself.

By beginning or continuing a given friendship or interacting with a friend in a way that might lead one to behave badly, is one treating different people differently with no good reason? Is one discriminating against them capriciously? One probably is not doing so if, again, one is acting in view of a genuine good—in this case, the good of friendship. But this still leaves open the second question one needs to answer to determine the consistency of a choice with THE GOLDEN

RULE: Would one be willing to accept a standard that permitted one to act in a way with the potential to lead to the kind of injury in question? For a reasonable standard would *also* be one that permitted anyone else in relevantly similar circumstances to act in the same kind of way. And acting in the same kind of way might involve behaving in a manner that led to injury, not to the third parties who might be adversely affected by one's own act, but, rather, to others, including not only third parties but also, potentially, oneself or one's loved ones.

If one *would* be willing to accept this kind of standard, then pursuing or maintaining the friendship, or interacting with the friend in the relevant sort of way, would be consistent with THE GOLDEN RULE. If, however, one realizes in the light of honest reflection that one *wouldn't* be willing to accept this kind of standard, then the relevant choice or pattern of choices wouldn't be consistent with THE GOLDEN RULE. And if one's choice or pattern of choices is consistent with all of the requirements of love in action, then it qualifies as a reasonable expression of love.

Consider an example. My friend Chris seems to specialize in treating others in a thoroughly catty way. And suppose I judge that, as a result of maintaining a friendship with Chris, *I* will, over time, come to treat other people less graciously. I may fear that I shouldn't be Chris's friend as a result.

Is remaining friends with Chris a reasonable way of loving? (*i*) I engage with Chris in view of the genuine good of friendship, so choosing to remain friends with him is consistent with RECOGNITION. (*ii*) I don't *intend* to become cattier or to injure people with my cattiness; no commitment precludes my being friends with Chris, so choosing to remain friends with him is consistent with THE PAULINE PRINCIPLE. (*iii*) Staying friends with Chris doesn't violate any serious plans or resolutions I've made, so it's consistent with COMMITMENT. (*iv*) It also doesn't involve any sort of ineffective pursuit of my goals, so it's consistent with EFFICIENCY. (*v*) Suppose I would be willing to accept a principle permitting my continued friendship with Chris, even if it meant that, in virtue of her friendship with another person, someone else was cattier with me or a loved one. In this case, while I would still have good reason to try to avoid inappropriate cattiness, remaining Chris's friend would be consistent with THE GOLDEN RULE. So, on the analysis I've offered, it would be consistent with the requirements of love in action for me to maintain my friendship with Chris.

It's also worth emphasizing that, even if it *wouldn't* be fair to accept a certain kind of influence from a potential or actual friend *in particular circumstances*, it doesn't follow that it would be unreasonable to initiate or continue the friendship. All that follows is that one should avoid the kinds of situations in which the relevant sort of influence would likely be exerted.

We should welcome opportunities to learn from friends. And that includes opportunities to learn about moral questions. To put it another way, we should not begin by assuming that, when we disagree with friends, when we take them to be disposed to believe and act wrongly, we're obviously right and they're obviously wrong, so that a friend's influence that pushes me in a new direction is in principle a *bad* influence. It's worthwhile to engage, observe, and discover, recognizing that we might sometimes find ourselves surprised. The humble realization that we might be wrong should provide reason to avoid fleeing a possible or existing friendship with someone out of fear that one might treat others badly because of her influence.

Worries about Negative Attitudes Shouldn't Prompt Rejection

One might be tempted to reject a friend in the fear that her sin, fallibility, and brokenness would encourage others to treat one poorly. Rejecting a friend on this basis hardly seems likely to be consistent with a genuine commitment to friendship. And it seems unlikely to square with THE GOLDEN RULE either, since one almost certainly wouldn't be willing to be rejected by a friend on the basis of *her* reputational worries. One might also worry that a friend's bad behavior might encourage one to think ill of oneself. But acceptance of oneself as a part of God's good creation, whose status is validated by divine love and grace, can make it less appealing to reject a friend in the interest of one's own self-image.[160]

Loyalty and Rejection

It may sometimes seem that we should reject morally flawed people as friends because we shouldn't find them *attractive*. But we may also think that we should say *no* to an actual or potential friendship with someone whose wrongdoing has injured someone else. Suppose, for instance, that Chris is friends with married partners Pat and Jean. Jean has an affair with Ray, going on to leave Pat and move in with Ray. Jean insists that Chris not be friends with Pat, while Pat insists that Chris not be friends with Jean.

Chris might well judge that Jean had acted wrongly (and perhaps also that in some other way, Pat had done so, too). But it would, at any rate, be entirely

160. O'Donovan, *Ethics as Theology* 3: 143.

consistent to judge that this was the case even while refusing to accept the demand issued by Pat to avoid friendship with Jean.

Chris's choice to remain connected with Jean despite Pat's objections (the same kind of analysis I offer here would apply to Chris's friendship with Pat despite Jean's objections) could be undertaken in pursuit of a real good, the good of friendship, and would thus be consistent with RECOGNITION. It need not be undertaken for the purpose of affirming Jean's choice to betray Pat or for the purpose of communicating the inaccurate message that this choice was acceptable or as any other sort of attack on Pat's well-being (or anyone else's). Chris could perfectly well be disappointed by this choice while still caring about and being loyal to Jean. Chris's continued friendship with Jean would thus be consistent with THE PAULINE PRINCIPLE. Presuming Chris has made no prior resolution that would bar continued friendship with Jean, persisting in the friendship would be consistent with COMMITMENT. Absent quite special circumstances, doing so would also be consistent with EFFICIENCY. There's also no reason the continued friendship would be inconsistent with THE GOLDEN RULE; Chris could perfectly well accept, and so act on, a standard permitting continued friendships not only in the case of Pat and Jean but also in all relevantly similar cases.

Perhaps Pat might object to the friendship on the basis that it communicated Chris's approval of Jean's betrayal. But it's a mistake to think that friendship involves any necessary endorsement of a friend's choices or character; two people can become and remain friends despite character flaws and wrongful choices—they need not regard each other as perfect. Chris can view Jean's actions as seriously wrong without treating Jean's wrongdoing as decisive where the decision to be Jean's friend is concerned. To the extent that that seems odd, it's only, I think, because of the prior assumption that a friend must seem uniformly attractive or that the decision to be someone's friend must involve a positive assessment of that person's character. Pat could not reasonably regard Chris's friendship with Jean as predicated on, and so as communicating, any endorsement of Jean's abandonment of Pat.

Chris's continued friendship with Jean need not facilitate Jean's abandonment of Pat, which has, of course, already occurred. And, since it need not convey any approval of Jean's actions, it need not make it less likely than would otherwise be the case that Jean will return to Pat (as Pat hopes). Chris *would* be disloyal to Pat by encouraging Jean to marry Ray or implying that Jean's relationship with Pat was beyond repair, but being friends with Jean need not involve doing these things. Even honestly acknowledging the positive aspects of Jean's relationship with Ray would be consistent with wanting Jean and Pat to reunite and gently conveying this hope to Jean.

Perhaps Pat might instinctively judge that Chris shouldn't be friends with Jean because Jean's betrayal merits retributive *punishment*. But retribution simply isn't warranted; no one deserves retributive punishment, which simply adds to the loss in the world. And perhaps Pat might simply *feel* hurt and resentful and betrayed by Chris's friendship with Jean. But either these feelings reflect damage to a real good or they don't. If they don't, then Pat can't reasonably object; the feelings are rooted in a fear of harm or a judgment that harm has taken place that just isn't warranted. Pat acts wrongly in making such feelings grounds for demanding that Chris stop being friends with Jean. Indeed, Chris would act wrongly in relation to Jean by acceding to Pat's demand.

This demand would not be unreasonable if Pat's feelings *did* reflect actual or threatened damage to a real good. However, this is unlikely to be the case. No actual good is injured by Chris's friendship with Jean. Rejection of or hostility to someone who has hurt a friend is not essential to or constitutive of a friendship. Neither rejection of nor hostility to someone can be seen as an aspect of *any* good; both are, in fact, *attacks* on goods (in this case, the good of friendship between Chris and Jean, perhaps among others).

Perhaps Pat thinks that close friendship means sharing the same reactions, attitudes, or beliefs. In this case, Chris is refusing to be a friend by not sharing Pat's hostility to Jean. But intimacy, closeness, shouldn't be confused with *sameness*. I can be your friend even while feeling, seeing, believing differently.

While Chris can be loyal to Pat even while remaining loyal to Jean, too, it's important to remember that loyalty to Pat doesn't mean denying that Jean has injured Pat. Chris should never seek to reinforce the negative view either friend might have of the other. Loyalty does not mean cheering when Pat *condemns* Jean. But being a loving friend absolutely does not mean, either, pretending that Jean always means well, exhibits appropriate self-control, and so forth. Chris can acknowledge genuinely harmful behavior, refusing to paper over it, without encouraging hostility or rejection or reinforcing Pat's angry or judgmental attitudes. "'Finding something nice to say' about someone is not practicing love." Assuring Pat that Jean "didn't mean it" can leave Pat "feel[ing] more isolated and alone."[161]

161. Hugh Prather, *Spiritual Notes to Myself: Essential Wisdom for the Twenty-First Century* (Berkeley: Conari 1998) 31.

Friends can and should signal and reaffirm their loyalty to each other, especially at difficult times. But Chris can be loyal, and can signal loyalty, by being present to and supportive of Pat. Loyalty to a friend is a matter of *benefiting* and *sharing life and oneself with* the friend, not of *injuring* someone else. That's true both because loyalty to one person doesn't inherently involve a negative stance in relation to anyone else and because injuring one person *can't* under that description constitute a benefit to someone else. No one is better off just because someone else has been harmed, even if a resentful person might unreasonably *feel* elated when an enemy is injured.

To be sure, I might injure a wrongdoer in the course of defending a victim—say, stopping an act of violence in a way that turns out to cause injury to the attacker. But what matters in this case is that the victim has been protected. *That*'s what's beneficial to the victim, not the injury to the attacker.

Loyalty is a vital aspect of friendship. And, in the case of a rupture like the one between Jean and Pat, showing loyalty to an injured friend can be absolutely vital. Sometimes, of course, that will mean choosing to prioritize one friend over another: Chris likely acts wrongly in relation to Pat by choosing to join Jean and Ray for a party if Pat desperately needs in-person emotional support at the same time. But choosing priorities isn't the same as choosing sides. And loyalty does not require Chris, or anyone similarly situated, to choose sides.

Pedagogical Rejection

It's never reasonable purposefully to facilitate someone else's harmful behavior or unreasonably to risk doing so—and of course that includes a friend's bad behavior. But simply being someone's friend is never a way of facilitating harmful behavior. So it's never appropriate to reject friends who've behaved badly in order to *persuade* them to behave better. To do so is both wrong and counterproductive.

It's wrong because it involves deliberate injury to a good, the good of friendship, *as a means* of affecting someone's behavior. And purposefully injuring a good as a means to some other end is inconsistent with THE PAULINE PRINCIPLE. It's important to emphasize, though, that refusing to reject a friend means keeping one's heart open to her and continuing to be willing to share one's life with her. It *doesn't* mean facilitating her bad behavior. Resisting the urge to reject a friend is entirely compatible with refusing to let her borrow one's car for an intoxicated joyride or to use one's pied-à-terre to cheat on her partner. Saying *no* to a friend isn't the same thing as rejecting her.

Rejecting a friend in order to improve her behavior is counterproductive because the injury done by rejection may be permanently wounding, leading to self-doubt, resentment, fear, and so forth. Instead of growing and thriving, the rejected person is likely to retreat into herself or to seek out destructive but validating relationships that she hopes will enable her to move past the pain of rejection but that will likely in fact encourage a spiral of self-destructive behavior. A friend's moral, spiritual, and emotional growth will likely be fostered most effectively by the recognition that one is absolutely reliable, that she can count on one's loyalty even when she behaves badly. And we might find the example of Jesus particularly telling: "Christ's friendship does not make the other's goodness a prior condition." This is not only because, we may assume, Jesus was not inhibited by the kinds of worries I've examined here but also because of friendship's positive potential to contribute to personal transformation. "The love of friendship is creative of personhood. . . . Love is God's way of creating and revealing goodness."[162]

A Model of Love

Love for friends despite their flaws is one aspect of Christian love more broadly. Friendship is not "the quintessential model for Christian love."[163] It is, rather, one of many forms such love can take. Christian love is not generic—owed, somehow, to everyone in just the same way and to the same degree. It is not best understood as abstract or necessarily impartial. Love is any positive orientation on its object.[164] Thus, we love in and through care, delight, desire, devotion, intimate knowing, loyalty, reciprocity, attachment, and respect. In the most general terms, someone loves when she acts with regard for some (existing or yet-to-be-realized) genuine aspect of flourishing, some authentic constituent

162. E. D. H. "Liz" Carmichael, *Friendship: Interpreting Christian Love* (London: Clark-Continuum 2004) 198.

163. As John Burnaby suggested it was; see Carmichael 163 (summarizing Burnaby).

164. See John B. Cobb Jr., *The Structure of Christian Existence* (Philadelphia: Westminster 1967) 127 (Cobb treats an affective element as integral here, as I do not). The merits or demerits of this account of love do not depend on the resolution of contested questions of biblical exegesis. But it's worth noting that the semantic ranges of *love* and its cognates in English are not terribly different from those of *agape* and its cognates in Greek. See, *e.g.*, James Barr, "Words for Love in Biblical Greek," *The Glory of Christ in the New Testament: Studies in Christology in Memory of George Bradford Caird*, ed. L. D. Hurst and N. T. Wright (Oxford: Clarendon-Oxford University Press 1987) 1–18.

of well-being, in her own life or another's. Our love is rightly focused and channeled in a variety of ways.

I suggest, then, unoriginally, that we represent the channeling and focusing of love for creatures using the image of a set of circles,[165] the outermost encompassing all the others and each of those either overlapping with or fully contained within one or more of the others. Each of these kinds of love is an expression of RECOGNITION, since love means being aware of what actually counts as well-being, and of EFFICIENCY, since any of our efforts to love should be undertaken in ways that don't disperse time, energy, and resources unnecessarily. The other ways of loving also come to expression in various ways in these kinds of love.

(*i*) In the most inclusive circle—the realm of universal love, of love for everyone without exception—love takes the form of sincerely willed respect, noninterference, and nonmanipulation. The kind of love expressed here is rooted in THE PAULINE PRINCIPLE's preclusion of purposeful (and thus of instrumental) injury to ourselves and others alike and in THE GOLDEN RULE's requirement of fairness to ourselves and others. This circle is home to the kind of love reflected at multiple points in the Decalogue's second table.[166] And it is the realm of crucial New Testament injunctions to love, especially a central aspect of love for enemies, the proscription of revenge and of any imagined right to engage in retribution (since revenge and retribution are ruled out by THE PAULINE PRINCIPLE and perhaps also THE GOLDEN RULE). It also comprehends prohibitions on various kinds of nonviolent but still actively objectionable conduct—assailing someone else's self-understanding through cruel insults, for instance. This kind of love is *peace*. Peace is sometimes invisible. It is quiet, unassuming, and in a sense passive. But it is the foundation of our relationships with everyone—including

165. Thanks to David Larson for the chance to discuss this topic. Stephen J. Pope has reflected helpfully on the question of love's structure (though he would doubtless question various things I say here); see Stephen J. Pope, *The Evolution of Altruism and the Ordering of Love* (Washington, DC: Georgetown University Press 1994).

166. Don't murder, don't (emergencies aside) interfere with others' justly acquired possessions, don't betray your spouse (obviously an egalitarian and otherwise modernized reading of the Seventh Commandment), and don't attempt to secure a conviction by perjury. (The Tenth Commandment's injunction against nurturing the desire, much less planning, to prey on others serves to support these protections. This is practically important; at the same time, it underscores the importance of sincerity, of genuinely *willing* that one's relationships be marked by peace.) Also in this first circle are the presumptive prohibition of lying to and defrauding others and the unqualified prohibition of torture.

those with near and distant strangers. It is thus the basis for the extended social cooperation that makes so much of our flourishing possible.

(*ii*) Love is often expressed as ordinary reciprocity—the willingness to return good for good (not bad for bad).[167] The gratitude implicit in the Fifth Commandment belongs here too. This kind of love, rooted in THE GOLDEN RULE, can't be offered to everyone, since it depends on the existence and nature of tangible interpersonal relationships, since we are not tangibly related to most people, and since not all such relationships are reciprocal. However, it can and should be a feature of our relationships with many people. We may respond to our intimates in part as a matter of reciprocity, though of course our intimate obligations extend well beyond those that might flow from reciprocity. But reciprocity is a vital element in our mutually supportive interactions with strangers. Among these strangers are the ones we meet face-to-face. But reciprocity is also crucial to our relationships with the strangers with whom we are linked in the process of extended social cooperation.[168] We will likely never know the names of these strangers or the precise role any individual person has played in enriching our lives. But we can nonetheless love them by returning good for good to those with whom we interact directly and who help to link us to and convey our support for more distant cooperating strangers. Reciprocity is also one reason for us to play our parts in keeping networks of cooperation thriving and in supporting the institutions that protect these networks.

(*iii*) Love is not only respect and reciprocity but also beneficence. In the third circle, it takes the form of what we might call *general* beneficence, beneficence to strangers, acquaintances, institutions, and in some cases, enemies.[169] This kind of love is shaped by THE GOLDEN RULE. Being beneficent on an ongoing

167. See Finnis, *Aquinas* 197.

168. See David Schmidtz, *Elements of Justice* (Cambridge: Cambridge University Press 2006) 73–103.

169. See, *e.g.*, Onora O'Neill, *Towards Justice and Virtue: A Constructive Account of Practical Reasoning* (Cambridge: Cambridge University Press 1996) 195–200; T. M. Scanlon, *What We Owe to Each Other* (Cambridge, MA: Belknap-Harvard University Press 1998) 224; Luke T. Johnson, *Sharing Possessions: Mandate and Symbol of Faith* (Philadelphia: Fortress 1981) 132–9; Finnis, *Law* 173–7; David Schmidtz, "Separateness, Suffering, and Moral Theory," *Person, Polis, Planet: Essays in Applied Philosophy* (New York: Oxford University Press 2008) 145–64; Neera K. Badhwar, "International Aid: When Giving Becomes a Vice," *Social Philosophy and Policy* 23.1 (Jan. 2006): 69–101; Alasdair MacIntyre, *Dependent Rational Animals: Why Human Beings Need the Virtues* (Chicago: Open Court 1999) 119–28; Liam Murphy, *Moral Demands in Nonideal Theory* (New York: Oxford University Press 2000); and Robert P. George, "Does the 'Incommensurability Thesis' Imperil Common Sense Moral Judgments?," *In Defense of Natural Law* (Oxford: Clarendon-OUP 1999) 94–100.

basis is a requirement of practical reasonableness. However, just which recipients one supports and at just what level are in significant part matters of free choice.[170] Particular ties of gratitude and loyalty, particular commitments, and vulnerabilities one has oneself created may all be relevant, as may the challenge of personal encounter. This kind of love provides needed support for valued institutions and for acquaintances and strangers in distress. Institutions that maintain social order, that uphold the common good—the framework that safeguards people's peaceful, voluntary cooperation—may also deserve support on the basis of love as general beneficence. (One's obligation to support such institutions may also flow from requirements of reciprocity and promise keeping that are integral to universal love.) General beneficence may also involve actively opposing predatory institutions and practices.[171] When active reconciliation with enemies is safe and otherwise reasonable, it will take its place here too.

(*iv*) In relationships marked by deep connection, love takes the form of more extensive beneficence, more thoroughgoing reliance (itself a gift of love) and invitations to reliance, and deeper loyalty. It also often includes desire of one kind or another. This kind of love might link one with friends, parents, children, and some colleagues, depending on how close one is to them. But it might also connect one to people one has committed to aiding in a sustained and substantial way—the students at a particular institution one is committed to supporting with philanthropic gifts or the patients at a mission hospital one is committed to assisting with one's medical skills during a period of service. Love of this kind is channeled by COMMITMENT and THE GOLDEN RULE—and sometimes also THE PAULINE PRINCIPLE. This kind of love will sometimes be a matter of fulfilling particular responsibilities, sometimes of creating space to nourish a relationship, sometimes a matter of sharing oneself openly and vulnerably—offering the gift of intimate presence. And it may be a matter of self-investment, as one chooses to spend time and resources and emotional energy on a relationship. This kind of love sustains and involves relationships that foster our own flourishing and that may in some cases help to shape our identities; at the same time, it involves substantial contributions to others' lives.

(*v*) Finally, there is love as devotion—to our closest friends, including lovers and spouses, and often enough, to children if we have them, as well as, perhaps,

170. O'Neill, *Towards Justice and Virtue* 197–200.

171. See Roderick T. Long, "On Making Small Contributions to Evil," Praxeology.net, 2008 <http://praxeology.net/SmallContributions-REVISED.doc>.

on occasion, to others who are fellow participants in some deeply valued common task. These are relationships that are richly constitutive of our identities, relationships with people for whose lives we would expect to give our own. Again, the kind of love evident in these relationships will include a mixture of respect, deep care, delight, desire, and attachment, as well as, often enough, the thoroughgoing intimacy of friendship. This is the kind of love we may sometimes think of as paradigmatic; but of course it is possible only in a very limited number of cases. It, too, is an expression of THE GOLDEN RULE, of COMMITMENT, and sometimes of THE PAULINE PRINCIPLE.

Love is a matter of realizing various goods, some individual and some shared, in our own lives and the lives of others. Friendship is a way of loving and, as a basic aspect of flourishing, a gift of love. Commitments channel and focus our participation in various goods, and so our loves. As a matter of following THE GOLDEN RULE, our promises and our implicit or explicit invitations to others to rely on us yield particular obligations. And THE GOLDEN RULE occasions assistance to others more generally.

Contributing to a friend's flourishing is essential to friendship; and of course doing so also, at the same time, is part of the friend's own flourishing (at minimum because it involves the friend's realizing the good of practical reasonableness by choosing well). Understood in this way, loving God and God's creation, and embodying and mediating God's love for creation, comes to expression in multiple ways. Friendship, involving the kinds of love in circles (*iv*) and (*v*), is not the only one of the ways; but it is distinctively valuable and worth affirming and treasuring.

Institutions concerned with law and justice are mechanisms for conveying the kind of love expressed in circles (*i*) and (*ii*), the realms of respect and reciprocity. Our support for those institutions is a matter of the kind of love expressed not only in circle (*ii*) (if we owe support as a matter of reciprocal obligation) but also in circle (*iii*), the realm of general benevolence. And the friendship group—bonded through the kinds of love expressed in circles (*iv*) and (*v*), the realms of rich connection and devotion—can help in various ways to enhance political processes and institutions. This is only one of the ways in which friendship and politics intersect. I will explore several of these ways in chapter 5.

5
Politics

Friendship is important for contemporary political life (though this importance is no excuse for idolatrous attitudes toward one's own political convictions), and it could be even more important in a more human-scale social and political order.

Narrowly construed, politics concerns the justified, systemic use of force to uphold or implement law. More broadly, politics is the process of seeking, characteristically in cooperation (and often dialogue) with others, to influence norms embraced and decisions made by or on behalf of institutions or groups. Yet more broadly, we might characterize as political any sort of critical reflection on and engagement with the exercise of significant influence in social environments.

The classical political tradition conceived of friendship as the ground and goal of political life.[1] "Friendship seems . . . to hold states together,"[2] Aristotle observed. "It is thought to be the special business of the political art to produce friendship."[3] Aristotle's way of linking friendship with politics may well catch us off guard.[4] We may be equally puzzled to find it echoed in the thought of Plato

1. See Hutter, *Politics as Friendship*.

2. Aristotle, *Ethica Nicomachea* 1155a <https://www.sacred-texts.com/cla/ari/nico/nico082.htm>.

3. Aristotle, *Ethica Eudemia*, trans. Joseph Solomon (London: Oxford University Press 1915) 1234b.

4. See, *e.g.*, *Ethica Eudemia* 1241a–2a; and *Ethica Nicomachea* 1161a–2b.

and Cicero,[5] among others. We don't tend to think of friendship and politics as relevant to each other in any meaningful way.

The political world of the Greek city-state was a small one. Only free, adult males could participate in political life—and there weren't terribly many of them. Given the relatively small size of a polis's enfranchised population, real face-to-face interaction would have been possible. Thus, friendly relations among political actors would have been an achievable goal, and individual groups of close friends within the city would have had meaningful opportunities to influence the political process directly.[6] (Even so, Athens itself was not governed by a single cadre of friends. The city's political class comprised "a *network* of *small groups* of friends."[7])

It's hard to imagine what it might mean to think of friendship as politically central in an age of mass politics in enormous, impersonal states, states that rule vast numbers of strangers. An understanding of friendship and politics as connected in various ways could form a significant element in a Christian political theology. But, in order to reappropriate this sense of the political significance of friendship, it may prove necessary to see friendship's potential in new ways and to reconsider the optimal shape of politics—while maintaining a clear sense of the *limitations* of politics.

I begin this chapter by examining links between friendship and political institutions—in particular, liberal politics—suggesting that friendship is a crucial and distinctive foundational element of a liberal society. Features of contemporary social life—social attitudes and especially norms evident in work life—pose serious risks to the maintenance of friendships; I argue that we should challenge norms and policies that threaten our intimate ties. While friendship is essentially focused and particular, it is surprisingly common to talk about the possibility of friendship (considered literally or metaphorically) for all of the members of various large groups, notably churches and political societies; I attempt to show why this kind of talk is problematic, why it makes no sense if friendship is understood literally, and why it is unhelpful to stretch the metaphorical use of friendship in ways that obscure friendship's particularity. I go on to highlight ways in which friendship can play a crucial role in motivating and sustaining political practice, preparing people to interact fruitfully despite

5. See Hutter, *Politics as Friendship* 93–4, 99, 133–74; and Cicero, *Lælius de amicitia*.

6. See Hutter, *Politics as Friendship* 25–55; and Brian Patrick McGuire, *Friendship and Community: The Monastic Experience, 350–1250* (Kalamazoo, MI: Cistercian 1988) xxxi–xxiii.

7. MacIntyre, *After Virtue* 146 (my italics).

political disagreement, and helping to put behavioral challenges to the status quo on display. I suggest that a decentralized, deterritorialized politics could create opportunities for friendship once again to play the political role that it did for classical authors. I argue that states qua states do not deserve any sort of loyalty that might trump our loyalty to friends. And I stress that friendship should not be sacrificed in the name of or threatened by an idolatrous reverence for political opinions or movements.

The Interdependence of Friendship and Politics

All human life is relational in character. Relationships, networks, communities, and societies link people with each other, overlapping in multiple ways. Friendship is a primary form of human sociality. But it is, in turn, intimately connected with the other varieties of sociality. In particular, friendship is related in various ways to political practice and the function of political institutions.

There is a good internal to a friendship and to a circle of friends. That good is the good of intimate connection—of friendship. And of course in a given case there may also be a shared commitment by friends to some good external to their relationship, but there need not be such a good. Friends seek to flourish first and foremost *as friends*, *in friendship*. So political goods are goods *external* to the practice of friendship.

Friends are joined by their love for one another and are thus committed to each other's good. And part of that good may be found in public and political life. Love for one's friend may impel one to join with her in political participation because her own good will be furthered, her own humanity realized, by displaying her qualities as a "political animal" or because—given that part of one's responsibility to her is to call her to moral accountability—she must fulfill political responsibilities. And political action in cooperation with a friend may be appropriate because her needs and interests are affected by the political environment and thus will be served by political involvement.

Friendship and broadly political institutions are related in that each contributes to the flourishing of the other. For instance, (*i*) political institutions can provide space within which friends can interact and support each other in public, if they engage qua friends in politics—whether narrowly or broadly construed. In addition, (*ii*) friendship helps to make political formation possible. (*iii*) The legal order and the security of person and property it makes possible allow friendships to develop and function. And, relatedly, (*iv*) political institutions help to secure a friendship's significance by sustaining the background of practices, events, and relationships against which a friendship is developed. To the extent that friends *do* things with, to, and for each other, their ability to do so depends on social order, which is in part sustained by institutions that maintain social order. Society more generally—the source of the language and symbols on which friends draw when communicating, the physical facilities within which they interact, the cultural products they enjoy together, and so forth—is safeguarded in part by the activities of such institutions.[8]

Persons are formed in intimate, personal relationships. Intimate contact is an irreplaceable good, one that also contributes to personal development: without such contact, people may tend to stagnate. Much of the wider culture's impact on personal development is mediated through intimate relationships. So political institutions that inhibit or undermine friendship, and thus prompt the stagnation of persons, are enemies of human flourishing.

Friendship and Liberalism

A liberal social and political order—one that welcomes individuality, diversity, experimentation, and peace, that features robust protections for civil liberties and open markets, and that is inhospitable to hierarchy and exclusion—makes it easy for freely chosen relationships like friendships to develop, and friendship offers valuable glue for a liberal society.

Nostalgia for Given Community

Aristotle's world is not ours. The relatively manageable political environment of the Greek polis has given way to an unimaginably complex political and economic order, one that leaves many people overwhelmed by a sense of vertigo. As a result, we sometimes find ourselves yearning for the recovery of lost forms of community.[9]

8. See McFadyen, *Call to Personhood* 255–6.

9. My analysis throughout the next few paragraphs is dependent on Marilyn Friedman, *What Are Friends For? Feminist Perspectives on Personal Relationships and Moral Theory* (Ithaca, NY: Cornell University Press 1993) 231–55; and Martha Ackelsberg, "'Sisters' or 'Comrades'? The Politics of Friends and Families," *Families, Politics, and Public Policy*, ed. Irene Diamond (New York: Longman 1983) 339–56.

What people sometimes seem to mourn when they reflect on the loss of many traditional ties is not just community and connection but a particular *kind* of community and connection—roughly speaking, *given* community and connection. That is, the sense of loss often seems to be an expression of dismay that people can *choose*, at least to some degree, whether or not to embrace particular ties. It reflects nostalgia for a world (real or imagined) in which people knew their places, in which social structures relieved them of the burden of choice, in which putatively unseemly links across traditional social barriers were unlikely to spring up, and in which traditional institutions didn't confront the threat that dissatisfied participants might exit, perhaps en masse.

Traditional forms of community undoubtedly provided their members with social support and reduced uncertainty. At best, however, they sustained a limited range of prescriptions that didn't respond flexibly to members' varied gifts and goals. More troublingly, in practical terms, the well-being of an institution often tended to be equated with the well-being of its dominant (typically middle-aged, male, wealthy) members, who benefited from existing arrangements in ways that others didn't.

Churches and ethnic, cultural, ideological, or neighborhood communities have often been experienced as oppressive. Patriarchal families have oppressed women and inhibited children's choices in marriage, employment, and religion. Churches have repressed dissenters and built high, impenetrable walls that have prevented contacts with outsiders. Communities united by language or ethnic heritage have often been similarly suspicious of those who don't sound or look right and have subjected their members to enforced conformity. Laments over the decline of community seem often enough, then, to reflect a perverse nostalgia for the dubious securities of a vanishing patriarchy or of exclusive enclaves. Some given communities obviously play valuable roles in empowering some people and constituting their identities. But this shouldn't obscure the rigidity they often exhibit or the hierarchies which often shape them and which they often help to sustain.

If concern for connection means concern for certain traditional forms of community, then the sense of rootlessness and chaos, of moral and existential vertigo, that has accompanied their decline may be a price we should be willing to pay. If the only alternative to the rootless flux and chaotic disconnection that seem—on bad days—to characterize our society is a return to the hierarchies of the past, we probably ought to settle for flux and disconnection.

Fortunately, conservatism and chaos are not our only options. We can construct and embrace forms of community that move beyond past hierarchies structurally and substantively, ones that respect individuality, that can be entered and reshaped by choice, and that protect participants' opportunities for voice and exit.[10]

Chosen Community

Normative social and political theories are characteristically concerned with (among other things) recognizing, affirming, and preserving connections of different kinds. So, for instance, for conservatism, the relevant connections are those among family members and, secondarily, among members of ethnic and religious communities. Similarly, for syndicalism, the relevant connections are those among workers in particular firms and economic sectors. For liberalism, the relevant connections are, I suggest, those among friends.

Chosen communities can help ground us when we find ourselves oppressed by or inclined to challenge given communities.[11] Thus, the foundations of a liberal society, which seeks to liberate individuals from oppressive traditional ties, lie *especially* in the friendship circle and similarly voluntary groups. Friendships and other kinds of chosen communities help to offer us *critical distance* from our given communities.[12]

To be sure, friendships aren't chosen with some sort of Godlike freedom.[13] Class, gender, circumstance, and mere propinquity can affect our friendship choices to a greater or lesser degree. But, of course, we can choose—albeit often at some cost—to transcend these constraints, something it's much harder to do where, for instance, kinship relations are concerned. Friendship's chosen character equips it to sustain and encourage the equality to which given communities sometimes appear indifferent. And communities of friends, "urban tribes,"[14] offer us social anchors that leave us free to develop our individual identities.

10. For the typology of voice and exit, see Albert O. Hirschman, *Exit, Voice, and Loyalty: Responses to Decline in Firms, Organizations, and States* (Cambridge, MA: Harvard University Press 1970).

11. Friedman, *Friends* 207–30.

12. Friedman 218–20.

13. Stephen R. L. Clark, *Civil Peace and Sacred Order* (Oxford: Clarendon-Oxford University Press 1989) 54–5, 63.

14. Ethan Watters, *Urban Tribes: Are Friends the New Family?* (New York: Bloomsbury 2003).

A Positive Liberal Vision

Pragmatically, liberalism has been motivated by the desire to reduce social conflict. But a positive liberal vision can and should be about more than just avoiding a replay of the Wars of Religion. A central element of such a vision is a recognition of the reality and value of genuine human variety, a variety that isn't captured by references to broad, general categories and that crosscuts social groupings defined by means of such categories. Liberalism seeks to foster the emergence and healthy development of social and political and legal institutions that welcome, rather than resisting or suppressing, this kind of variety.[15]

While some liberals are subjectivists who deny that there are even *potentially* correct answers to questions about good lives and while others stress the difficulty of assessing the merits of such answers, liberalism is perfectly compatible with a robust, positive vision of the good life. On a view of Christian love that emphasizes flourishing, there are multiple human goods and many reasonable ways of participating in these goods. Open institutions facilitate individual and social experimentation and thus the exploration and evaluation of (explicit or tacit) proposals regarding human flourishing. And there are good reasons to limit the use of physical force to those cases in which it is necessary to prevent, end, or remedy the misuse of physical force by others. Thus, even when people make choices that result in harm to themselves or when they injure others *nonviolently* (as, say, when one spouse betrays another), there are good reasons to avoid using force to constrain their choices. There will also not infrequently be reasons to limit the use of social pressure to inhibit choices that don't involve the misuse of physical force, too. And these reasons to limit force and social pressure are reasons that can be discerned from *within* a rich conception of the good life: they don't, that is, depend on a thin theory of the good, on subjectivism, or on skepticism.

15. See Deirdre Nansen McCloskey, *Why Liberalism Works: How True Liberal Values Produce a Freer, More Equal, Prosperous World for All* (New Haven, CT: Yale University Press 2019); Chartier, *Flourishing Lives* 1–29; and Gary Chartier, "Radical Liberalism and Social Liberation," *The Dialectics of Liberty: Exploring the Context of Human Freedom*, ed. Roger E. Bissell, Chris Matthew Sciabarra, and Edward W. Younkins (Lanham, MD: Lexington-Rowman 2019) 255–74. While liberalism is sometimes seen as inhospitable to Christianity, Gilbert Meilaender has rightly emphasized the degree to which an Augustinian sensitivity to human limitations and pretensions should yield a Christian preference for something like liberal politics even on the view that liberalism embodies an impoverished conception of ethics. See, *e.g.*, Gilbert Meilaender, *The Way That Leads There: Augustinian Reflections on the Christian Life* (Grand Rapids: Eerdmans 2006) 77–116.

Liberalism doesn't depend on skepticism, on any sort of denial that there is or could be a reasonably accurate understanding of what makes for a good life. It *is*, however, deeply suspicious of *authority* as a means of *gaining* this sort of understanding. Liberalism embraces the insight that experiment, debate, and the exploration and critique of alternatives can be seen as most likely to facilitate our approach to truth, just as experiment and the provision of alternatives in the market can be seen as most likely to give people access to the genuine goods they've opted to pursue.[16] Liberalism is "a political position which affirm[s] the value of individual existence in all its variousness, complexity, and difficulty."[17] And it thus seeks to limit power not only to make room for experimentation and discovery but also in light of the recognition that "some paradox of our nature leads us, when once we have made our fellow men the objects of our enlightened interest, to go on to make them the objects of our pity, then of our wisdom, ultimately of our coercion."[18]

Liberal Friendship

There is a natural interdependence between friendship and liberalism.

(*i*) Liberalism creates and protects space for friendship to develop and thrive.

(*a*) It reduces the social centrality of social institutions alternative to friendship, institutions that constitute or sustain *given* forms of community. It reduces both the time demanded by such forms of community and the claims they make on people's loyalties. In so doing, it enables people to devote greater attention to friendship, to crafting communities of friends.

(*b*) At the same time, liberalism reduces social and political barriers to the formation of friendships. By emphasizing individual diversity, liberalism resists attempts to *reduce* people to membership in groups characterized in virtue of national ties, work, religious beliefs, or phenotypes (though of course there may be pragmatic reasons in particular circumstances to affiliate with others based on membership in groups defined by these categories).[19] If we assume the value

16. See Gary Chartier, *An Ecological Theory of Free Expression* (New York: Palgrave 2018); and Chartier, *Good Life in the Market* 47–111.

17. Lionel Trilling, "Art and Necessity," *The Moral Obligation to Be Intelligent: Selected Essays* (Evanston, IL: Northwestern University Press 2008) 511.

18. Lionel Trilling, "Manners, Morals, and the Novel," *Obligation* 118.

19. While liberalism strongly resists *defining* people with reference to these sorts of characteristics, of course observant liberals recognize that these characteristics can be *used* by bigots and other illiberals as bases of exclusion and subordination and that there can thus be good reason

of friendship, then liberalism's positive relationship with friendship can serve as one reason to embrace liberalism.

(*ii*) Friendship provides a vital form of community in liberal societies. Humans need connection, but liberalism—fortunately—tends to undermine rigid and stultifying *varieties* of connection. Rootlessness and disconnection can lead to alienation and, indeed, to support for populist movements and demagogues. Friendship offers a powerful alternative source of connection. It thus serves as a means of *support* for liberalism.

(*iii*) If liberals wish to recapture the traditional political importance of friendship, their intent to do so can help to define the proper *institutional framework* for liberalism. A liberal concern with friendship can provide, among other things, a basis for liberals to explore the merits of networked politics (a topic I explore below).

(*iv*) Liberalism makes it easier for people to create and sustain friendships despite religious, political, or other sorts of ideological disagreements. It creates opportunities for interactions across traditional barriers and encourages cultural attitudes that lead people to view such barriers skeptically.

Friendship, Politics, Norms, and Work

Liberalism can seem to be associated with social shifts that increasingly detach people from each other and that undermine friendship and other intimate ties. But liberal principles can also help to facilitate such ties in the face of contemporary work-related challenges.

Economic Pressures on Intimate Connections

We experience combined pressures for social, organizational, and geographic mobility.[20] As a result, interpersonal relationships are increasingly transitory. Even when someone is simply reassigned within a given organization, friendships

---

not to ignore them. Solidarity among those singled out for mistreatment and marginalization on the basis of particular features can be pragmatically important, sometimes essential to survival, even when those features, like the ones taken to make up "race," have been grouped arbitrarily and when arbitrary groupings can be used to obscure individual differences.

20. Of course, during periods of recession or depression, such relocation may seem not only attractive but, indeed, essential to personal or familial survival. Cp. Alvin Toffler, *Future Shock* (New York: Random 1970) 92–6.

can be ruptured.[21] People can find themselves encouraged to view their friendships in strictly instrumental terms and to embrace fluid selves marked by limited coherence, integration, and commitment.[22] The end result is that, as John Barth remarks melancholically, "our friends float past; we become involved with them; they float on, and we must either renew our friendship—catch up to date—or find that they and we don't comprehend each other any more."[23]

Forging new social connections and severing old ones are seen as necessary concomitants of upward mobility. The ability to sit light to personal ties is "richly rewarded."[24] Thus, an executive can observe with exceptional cold-bloodedness that the wife of a newly promoted manager "can be downright dangerous if she insists on keeping close friendships with the wives of her husband's subordinates. Her friendships will rub off on him, color his judgment about the people under him, jeopardize his job."[25]

Friendship and the Reconfiguration of the Workplace

Shifts in governance processes can help to reduce workplace pressures on friendship.

There is no single model of workplace governance that is right for every firm; and even if one were convinced that there were such a model, actual or threatened physical force shouldn't be used to impose it. The law cannot and should not mandate particular governance patterns. However, liberal policies can foster the emergence of participatory patterns in more than one way.

(*i*) They can do so by eliminating privileges that prop up workplace hierarchies and minimize opportunities for self-employment.[26]

Most people would prefer not to work in hierarchical environments because such environments are frustrating, disempowering, and marked by persistent assaults on autonomy and dignity. In addition, knowledge is distributed throughout any organization; but hierarchical structures keep most workers from using

21. Toffler 97–100.

22. Toffler 86–9, 97; cp. Anthony Giddens, *The Transformation of Intimacy: Sexuality, Love and Eroticism in Modern Societies* (Cambridge: Polity 1992) 61–4; and Robert Bellah *et al.*, *Habits of the Heart: Individualism and Commitment in American Life* (Berkeley: University of California Press 1985).

23. John Barth, *The Floating Opera* (New York: Avon 1956) 13–4, qtd. Toffler, *Shock* 96–7.

24. Toffler, *Shock* 105. See 105–7.

25. Qtd. Toffler 106–7.

26. For much of what follows, see Kevin A. Carson, *Organization Theory* (Charleston, SC: BookSurge 2009).

their local knowledge to make effective decisions. And ownership and compensation structures reduce workers' incentives to improve organizational performance. As a result, hierarchical organizations are deformed in ways that limit their efficiency; and *large* hierarchical organizations exhibit not only economies but also *diseconomies* of scale.

As a result, we might expect that small, nimble organizations would outcompete corporate behemoths and that clumsy giants would thus tend to vanish from the marketplace. However, politically secured privileges help to insulate large firms with top-down structures against the deleterious effects of hierarchy and size. These include provisions of the tax code that reward organizational size, regulations with which it's efficient only for large organizations to comply, various direct and indirect subsidies, policies that limit the availability of capital and increase start-up costs, licensing requirements that raise the cost of self-employment, and rules that increase individual living costs and thus make it harder for people to risk losing income while pursuing their own work-related projects. A liberal legal order, resistant to these privileges for the sake of workers and consumers alike, that eliminated such props to corporate size could significantly increase the likelihood that firms would be smaller and flatter and that there would thus be more opportunities for meaningful, effective participation by workers in workplace governance—not least because it would be easier to organize smaller firms as producer cooperatives and partnerships.[27]

In smaller and more participatory firms, there would be more room for groups of friends to influence decision-making, and so to exercise political—planning, leadership, persuasion—skills. For those who worry that workplace commitments might inhibit the formation and maintenance of friendship, more participatory structures create more opportunities to craft policies that don't undermine friendships. Worker cooperatives, inclusive partnerships, and, for that matter, sole proprietorships will likely involve fewer barriers to creating and maintaining workplace friendships than will hierarchical corporations. Loyalty among friends can actually contribute to productivity in organizations that leave space for intimate ties to flourish. And, to the extent that climbing a corporate hierarchy leads to detachment from friends, decreasing the prevalence of workplace hierarchies can be a way of reducing stresses inimical to intimate ties.

27. It is often assumed that such structures must be inherently inefficient. But see David Prychitko, *Marxism and Workers' Self-Management: The Essential Tension* (Westport, CT: Praeger 1991); and David Prychitko, "Context Matters: Finding a Home for Labor-Managed Enterprise," Bissell, Sciabarra, and Younkins, *Dialectics of Liberty* 175–83.

(*ii*) They can also do so by eliminating arrangements that allow individuals and firms to externalize transportation costs on others.[28] Among these policies are highway funding strategies that don't place full funding responsibilities on users, the use of eminent domain to acquire property for roads and airports, railroad and airport subsidies, and the insulation of railroads from tort liability. These and other policies ensure that inaccurate signals regarding the real costs of transportation are sent to the market, that expenses by end-users of transportation infrastructure don't reflect the actual costs of that infrastructure, and that the public must bear costs that users should have paid. The end result is that there is, in effect, a subsidy to geographic mobility, with the result that people opt for mobility when they might not otherwise do so and that they don't consider or push for alternatives.

(*iii*) They can do so, further, by eliminating legal rules that privilege or require face-to-face engagement (for instance, ones that preclude or limit telemedicine and virtual psychotherapy). Again, such rules can increase pressures to move and can thus reduce opportunities for stable face-to-face relationships among friends.

Critical Conversation about Social Norms

Law and regulation definitely play significant roles in encouraging a kind of mobility that undermines the stability of friendships. And these are rightly the concern of politics narrowly construed. But politics understood more broadly can help to shape the attitudes that inform social norms. And such norms obviously play crucial roles in facilitating or undermining friendships.

There is always the risk that work-related demands will swallow our individuality and deprive us of the time and energy we need to nourish intimate ties. Public conversation should therefore focus especially on social norms that determine how work will affect such ties. These include ones of several kinds.

Consider, for instance, (*i*) norms concerned with loyalty. How should one treat one's friends when one is promoted? What does loyalty demand when a friend is targeted for unreasonable treatment?

Also important are (*ii*) norms concerned with geographic stability. For many people, it's obvious that one should move when a more prestigious or rewarding

28. Thanks to Kevin A. Carson, "The Distorting Effects of Transportation Subsidies," FEE, Oct. 22, 2010 <https://fee.org/articles/the-distorting-effects-of-transportation-subsidies/>, for insights reflected here.

job becomes available. But what if a move undermines opportunities for regular face-to-face connections with friends?

(*iii*) Norms concerned with the propriety of workplace friendships matter, too. Such friendships might be frowned upon as, for instance, potential sources of dissent or occasions for disruptive favoritism or as breeding grounds for turbulence-inducing romantic or sexual conflicts. However, work is likely to be the occasion for a disproportionate number of close connections. As a result, discouraging such friendships will meaningfully reduce people's access to such connections. And this ought to matter as regards the norms we do and don't want to sustain.

Also significant are (*iv*) norms concerning the acceptability of limiting time in the workplace—not only in the interest of family ties but also as a means of nourishing friendship. Do coworkers look askance at someone who leaves at the end of a normal workday rather than working late into the evening? Is someone overlooked for promotion because, while investing reasonable effort in the fulfillment of her responsibilities, she continues to prioritize her friendships?

And then there are (*v*) norms related to remote work.[29] In-person engagement may be important on occasion, but attachment to it in other cases may be a matter more of fetish, taboo, and habit than of rational analysis. And leaving open remote working options is, very importantly, a way of reducing pressure on people to change their places of residence in search of employment and thus of leaving them free to nourish direct contacts with friends.

Public conversation generally will not alter these norms on its own. And even explicit exchanges in a given workplace can hardly be expected to guarantee the adoption of friendship-friendly norms. But exchanging ideas can affect attitudes in important ways. If friendship matters, then it's worth talking in public (in the various relevant senses of "public") about how much it matters and about how institutional dynamics can support or undermine it.

Quasi-Friendship at Work

Both structural changes and changes in norms can help to address another problem that suffuses the contemporary workplace. The contemporary workplace

29. See Alvin Toffler, *The Third Wave* (New York: Morrow 1980). Predicting the development of a "home-centered society," he suggests that people who work at home will be able to plant their roots more deeply in the communities where they live (220–1; cp. 237–9).

can provide fertile ground for the development of authentic friendships.[30] And it is important to resist workplace policies that inhibit friendship formation. But rich personal ties can also be crowded out by the pressure to treat everyone in the workplace as a friend, not only at work but also at home and in other social settings.

Addressing this problem is partly a matter of altering social norms (related to politics in the broad sense) and partly a matter of increasing the range of available work options. People who don't want to confront this sort of pressure in the current work environment may have little choice but to tolerate it and submit to it. Even in a society of small, flexible, flat firms—partnerships, worker cooperatives, and so forth—there could still be pressure to behave this way. But, at least in an environment no longer riddled with privileges that propped up hierarchies, raised living costs, and made it legally and financially difficult to take the risks associated with self-employment, people would find it easier to resist the push for faux friendship and to leave overly clubby work environments in pursuit of alternatives. The availability of options created by the abolition of such privileges could leave people freer to focus on real friendships rather than imposed work-related substitutes.[31]

Escaping the Pressure to Work

In addition to the specific pressures related to friendship that people often experience at work, the need to work for many hours each week makes maintaining friendships more difficult. The inability to depart the rat race keeps people from focusing on creating friendships and enjoying their friends. Legal rules all too frequently make and keep people poor and raise living costs for poor and middle-class people alike.[32] These rules also predictably increase the pressure to work—and in particular to accept demanding and demeaning jobs.[33] They thus

30. See Shasta Nelson, *The Business of Friendship: Making the Most of Our Relationships Where We Spend Most of Our Time* (Nashville: HarperCollins Leadership 2020).

31. Thanks to Kevin Carson for this point (personal comm., Oct. 21, 2020).

32. See, *e.g.*, Charles W. Johnson, "Scratching By: How Government Creates Poverty as We Know It," *Markets Not Capitalism: Individualist Anarchism against Bosses, Inequality, Corporate Power, and Structural Poverty*, ed. Gary Chartier and Charles W. Johnson (New York: Minor Compositions-Autonomedia 2011) 377–84 <http://radgeek.com/gt/2011/10/Markets-Not-Capitalism-2011-Chartier-and-Johnson.pdf>. See Chartier and Johnson 323–75.

33. Thanks to Kevin Carson for helping me in multiple contexts see the importance of this point. See, *e.g.*, Carson, *Theory* 111–8.

reduce opportunities for leisure and thus for the formation and nourishment of friendships, especially ones outside the workplace. Eliminating these rules would offer people more space to redirect their attention from work—whether their work environments were humanizing or not—and focus on aspects of life they found directly rewarding, like friendship.[34] By increasing exit options, ending these rules would also increase pressures on existing workplaces to embrace more humane policies and attitudes in order to retain workers.

Friendship for Everyone?

Workplaces aren't the only settings, of course, in which we can confront the expectation that everyone should be friends with everyone else. The idea that we must be is in tension not only with liberal values but also with friendship's character as a particular, preferential relationship.

Liberalism emphasizes the importance of choice, which is one reason friendship is arguably the liberal social tie par excellence. Friendship is necessarily limited by our choices. And those choices, in turn, are constrained by our time, our energy, and our preferences.

Benjamin Jowett urges us to think of "Christian friendship" as "not a friendship of one or two, but of many," suggesting that "it is less personal and individual, and more diffused toward all men."[35] But, whatever the appeal of this sort of rhetoric, the vast majority of people in almost any group to which we belong can't be, won't be, shouldn't be expected to be our friends. We can treat every acquaintance and stranger with respect and appropriate regard; we ordinarily can and should, indeed, be *friendly*. But not every acquaintance or stranger is a potential friend, both because we may not connect in the right way or share the right kind of history with every stranger and because the number of friends with whom we can link ourselves deeply and richly is relatively limited. But some approaches to politics—broad and narrow—seek to undermine and ignore the essential particularity of friendship by calling for universal friendship of one sort or another.

34. See Carson 400–22.

35. Benjamin Jowett, *Sermons on Faith and Doctrine*, ed. W. H. Fremantle (London: Murray 1901) 352 <https://ccel.org/ccel/jowett_b/faith/faith.iii.xix.html>. Thanks to Liz Carmichael for calling this passage to my attention.

Limitation and Friendship

Friendship typically requires active engagement, deep knowledge, initiation through significant appreciation of a friend's qualities, perceptive responses to the friend's particularity, meaningful knowledge and appreciation of me by the friend, and a substantial history of interaction. And these requirements can only be met in a very limited number of cases.

My actions may have microscopic effects on the lives of a larger number of people, but I can only engage actively—in a way that impacts someone's life, that involves my responsiveness to that person, that prompts that person's responsiveness to me, that makes mutual knowledge and understanding possible—in the case of a small number of people. In order to become friends, we have to see each other (at least ordinarily), and we have to spend time together. In the course of spending time together, we need to discover that we like and trust each other. My discovery of another's qualities, a potential friend's awareness of who I am, the mutual evocation of trust, and bonding in the course of ongoing engagement all require substantial time, which I can invest in interactions with a limited number of people, only a subset of whom will finally become my friends.

Prejudice may keep me from considering someone a possible friend. And I should, indeed, let go of false beliefs about people. But, of course, even if I no longer hold a false belief about someone I once ruled out as a friend because of that false belief, I may still ultimately not become that person's friend. Not everyone can or should become friends with everyone else.[36]

The limitations imposed by human finitude make it seem implausible that any finite person should be described as the friend of every other finite person. Our time and energy are limited.[37] If the ideal form of friendship is one in which the friends' sharing of lives can reasonably be described as "living together," then there will likely be "a fixed number" of persons with whom one can be close friends—"perhaps the largest number with whom one can live together . . . ; and that one cannot live with many people and divide oneself up among them is plain."[38]

36. On choosing friends via algorithm, see Gilbert, *Human Relationships* 73–4.

37. See Aristotle, *Ethica Eudemia* 1245b.

38. Aristotle, *Ethica Nicomachea* 1171a <https://www.sacred-texts.com/cla/ari/nico/nico105.htm>.

These are all commonplaces, but it seems important to highlight them because calls for friendship with everyone seem so commonly to form elements of various kinds of religious and political rhetoric.[39] But, because of what it involves, friendship is simply not possible with the vast majority of one's fellow humans, fellow Britons, fellow members of Christ the King Lutheran Church . . .

Sometimes, of course, "friend" is used simply as the opposite of "enemy." And in this sense, one can, indeed, seek to view and treat all people as friends. Similarly, one can in the broad sense behave toward most people—those whose behavior doesn't require one to flee or to defend oneself or others—in a friend-*like*, a *friendly*, manner rather than a cold or dismissive one. But the rhetoric of universal friendship can seem to urge us to extend to many, many others that welcome, trust, intimacy, and focused, extensive positive concern that only really make sense where actual friends are concerned.

Fellow Citizenship Is Not Friendship

So, for instance, Pope Francis calls for "a social friendship that excludes no one" and "forms of social friendship that include everyone."[40] And G. A. Cohen famously argued that people belonging to a given political community should treat the other members of that community on the basis of the principles and moral intuitions that would guide their behavior if all of them were friends on a camping trip.[41] On this view, the sharing and solidarity that friends in such a setting should exhibit should be reflected in the basic structure of the state and the community spirit evident within it.

In fact, however, we typically don't interact in ordinary life even with close friends in the way we would with those friends on a camping trip. The environment itself is out of the ordinary, not typical of the ones in which social interaction ordinarily occurs.

In addition, we don't choose to go on a camping trip with just anyone, so by structuring a camping trip *with friends* we've implicitly decided what norms we'll follow. The preexisting trust and commitment characteristic of friendship

39. See, *e.g.*, Ælred, *Spiritual Friendship* 3.134.

40. Pope Francis, *Fratelli tutti* (Vatican City: Holy See 2020) ¶94, ¶180 <http://www.vatican.va/content/francesco/en/encyclicals/documents/papa-francesco_20201003_enciclica-fratelli-tutti.html> (Oct. 22, 2020).

41. See G. A. Cohen, *Why Not Socialism?* (Princeton, NJ: Princeton University Press 2009).

will create a dynamic very different from the one likely to prevail if one found oneself camping with strangers.

Not only levels of trust and commitment but also degrees of knowledge and influence distinguish friends from fellow citizens or subjects of a state. We know friends well, and our knowledge of them allows us to anticipate what they will do in particular situations and hold them accountable if they behave badly. Similarly, friends' appreciation for each other's opinions, concern for each other's welfare, identification with each other, and vulnerability to each other enable them to influence each other in ways that it's not possible, ordinarily, to influence strangers.

Talk about various sorts of putatively universal friendship can make it harder for us to see particular relationships for what they are. A state is not a society of friends.[42] Thinking and speaking as if it were such a society encourage us to elide the differences between friendships and relationships of other kinds and thus to assign actual friends unduly low priority in our decision-making. It encourages us to view our relationships with strangers unrealistically and to frame practices and policies as if we were close to and responsible for them in ways in which we're not. It also obscures the significance of the information gaps that obtain between fellow citizens but not, in general, between friends and that enable friends to make reasonable judgments about each other's characters, circumstances, and needs.

If you think people should treat fellow citizens or subjects in the way they would treat their friends on a camping trip, it can't be because you actually believe they are indistinguishable from friends on a camping trip. They're obviously not. Some additional rationale seems required. And, given that there are quite specific reasons for treating friends in ways different from those in which we ordinarily treat others, such a rationale seems unlikely to be forthcoming.

Avoiding hostility and embracing friendliness are important expressions of the regard that others merit just as such. And they also can lay the groundwork for the establishment of genuine friendships.[43] Recognizing their importance need not obscure the distinction between friendship and less intimate relationships.[44]

42. See Meilaender, *Friendship* 72–5.

43. Neera Badhwar makes this point very nicely in "Friendship and Commercial Societies," *Politics, Philosophy and Economics* 7.3 (2008): 301–26. See Nehamas, *On Friendship* 108.

44. See Olthuis, *I Pledge You My Troth* 120–3.

National Affinity Is unlike Friendship

Even if the members of a given society are not, just as such, friends, one might imagine that something like an attenuated version of friendship united the subjects of a given state. On this view, it would be reasonable, perhaps even obligatory, for someone to prefer the good or the company of others just because they were fellow citizens.

Friendship is a good, an aspect of well-being, the pursuit of which renders a choice intelligible and potentially reasonable. Shared rule by a given set of political institutions is not. Fellow subjects of a given state do not, just as such, form a community: they need not embrace common purposes, and there is no reason to think that they necessarily identify with each other. Friends know and interact with each other, while subjects of a given state need not, as a general matter, be aware of each other as particular persons, respond to each other individually, or understand each other's needs, desires, or circumstances.

Friendliness toward fellow citizens or subjects is, of course, an expression of practical reasonableness, just like friendliness to all people. And in particular cases, fellow citizens may, because of their shared political environment, embrace particular concerns or frustrations in common. Their doing so may provide the basis for joint political action, and it may even provide the occasion for friendship to develop. But the relationship of fellow subjecthood or fellow citizenship does not as such contribute to or constitute anyone's good any more than being fellow patients at a given dental practice might do so.

National populations are "nebulous groupings" that "are so big and arbitrary"[45] that they can experience and exhibit, at best, an "imagined fraternity."[46] The notion that bonds with strangers with whom we might share nothing but rule by the same political structure *are* somehow enriching is hard to understand apart from propagandistic efforts by states and their supporters which create the illusion on the part of their subjects that they are themselves responsible for political decisions that are in fact made by largely unaccountable elites.

Also at the root of the illusory fellow feeling often associated with citizenship is the seemingly irresistible tendency on the part of humans to sort themselves into teams. But identifying with fellow fans of a sports team, a television show,

45. Summers, *Friendship* 122.

46. Kwame Anthony Appiah, *The Ethics of Identity* (Princeton, NJ: Princeton University Press 2007) 237, qtd. Summers, *Friendship* 122.

or a band seems both more reasonable and far less dangerous than identifying with fellow citizens. It seems more reasonable because doing so is based on genuine common interests and experiences and is likely to lead to connections with people capable of becoming friendly acquaintances or full-blown friends. It appears far less dangerous than identifying with fellow citizens because identifying with fellow citizens runs the serious risk of leading people to, for instance, treat a military campaign like a sporting event and military actors as worth cheering just because of their team identifications.

Postmortem Universal Friendship?

Friendship in this life cannot meaningfully be enjoyed by everyone with everyone. But some Christians have suggested that we can look forward to universal friendship beyond death.[47] This idea is implausible. But thinking about it matters if it is advanced with an eye to undermining our appreciation for and commitment to the particularity of the friendships in which we participate in the present.

Even with endless time at her disposal, a person enjoying life beyond death could maintain friendships with all other created persons only if her cognitive resources permitted her to remember and respond to each of them on an individual basis. But we cannot suppose that the limitations of finite creatureliness will somehow vanish after death; and it would require something closer to the infinite divine mind than to any creaturely mind we know or could imagine to perform the requisite task.

It is distinct, particular persons who experience life beyond death. Those individuals have been shaped, and will continue to be shaped, by particular interactions with others. And their interests and commitments will continue, we may suppose, to differ with their histories and personal characteristics. Persons alive beyond death may be inclined to learn and grow in thoroughly new ways. But there is no reason that differences in disposition should not continue. So, if friendships initially form on the basis of common interests or individually shared experiences (even while transcending concern with them over time), people could still be expected to sort themselves into different relationships postmortem. It seems more probable that the individuality and particularity of human persons will be *enriched* and *increased* in postmortem life than that they will exhibit a generic uniformity. And, if they do, belief in universal friendship

47. Augustine and Ælred, for instance; see McGuire, *Friendship and Community* 323.

beyond death cannot be grounded on an appeal to a commonality that leads to the transcendence of individual differences.

None of us can accurately characterize life beyond death, of course. But the notion of universal friendship can be invoked as a kind of asymptotic limit point toward which all human relationships should be tending. It can thus, like other conceptions of eschatological existence, be used as a means of affirming or criticizing some feature or features of contemporary created existence. It is important, then, to show that even our life beyond death cannot involve the universalization of friendship. The anticipation of universal postmortem friendship cannot become the basis for criticism of the present particularity of our friendships.

Even if one deemed universal friendship to be a future reality, one would really not be justified in treating particular friendships as inappropriate to the current condition of humanity. For, if universal friendship *were* possible, radical changes in the moral and metaphysical constitution of human beings would be required to make this kind of friendship a reality. And if these changes are not to be expected in this life, then we cannot live as if they were already real.

If universal friendship were, per impossibile, to be expected, it could not be created whole cloth. (*i*) Bringing it into being ex nihilo would violate the freedom and authenticity that are essential to friendship. (*ii*) Creating friendship ex nihilo would also involve a kind of divine action that there is no reason to expect, given that divine action is mediated in and through the actions of creatures and that it is constrained by the freedom of creatures and the integrity of natural processes. (*iii*) Friendship is a historical phenomenon. The self of my friend is a self that has been shaped through, among other things, a series of interactions with me. Our relationship has developed over time. But a series of historical interactions cannot simply be created. To be authentic, such interactions must actually occur in time, as free persons engage with each other. It is hard to see how the conditions of life beyond death could lead to a change in this feature of friendship.

Thus, postmortem persons could at most be situated in circumstances in which the development of such histories of interaction was particularly facilitated. At that point, however, friendship formation would have to proceed in essentially the way it does in this life. And this means, in turn, that there would be no guarantee that friendship would occur in any particular instance. At most—even ignoring limitations in people's cognitive capacities and the specificity of their personal interests—universal friendship might be an object of hope.

Friendship and the Church

Maintaining a flourishing community life within the church—by which one might mean the Christian church as a whole or some particular array of Christians—is a valuable aspect of an authentically Christian politics. The church can serve as a laboratory within which experiments in conviviality can be conducted, and the shape of its common life can serve as an enacted challenge to dominant ideals of subordination and exclusion. Using "friendship" as a *metaphor* for church membership can underscore the social equality of church members and inappropriateness of ecclesial hierarchy.[48] However, *equating* church membership with friendship is no part of a reasonable ecclesiology.

The church has a more focused, specific identity than a state or an ethnic assortment. And membership in the church is often a matter of *choice* to a greater degree than membership in either kind of social group.[49] It might, as a result, seem more tempting to think of friendship as what unites fellow members of the church, to agree with Richard Bentley in maintaining that "Christian friendship or charity, in the same degree of affection, is extended to the whole *household of faith*."[50]

Friendship *may*, of course, contingently unite *particular* members of the church. I might happen to be friends with the person in the pew next to me. As in the case of political community, friendship might serve as an analogy or metaphor for a relationship within the church that wasn't actually a friendship. Openness of a certain kind matters among church members, whose relationships should, of course, be friendly, warm, and supportive;[51] these relationships can acknowledge and appreciate members' particularity even in the absence of the intimacy and preference characteristic of friendship in the primary sense. But, again, they lack the intimacy, the intensity, the focus, the preferential

48. See Elizabeth Moltmann-Wendel, *Rediscovering Friendship: Awakening to the Power and Promise of Women's Friendships* (Minneapolis: Fortress 2001) 13.

49. See Jürgen Moltmann, *The Church in the Power of the Spirit: A Contribution to Messianic Ecclesiology* (London: SCM 1977) 115.

50. Richard Bentley, *The Works of Richard Bentley, D. D.* 3: *Theological Writings*, ed. Alexander Dyce (London: Macpherson 1838) 418–9. Bentley suggests that Christian friendship extends "in true good-will and beneficence to all the race of mankind" (419). Thanks to Liz Carmichael for calling Bentley's work to my attention.

51. See Moltmann, *Church* 316–7.

character[52] that differentiate friendship from other relationships. A Christian congregation (much less a Christian denomination) is not just as such a "community of friends."[53]

Blurring Distinctions

"Christian friendship," Jürgen Moltmann maintains, "cannot be lived in the inner circle of one's equals but only in open affection and public respect for other people."[54] Moltmann is describing a kind of interaction that matters. But it is not clear that what Moltmann is talking about is helpfully described as a variety of friendship.

In older cultures, he asserts, friendship "was forged through alliances and publicly proved through loyalty."[55] Of course, it doesn't follow either that we should want to emulate those cultures or that the characteristics he identifies couldn't be exhibited by friendship as a genuinely intimate and thus necessarily preferential relationship. Even if it is *also* true in a different way of church membership, we are not required to equate the two kinds of relationship.

We can certainly hope that friendship will enjoy "public respect,"[56] at least if that means that friendship is supported and sustained by public recognition, including recognition and support by the church. But can it not be precisely friendship as an intimate relationship of mutual love and commitment which can find public sustenance and expression?

What *doesn't*, by contrast, seem to be helpful is an expansion of the boundaries of friendship in such a way that it includes everyone and *focuses* on public concerns. This sort of conception dilutes friendship while also, effectively,

52. Olthuis, *I Pledge You My Troth* 124–5; cp. Diogenes Allen, *Love: Christian Romance, Marriage, Friendship* (Cambridge, MA: Cowley 1987) 57–60.

53. L. Gregory Jones, *Transformed Judgment: Toward a Trinitarian Account of the Moral Life* (Eugene, OR: Wipf 2006) 130. Moltmann (*Church* 316) seems to recognize the problems with the metaphor, which he employs enthusiastically, when he observes that ordinary friendship is terminable but that there is an aspect of unconditional loyalty and love to church membership. This isn't the only—or, indeed, the most important—difference between church membership and friendship, it seems to me (not least because one can imagine a variety of close friendship that is rooted in unconditional loyalty).

54. Moltmann, *Church* 120.

55. Moltmann 120.

56. Moltmann 121.

placing greater demands on the church than it is likely to be able to bear. Further, if we treat the church as a gathering of friends, its other foci may be obscured.[57]

It is confusing to overlook the distinctions among terms like *sisterhood*, *brotherhood*, *friendship*, and *friendliness* and the social realities to which they correspond without paying significant attention to the distinctions between them. It also makes it much too easy to pressure church members to engage with others in ways that don't interest them, that feel intrusive or demanding, that demand investments of time people are unprepared to make.[58] Pressuring people in this way may drive them out of church fellowship because the expectations associated with it are too great.

Church membership in general unites people in ways that transcend a broad range of social divisions.[59] Church members are united by a common creatureliness, rooted in God's creative activity, the illuminating work of the Logos, the inspiration of God as Spirit. Members of a specific church community are linked by their embrace of the group to which they belong and their immersion in the narrative it relates.[60] One's unique relationship with a friend, by contrast, is the outcome of an ongoing, distinct history involving irreplaceable particular interactions. "Group friendship" is not friendship, however admirable a form of community it might in limited circumstances prove to be. Friendliness and respect among all church members can be a powerful element of the church's testimony. The attempt to make all church members actual friends, by contrast, seems like a recipe for cultishness.

Friendship and Political Engagement

Friendship can help people be political, perhaps in surprising ways. Friendship can help people learn how to engage with those who are different in public conversations about issues that matter. It can empower people to nourish and express dissenting views. It can support friends who put dissenting patterns of life on display for others. And it can participate in and support the church's political witness, which should, in turn, support fidelity and openness in friendship.

57. Olthuis, *I Pledge You My Troth* 125.

58. Allen, *Love* 59–60.

59. Allen 58–9.

60. Paine, "Exploratory Analysis" 133.

Friendship and Interaction in the Public Square

Friendship can be politically important as a way of helping people learn how to understand others who are different from themselves, recognize that goods they do not themselves seek to realize may nonetheless be goods, communicate effectively with those who see the world differently, and coexist peacefully, respectfully, and appreciatively with people whose beliefs and ways of living aren't theirs.[61]

There's nothing magical about this possibility; there's no guarantee that it will eventuate in any particular case. Frequently enough, people participate in political activity, broadly conceived, in order to achieve immediate institutional goals or personal objectives. At least sometimes, however, they may do so for expressive reasons, to stake claims to particular identities and to be acknowledged as embracing—and, they may hope, validated for embracing—the positions they do.

To achieve their goal of self-communication, political actors motivated by the desire to express themselves must seek encounters with those who do not yet know them, those whose views differ from theirs, and those who can grasp what they wish to convey about themselves in the terms in which they wish to express it. The public square presents an invigorating challenge to anyone who wants to express herself and be understood, given the diversity of perspectives in evidence there.[62] Confrontation with different views and disagreeing people—a kind of confrontation fostered by political engagement—can help someone to feel confident about his or her self-forged sense of meaning and identity. Political interaction can foster this kind of engagement.[63] And friendship can help to prepare one for political interaction.

Despite the possibility of integrating the friend with the self, the friend remains *other*, and the very otherness of the friend is both a preparation for and a useful reminder of the gap between the self and *every* other it encounters.[64] Friendship provides a distinctive context for recognizing the alien character of the other. By contrast with impersonal and superficial relationships, friendship

61. See Stephana J. Landwehr, "Friendship: The Forgotten Meaning of a Vital Nexus in Political Life" (PhD diss., University of Missouri–Columbia 1972) 277.

62. Landwehr 306–7.

63. Landwehr 321.

64. Karl Barth, *Ethics*, ed. Dietrich Braun, trans. Geoffrey W. Bromiley (Edinburgh: Clark 1981) 188–90.

forces me to grant both that I am interacting with another self and that that other self is irreducibly different from me.[65]

While friendship's intimacy makes it seem special and distinctive, successful friendship may properly be seen as a school for social life generally. Friendship can—though it need not[66]—serve to open the self to the wider world: love for friends can help one learn to acknowledge the reality and value of others as well.[67] Having formed a character marked by the virtues necessary for friendship, someone may well find herself increasingly open to others, increasingly unable to restrict to a narrow corner of her life her commitment to integrity and truthfulness and the other virtues required for friendship. So it is unsurprising that "the failure to develop and maintain friendships is taken as an index of psychopathology in most systems of classification."[68]

We discover who we are in the course of our interactions with friends, as we learn about ourselves through what they are able to tell us and see ourselves implicitly in their reactions to us.[69] In addition, of course, the ways in which friends choose to engage with us can encourage particular ways of being and discourage others. And friends can help us understand alternative conceptions of the good life more clearly by embodying them and thus putting them on display for us to consider.[70]

By narrowing the scope within which force is employed, narrowing the scope of issues regarding which conscious collective decision-making is needed, and maximizing ease of exit from decision-making institutions, genuinely liberal political institutions can minimize the need for people to debate with each other regarding the disposition of shared resources and the use of coercive power. But that doesn't mean that, even in a liberal society, there wouldn't be considerable room for politics in the broad sense in a variety of institutional settings. And of course our institutions at present *aren't* those of a genuinely liberal order—a fact which makes dialogue about politics even in the narrow sense more important.

Effective politics can certainly be seen to depend on conversation. And conversation will be effective when people with divergent accounts of the good

65. See Wadell, *Friendship* 156–8.

66. Badhwar, "Guided by the Best" 484–5.

67. See Bernard Williams, *Morality: An Introduction to Ethics* (Cambridge: Cambridge University Press 1973) 24–6; cp. Steve Duck, *Friends, for Life: The Psychology of Close Relationships* (Brighton: Harvester 1983) 15–22.

68. Davis and Todd, "Assessing Friendship," 21.

69. See Jones, *Transformed Judgment* 80–3.

70. Jones 83.

life can engage with each other empathetically, courteously, and in a manner marked by openness to discovery, self-disclosure, and, indeed, the possibility of change-inducing realization.[71] Friendship can function as a school for this kind of conversation.

Furthermore, friendship between persons of divergent political views is arguably among the most satisfactory bases for political dialogue. And I have authentic, close friendship in mind here, not merely civic amity: I am not sure that civic amity could make possible genuine trust and self-disclosure about the things that really matter in a way that prepared people for political dialogue. Obviously, such friendship will not extend to every individual exponent of any opposing viewpoint, but it may exist to a degree sufficient to ensure that persons are exposed to alternative positions as humanly embodied and challenged to confront them in ways they might otherwise have avoided.

Moral and political views are obviously interrelated. And awareness of this fact leads to the realization of yet another deficiency in the stereotypical notion of character friendship. If our loyalty and responsibility to our friends derive not from commitment to our friendships but, rather, from shared dedication to some external agenda, our friendships will be less likely to break down barriers that impede understanding and, thus, to help us avoid becoming mired in ideological conflict. One should not, of course, use diversity as a rigid criterion of friendship selection any more than uniformity. But by actively affirming the quality of friendship as a gift—by accepting the results of the random processes and providential workings that bring friendship into being, along with the willingness to respond to a wide range of appealing features when selecting friends—one makes it possible to build bridges across various political chasms.

Friendship performs another indirect political function, too. Even where overt political disagreement is not addressed in the conflict of friendship, the diversity of one's friends requires one to develop an openness to alternative views and lifestyles which one can bring into the political arena as an invaluable resource for political interaction. Further, the trust that is required if one is to engage in self-revelatory political discourse can perhaps be most effectively developed as one discloses oneself to one's friends, whether or not the dimensions of oneself thus initially revealed are political.

In addition, in the settings provided by their friendship groups, people learn how to negotiate difference and resolve challenges related to power.[72] Because

71. Landwehr, "Friendship" 321–2; cp. McFadyen, *Call to Personhood* 206–8.

72. Hutter, *Politics as Friendship* 11.

as a friend one comes to understand how and when power is to be used and renounced, how trust occasions and limits power, how fear is to be overcome,[73] how to describe and defend options and help to make decisions,[74] we discover in the practice of friendship metaphors and analogies which we can bring to bear to inform our public and political activity.

Commerce, Friendship, and Social Barriers

People often instinctively suppose that business relationships are arm's-length connections, perhaps even cynically manipulative. And of course they can be. But commercial interactions can ultimately yield rich personal connections.[75] Commercial engagement tends to generate and reinforce trust among strangers.[76] And it also has the capacity to nourish relationships that, while they may begin as instrumental ones, can become genuine friendships. The emergence of such friendships can not only enable the individual participants to bridge cultural, religious, and ethnic barriers but also lead, thanks to the participants' self-reports and examples, to reductions in such barriers between other people as well.

Dirigiste regimes may put in place constraints on commerce that inhibit the formation of intergroup friendships—by, for example, raising barriers to entry into various kinds of economic activity that disproportionately affect new and undocumented immigrants and other people affiliated with disfavored groups.[77] A liberal order can foster friendship formation in part precisely by razing barriers to entry into economic life.

73. Hutter 12–3.

74. See Carole Pateman, *Participation and Democratic Theory* (Cambridge: Cambridge University Press 1970) (arguing for workplace democracy as an essential prerequisite to effective participation in democratic political life).

75. Badhwar, "Societies" 311–2.

76. See Joseph Henrich *et al.*, "'Economic Man' in Cross-Cultural Perspective: Behavioral Experiments in Fifteen Small-Scale Societies," *Behavioral and Brain Sciences* 28 (2005): 795–855 <https://www.econ.uzh.ch/dam/jcr:ffffffff-9758-127f-0000-00004de60616/Henrich_et_al_in_BBS_Dec_05.pdf>; and Badhwar, "Societies" 318–9.

77. It is unsurprising that political power is used for the benefit of those with political power and access and to the detriment of the excluded and subordinated; see, *e.g.*, W. H. Hutt, *The Economics of the Colour Bar: A Study of the Economic Origins and Consequences of Racial Segregation in South Africa* (London: IEA-Deutsch 1964) <https://cdn.mises.org/The%20Economics%20of%20the%20Colour%20Bar_2.pdf>.

This includes, of course, not just eliminating regulatory burdens but also ending barriers to immigration.[78] These barriers make it much more unlikely that immigrants will reap the benefits of new commercial relationships and share their newfound resources with relatives and friends, of course. But they also substantially limit opportunities for friendships to develop between immigrants and others in the immigrants' new home societies. Such friendships can be beneficial in virtue not only of friendship's inherent value but also of their ability to reduce cross-cultural suspicion and hostility.

The more people are free to participate in commerce, the more likely it is that they will be able to connect with each other and to develop fruitful relationships, including ones that cross traditional boundaries.[79] Liberal institutions can thus foster personal flourishing for individual economic actors even as they also promote social peace and harmony.

Friendship and Dissent

Friendship circles play practical roles in on-the-ground politics, narrow and broad alike. Legislators, for instance, are linked not only by ideology or strategic calculation but also by personal relationships,[80] and friendships help to foster consensus and conflict resolution among them.[81] The same is true of union members, for whom friendship groups can serve as springboards for involvement in union affairs as well as means of influencing union policies.[82]

Arguably, however, a more important way in which friendship both reflects the values of a liberal culture and helps to reinforce those values is by providing a standpoint from outside the societal mainstream from which conventional

78. An excellent recent case for this position is the following: Bryan Caplan and Zach Weinersmith, *Open Borders: The Science and Ethics of Immigration* (New York: First Second-Roaring 2019).

79. See Badhwar, "Societies" 318.

80. Gregory A. Caldeira and Samuel C. Patterson, "Political Friendship in the Legislature," *Journal of Politics* 49 (1987): 952–75.

81. Caldeira and Patterson 967–70. Caldeira and Patterson reference Ross K. Baker, *Friend and Foe in the US Senate* (New York: Free 1980) 6.

82. Sidney Verba, "The Small Group and Political Behavior," *The Small Group in Political Science: The Last Two Decades of Development*, ed. Robert T. Golembiewski (Athens: University of Georgia Press 1978) 85.

ideas and behavior patterns and institutions can be subjected to critique.[83] In short, friendship can serve as a crucial source of support for dissidents.[84]

The support provided by friendship groups is often vital to survival on the margins of politics.[85] Friendship can provide someone with a critical perspective on the mainstream together with the personal strength and self-confidence to act on the basis of such a perspective,[86] perhaps alone (supportive friends may not be political allies), perhaps precisely as a member of a friendship group,[87] drawing on the resources shared action provides.[88]

This isn't coincidental. Some display of deviance from social norms can sometimes help a friendship to form. To become a potential friend, one must often be selected from among the members of a larger social group; and one must thus display one's individuality. A potential friend needs to believe that she is seeing not just the self I present in public but a self which is more authentically mine and which I want her, in particular, to see. And to do this I may need to act in a distinctive way. One way of acting distinctively is to act rebelliously, to flout social conventions.[89]

Friends need not be dissenters. But there is a natural fit between friendship and dissent. And, when a friendship begins in dissent, the nature of its origins may tend to reinforce a tendency to engage in dissent in the future. To be sure, when friends challenge propriety, their challenges may often be trivial;[90] but this needn't be the case. Friendship thus has the potential to be subversive.

Indeed, judging oneself to be a political outsider may be among the reasons someone might choose to enter a circle of intimate friends. Such circles offer people settings within which they can express dissenting views as well as the confidence to voice those views publicly.[91] This need not be because the friends share a dissenter's views; what matters is that they are willing to accept her. In

83. Hutter, *Politics as Friendship* 9; cp. Michael Novak, *A Theology for Radical Politics* (London: Herder 1969) 40.

84. Friedman, *Friends* 219, 248–9; Janice Raymond, *A Passion for Friends: Toward a Philosophy of Female Affection* (Boston: Beacon 1986), ctd. Friedman, *Friends* 249.

85. See Hutter, *Politics as Friendship* 18–9.

86. See Kerney, "Theology of Friendship" 42.

87. Hutter, *Politics as Friendship* 9.

88. Verba, "Small Group" 90–2.

89. Suttles, "Friendship" 116.

90. Suttles 118.

91. Ada Finifter, "The Friendship Group as a Protective Environment for Political Deviants," Golembiewski, *Small Group* 132, 152.

virtue of its relative independence and its capacity to serve as a counterweight to other social forces, the friendship group can turn out to be countercultural, even potentially revolutionary, even if it didn't form initially because its members were political dissenters or in order to encourage dissent.

Friendship groups can welcome members with diverse political views. But a friendship group seems likely often not only to protect but also to help shape its members' political beliefs. Certainly, the political affiliations of participants in friendship groups can affect members' voting patterns and prompt people to abandon their families' traditional political loyalties.[92]

Friendship can also help to create awareness of the possibility of social equality, to model this kind of equality, and thus to encourage greater equality in practice. It is necessary for people to transcend their social roles in large measure if they are to be friends. The possibility of friendship is therefore the possibility that such roles, and hierarchical power structures dependent upon them, will be relativized.[93] A friendship group can give people the general experience of interacting with social equals. And if one engages as a friend with someone who might otherwise be viewed as occupying a different rung on the social ladder, interaction with that person as a friend can lead to greater equality in one's relationship with her outside the friendship group.

Friendship and Experiments in Living

Friendship groups can contribute to insight and discovery in and through their participation in and support of what John Stuart Mill termed "experiments in living."[94] When people try out alternative ways of being human and put them on public display, others (and the experimenters themselves) can learn more about the attractions and liabilities of these ways of living, which can be more readily considered as live options for adoption or rejection in the wider society. Simply demonstrating the possibility of alternatives to established patterns of behavior—say, the possibility of friendship across racial barriers in apartheid-era South Africa[95]—can be powerfully disruptive to the status quo.

92. Herbert McCloskey and Harold E. Dahlgren, "Primary Group Influence on Party Loyalty," Golembiewski, *Small Group* 121.

93. Hutter, *Politics as Friendship* 10.

94. See John Stuart Mill, *On Liberty* (London: Parker 1859) 103–39. See Mentinis, "Friendship" 74–6.

95. See, *e.g.*, Carmichael, *Friendship* 1–3.

Some experiments will be dismal failures. But voluntary social experiments of all kinds, perhaps sometimes especially the disastrous ones, can help the participants and the observers understand human possibilities more satisfactorily. As Mill put it,

> In this age, the mere example of nonconformity, the mere refusal to bend the knee to custom, is itself a service. Precisely because the tyranny of opinion is such as to make eccentricity a reproach, it is desirable, in order to break through that tyranny, that people should be eccentric. Eccentricity has always abounded when and where strength of character was abounded; and the amount of eccentricity in a society has generally been proportional to the amount of genius, mental vigour, and moral courage which it contained. That so few now dare to be eccentric, marks the chief danger of the time.[96]

Friends can join each other in deliberately choosing to live visibly in ways that challenge the status quo. Engaging in a voluntary social experiment with friends will often be easier than doing so with strangers and will involve fewer conflicts of the kind often brought about by the friction that can arise between people who don't know each other well. Even when she doesn't opt for an experimental way of life, someone can provide moral and, sometimes, financial support to friends who do choose to experiment with alternative models of existence. (Many such experiments won't require outside funding, of course.)

It can be particularly important for those engaged in experiments in living to be aware of the validating affirmation of friends who are not among their coexperimenters but who regard their experiments as interesting, potentially fruitful, and worth undertaking. In addition, someone who observes a friend's experiment in living can provide critiques more likely to be heard and understood than ones offered by strangers. And friends can help to publicize the results of social experiments—sometimes again, perhaps, with more credibility than the actual participants. In so doing, as they engage in politics of a particularly quiet kind, friends can foster the adoption or retention of fertile patterns of life.

96. Mill, *On Liberty* 120–1.

The Church Witnesses by Supporting Friendship

At its best, the Christian church is engaged in an ongoing experiment in living, which is a crucial aspect of its participation in political life. Liberalism rightly seeks to rule out the use of coercive force by religious communities. But nonviolent action by the church can be highly significant politically.[97]

For instance, in a culture in which friendship is too often trivialized and devalued, the church can witness powerfully by occasioning, sustaining, and nourishing intimate ties. The church can effectively put on display a style of life that may diverge in important ways from the pattern of behavior encountered in society generally. Taking people's friendships seriously is itself *part* of such a style of life. And healthy friendships can contribute in multiple ways to other aspects of the church's witness.

In the wider culture, friendship is often treated cavalierly, with friendships abandoned as people move up corporate ladders, change jobs, or relocate. The church can testify to the value of loyalty by modeling in practical ways a recognition of friendship's value in the face of pressures to abandon or deemphasize rich personal connections.[98]

It can do so in part, perhaps, by formally recognizing the existence, value, and seriousness of close friendships using celebratory rituals and other institutional practices. People who might be uncomfortable with formalizing friendship *legally* might well regard ritual acknowledgment by the church as worthwhile and nonthreatening. In addition, congregations, denominational institutions, and parachurch organizations can actively embrace norms hospitable to and supportive of the maintenance of friendships in difficult circumstances. Whatever might be true of attempts to foster such norms in the wider culture, Christian groups can find such norms particularly worth affirming as expressions of a broader sensitivity to the profound importance of fidelity. Like marriage, friendship provides ample opportunity for the display of potentially heroic fidelity. While friendships may be more fluid than marriages, the church

97. The notion that witness is a key kind of political action by the church has been developed and expounded at multiple points by Stanley Hauerwas. In addition to the other texts by Hauerwas I cite in this book, see, *e.g.*, Stanley Hauerwas, *In Good Company: The Church as Polis* (Notre Dame, IN: University of Notre Dame Press 1995).

98. These observations are inspired by Hauerwas's discussion of the church's affirmation of marriage and marital fidelity as politically important; see below.

can acknowledge the genuine value of reliability, trustworthiness, and loyalty in friendship, honoring those who maintain friendships even under pressure.

Thus, the church can help people sustain friendships despite political, religious, and other sorts of potentially divisive disagreements. It can enable people to step back from disagreement and to resist the temptation to resent or dislike others on the basis of such disagreement. It can do so by emphasizing that each person is uniquely cherished by God and embraced by divine love, that the church itself is a place in which that love can be exhibited, that no person possesses God's omniscience and infallibility, and that no creaturely project deserves anything like absolute importance or loyalty. The church can model a kind of life in which the intensity and vitriolic character of political, religious, and similar disputes are minimized. That does not mean, of course, that the church cannot take strong stands. Taking such stands, however, is quite compatible with affirming and supporting friendships with people who, even if profoundly and destructively mistaken, remain God's beloved children.

This kind of affirmation coheres not only with the church's conviction that fidelity matters but also with its hope that divine grace will foster healing and transformation even in difficult relationships.[99] The church can and should do this with the recognition that, in supporting friendships, it is not only benefiting individual members but also giving visible, shared expression to convictions with transformative value for the wider society and offering thoroughly practical expression to the divine faithfulness it celebrates.

By valuing and embodying relationships that are not manipulative or instrumental, the church can help people see the real possibility of genuine friendship.[100] Of course concern with respectful patterns of interaction isn't and shouldn't be limited to friendships; however, if people can learn in church how to value others in their particularity, they will have discovered something important about how to be friends.[101] A church that recognizes God as revealed in the crucifixion of Jesus must be alert to the value of nondomination, the value of acknowledging otherness even when it's disturbing and unsettling and threatening.

99. See Stanley Hauerwas, *A Community of Character: Toward a Constructive Christian Social Ethic* (Notre Dame, IN: University of Notre Dame Press 1981) 190–4. Hauerwas's concern is with marital fidelity as an aspect of the church's witness, but I think the same point can readily be made with respect to friendship.

100. On the contribution of the church to friendship, see Rodney Clapp, "The Celebration of Friendship," *Reformed Journal* 39.8 (Aug. 1989): 11.

101. Clapp 11.

Perceiving the friend as distinctively *other* than oneself is crucial to genuine friendship; and the stance of attentive openness fostered by the church's proclamation can help one to recognize that friendship *realizes*, *embodies*, goods rather than simply helping to *produce* them. And the practice of eucharistic fellowship in the context of the church inculcates in us the disposition to be forgiving—crucial to friendship between fallible, sinful people.[102]

As Justin Martyr observed, Christ "is the Word of whom every race of men were partakers; and those who lived reasonably are Christians, even though they have been thought atheists."[103] The church can bear witness to the universality of the presence and activity of the Logos by being open, and encouraging individual members to be open, to the insights offered by those affiliated with non-Christian traditions or with none at all. The church can also convey its commitment to friendship by helping members to enrich the lives of their unchurched friends, by offering them not only personal nurture but also ideas and perspectives that can helpfully challenge the shibboleths of contemporary culture.

The church can bear political witness in part, then, through its ability to embrace people who don't share its convictions and to help friends love each other despite difference and wrongdoing. The life of the church can thus be a contributor to friendship's flourishing. Friendship can be, in turn, a contributor to the church's fulfillment of its mission.

Friends Support the Church's Political Witness

If being a distinctive kind of community is a crucial political act on the church's part, then *helping* the church to be this kind of community must likewise be politically significant. In the context of a relatively small community like a congregation, the political impact of the friendship group is likely to be greater than it might be were its only influence on the wider society exerted without mediation. So friendship within the life of a congregation—or, for that matter, a small denomination—has the capacity to make a distinctive political contribution. Friends can help the church be the church by actively encouraging their

102. Clapp 12.

103. Justin Martyr, *The First Apology*, trans. Marcus Dods and George Reith, *Ante-Nicene Fathers*, ed. Alexander Roberts, James Donaldson, and A. Cleveland Coxe, 10 vols. (Buffalo, NY: Christian Literature 1885) ch. 46 <http://www.newadvent.org/fathers/0126.htm> (ed. Kevin Knight; Aug. 25, 2020); cp. Clark, *God's World* 59–87.

congregations and denominations to witness in various ways. They can also do so by modeling the kind of support of friendship that church entities should provide and the kind of fruitfulness on the part of friendship groups generally that church entities should recognize and celebrate.

The friendship group can't bear just the same kind of witness as the church, since there is a givenness about ecclesial relationships that does not characterize relations between friends, a givenness which requires the church to integrate diverse perspectives and practices into a flourishing whole. But, while the friendship group need not always take account of the kind of diversity to be found within the church, it can nonetheless model a kind of egalitarian mutuality that stands in sharp contrast with the hierarchicalism and exploitation characteristic of many kinds of political structures.[104] It can also help to support and exemplify insightful approaches to "civility and the intellectual and moral life"[105] in ways that influence the practices of others, including the practice of the church itself—too often given, as it is, to embracing hierarchy (internally and in the wider society).

A fruitful, creative tension can exist between the church and the friendship circle. The church at its best can induct a member into a public tradition, with an extensive history of reflection on and critical engagement with the wider society. At the same time, however, it can ossify; and conventional assumptions can remain unchallenged—reinforced, in fact, in virtue of the desire to conform and belong and of fear of institutional censure.

A friendship group within the church can serve to offer support for courageous dissent while also helping to anchor people in their ecclesial community. Friendship circles that connect church members with those outside the church can offer participants in the life of the church perspectives they might be less likely to gain from other members and can enable them to develop critical perspectives on beliefs and practices that the church might be inclined to take for granted.

Friendship and Networked Politics

Networks, essentially voluntary, consensual, and nonaggressive, can be *peaceful* in ways that territorially monopolistic states are incapable of being. There is reason to prefer networks to states as sources of social order, and the emergence

104. See Hunt, *Fierce Tenderness*.

105. MacIntyre, *After Virtue* 263.

of a network-based politics could help to render friendship politically significant in new ways.

Human flourishing involves communication, and the core of communication is face-to-face encounter. The exercise of personal voice is a crucial element of personal empowerment in a variety of institutional contexts. Freedom of exit is absolutely crucial, and reducing the costs of exit can make things much easier for dissidents and others unhappy with the way in which institutions are structured. At the same time, however, there will often be good reasons for dissidents to remain connected with institutions they wish to challenge—sometimes instrumental, sometimes identity-constitutive. And this means, in turn, that *voice* matters, that people need to know that they can influence policies not only by leaving unsatisfactory institutions but also by helping to reshape them. This matters not only because continued membership in a particular institutional community may be important but also because of the value of being *heard* and of being *validated* through the responses of others to one's voiced concerns and one's arguments for new policies.[106] One crucial way in which voice can matter is in the course of direct, interpersonal exchange.[107] This matters both because one-on-one personal relationships themselves matter and because individual persuasion can be an effective and important means of making change happen in a human-scale environment.[108]

This kind of engagement matters in the context of many different institutions—churches, schools, workplaces, clubs. It matters, that is, in relation to politics in the broad sense. But it can and should also be significant as regards politics in the narrow sense, the realm of enforceable legal rights. Changes in this arena could foster the recovery of—a contemporary version of—friendship's classical political significance.

Small-Scale Democracy

A common approach to encouraging the emergence of human-scale politics has been to argue for local democratic structures, perhaps even at the neighborhood level, with large-scale ones compounded out of smaller ones.[109] In such

106. See McFadyen, *Call to Personhood* 206, 256, 314.

107. McFadyen 257.

108. See McFadyen 259.

109. See, *e.g.*, G. D. H. Cole, *Essays in Social Theory* (London: Macmillan 1950) 94–5; Verba, "Small Group" 96 (my source for the Cole citation); and Martin Buber, *Paths in Utopia* (London: Routledge

a political order rooted in small-scale democracy, friendship could achieve a public importance it has arguably lacked since the days of the polis.

A decentralized political system rooted in something like face-to-face democracy need not be seen as a throwback to a simpler political era without contemporary applicability. In fact, Hannah Arendt argued that just such a system had spontaneously and repeatedly arisen—the work not of professional revolutionaries but, rather, of ordinary people—in the course of revolutionary movements throughout the modern period.[110] While Thomas Jefferson argued on theoretical grounds for wards as loci of face-to-face democracy, such bodies actually appeared during the French Revolution, the 1917 Russian Revolution, and the 1956 Hungarian Revolution.[111] Arendt maintained that implicit in the ward system where it emerged was the conviction, which today we might call broadly republican, "that no one could be called either happy or free without participating, and having a share, in public power."[112] Deliberative bodies emerged in neighborhoods, among fellow combatants, among writers and artists, among students, among people working in particular factories, among military personnel, and elsewhere.[113] What seemed to develop was a model of nested councils selecting representatives to more inclusive bodies, all the way up to the national level.[114]

Arendt paints a rosy picture of the political possibilities of government-by-council because she believes it makes possible the kind of fulfillment derived from "having a share in public business."[115] She sees it as a reasonable way to distribute and limit power.[116] And she wonders whether councils would inhibit the rise and diminish the influence of potentially bigoted, oppressive, and irrational mass movements and allow the emergence of political decision makers acknowledged as capable by their peers and demonstrably equipped to address public concerns.[117]

1949) 133–7.

110. See Bhikkhu Parekh, *Hannah Arendt and the Search for a New Political Philosophy* (London: Macmillan 1981) 168–71; and Hannah Arendt, *On Revolution* (London: Faber 1963) 252–70.

111. See Arendt, *On Revolution* 258–9.

112. Arendt 259.

113. Arendt 270.

114. Arendt 271, 282–3, citing Oskar Anweiler, "Die Räte in der ungarischen Revolution 1956," *Osteuropa* 8.6 (June 1958): 393–400.

115. Arendt, *On Revolution* 115.

116. Arendt 282.

117. Arendt 283; cp. Buber, *Paths* 136.

By altering the *scale* of day-to-day politics, a system to which small, local democratic assemblies were central could make it possible for the individual friendship circle to play a significant political role as it did in classical Greece. In such a system, with the number of political actors in any given jurisdiction quite limited, groups of friends could exert meaningful influence. And, indeed, involvement in local deliberative democracy could help to form new friendships as well.

Concerns about Councils

Council democracy has evident advantages over mass democracy as regards personal empowerment. It is realistic to imagine that one could exert meaningful influence over a small, local deliberative body. Involvement in small decision-making bodies might contribute significantly to members' political education. Such bodies could enforce greater accountability on the part of decision makers. And the exercise of responsibility by such bodies might encourage concern for other people and for communal institutions.[118] But a network-based model would, I think, be preferable.

Local assemblies responsible for making rules for small, defined geographic areas might prove to be magnets for busybodies and authoritarians interested in regulating the lives of their neighbors. And assembly participants' personal knowledge of each other and awareness of each other's votes might tend to lead to the suppression of dissenting views and to disregard for minority rights and interests.[119]

The most arguably problematic feature of small, local assemblies is that they seem likely to retain the power to exclude alternatives.[120] If a council is the sole decision maker regarding the definition and enforcement of legal rights in a coherent geographic area, it qualifies as a territorial monopolist, able to exclude

118. Jane J. Mansbridge, *Beyond Adversary Democracy* (New York: Basic 1980) 298, citing Benjamin R. Barber, *Political Participation and the Creation of* Res Publica (Bloomington, IN: Poynter 1977); C. B. Macpherson, *The Life and Times of Liberal Democracy* (Oxford: Oxford University Press 1977); Sara M. Shumer, "Machiavelli: Republican Politics and Its Corruption," *Political Theory* 7.1 (1979): 5–34.

119. See Mansbridge, *Beyond Adversary Democracy* 292.

120. Arendt's own observations complicate things in this regard, since she discusses a variety of *functional* rather than geographically localized deliberative bodies. The more responsibility is dispersed among such groups the better. But as long as territorial monopolists remain in operation, the problems I note in the text remain, even if they aren't the only decision makers.

others from making at least some decisions about rights in that area. A monopolistic council can impose rules on people without the consent of those people. It is thus, in effect, a *state* (perhaps a city-state or a neighborhood-state). And suppose a set of geographically proximate local monopolistic councils in a given region were in some way nested within or overseen by a more inclusive assembly that was exclusively responsible for that region. In this case, the assembly would be even more clearly a monopolist able to make decisions for the smaller regions governed by the assemblies under its umbrella. Such an assembly would thus be even more state-like than its constituents.

We might want to look critically at states, even local microstates, for several reasons.[121]

(*i*) States in the contemporary world are often viewed as authoritative—as entitled to obedience in at least partial independence of the *contents* of their laws, regulations, policies, and executive decisions—in virtue of the consent of the governed. But, as is widely recognized,[122] their claims to authority cannot be supported by appeals to consent. The governed have not, at least in the vast majority of cases, given their actual consent to state institutions or authorities. In the small number of cases in which the governed *have* consented, they have generally done so under explicit duress or with the threat of force in the background.[123] States thus lack consensual grounding.

121. See, *e.g.*, Chartier, *Anarchy and Legal Order*; and Michael Huemer, *The Problem of Political Authority: An Examination of the Right to Coerce and the Duty to Obey* (New York: Palgrave 2013).

122. See, *e.g.*, Chartier, *Anarchy* 161–2; Clark, *Peace* 71–92; Clark, *Political Animal* 23–39; Jan Narveson, *You and the State: A Short Introduction to Political Philosophy* (Lanham, MD: Rowman 2008) 183–201; Aeon Skoble, *Deleting the State: An Argument about Government* (Chicago: Open Court 2008); Leslie Green, *The Authority of the State* (Oxford: Clarendon-Oxford University Press 1990); Joseph Raz, *The Authority of Law: Essays on Law and Morality* (Oxford: Clarendon-Oxford University Press 1979); and M. B. E. Smith, "Is There a Prima Facie Obligation to Obey the Law?," *Yale Law Journal* 82 (1973): 950–76. See polling data from 2018: "Most Say Government Doesn't Have Consent of the Governed," Rasmussen Reports, Aug. 20, 2018 <https://www.rasmussenreports.com/public_content/politics/general_politics/july_2018/most_say_government_doesn_t_have_consent_of_the_governed>. For some self-consciously Christian responses to the relevant phenomena, see, *e.g.*, Sam Underwood and Kevin Vallier, "Christian Anarchism," *Routledge Handbook of Anarchy and Anarchist Thought*, ed. Gary Chartier and Chad Van Schoelandt (London: Routledge 2020) 187–204; Vernard Eller, *Christian Anarchy: Jesus' Primacy over the Powers* (Grand Rapids: Eerdmans 1987); and Jacques Ellul, *Anarchy and Christianity* (Grand Rapids: Eerdmans 1991).

123. See Charles W. Johnson, "Can Anybody Ever Consent to the State?," *Rad Geek People's Daily* (blog), Jan. 8, 2009 <http://radgeek.com/gt/2009/01/08/can_anybody>.

(*ii*) States reduce diversity. They attempt to make decisions for all members of the populations they seek to govern. If problems are addressed uniformly, mistakes are much more costly than they would be if made by smaller entities with narrower scopes of activity, and the range of people's preferences and needs is ignored.

(*iii*) States raise the cost of selecting congenial legal rules and institutions. As long as states rule the world's territories, the easiest way to ensure that one lives in a more congenial policy environment will be to leave one state and move to another.[124] However, moving is often costly, even for relatively short distances. There aren't many states from among which to choose in today's world. And the exercise of monopolistic powers even by local assemblies would significantly reduce the number of options—as regards legal rules and institutions—from which people could select. If foot voting is someone's only option, then, it's much less likely that alternative rules and structures will be tried out or made available to those who might wish to experiment with them.

(*iv*) States pose serious risks to ordinary people's welfare.[125] For instance, (*a*) they initiate and perpetuate profoundly destructive wars and other policies that lead to mass death.[126] (*b*) State actors often enjoy special immunity from liability, with the result that they act with relative impunity and that they fail to internalize the costs of their decisions. (Police violence is an obvious, and especially disturbing, example.) (*c*) The ability of states and state actors to externalize the costs of their choices on others—notably on taxpayers—means that they can be expected to behave irresponsibly or worse. In particular, they can implement some people's prejudices at little cost to the prejudiced—by acquiring funding from the public as a whole. As a result, they can undertake unjust, destructive programs of activity, such as South African apartheid, Jim Crow in the post–Civil War South, the criminalization of same-sex sexual activities in many parts of the world, and the racist War on Drugs. (*d*) States implement

124. On foot voting, see, *e.g.*, Ilya Somin, *Free to Move: Foot Voting, Migration, and Political Freedom* (New York: Oxford University Press 2020).

125. See Chartier, *Anarchy* 208–32.

126. See, *e.g.*, Max Roser, "War and Peace," Our World in Data (Global Change Data Lab), 2016 <https://ourworldindata.org/war-and-peace>; Micheal Clodfelter, *Warfare and Armed Conflicts: A Statistical Encyclopedia of Casualty and Other Figures, 1492–2015*, 4th ed. (Jefferson, NC: McFarland 2017); R. J. Rummel, *Death by Government: Genocide and Mass Murder since 1900* (Piscataway, NJ: Transaction 1994); and Milton Leitenberg, *Deaths in Wars and Conflicts in the 20th Century*, 3d ed. (Ithaca, NY: Cornell Peace Studies Program 2006) <https://www.clingendael.org/sites/default/files/pdfs/20060800_cdsp_occ_leitenberg.pdf> (Nov. 6, 2020).

programs of large-scale depredation, such as the theft of land from peasants and its transfer to well-connected elites. (*e*) States serve as mechanisms for creating and maintaining privileges for state actors' cronies and thus for channeling resources from the public to the wealthy and well connected.

(*v*) Consensual institutions can maintain social order reliably while occasioning fewer risks, at lower costs, and with greater accountability than inherently monopolistic states.[127]

Acknowledging the difficulties I've noted does not mean, of course, that it's always wise or fair to flout state edicts. State-made laws may, for instance, embody preexisting moral duties (to avoid murder or theft or fraud, say). And, even if they don't, it may be prudent to follow them because of the consequences of disobedience for oneself or others. But these difficulties do give us good reason to consider alternatives to monopolistic states.[128]

127. See, *e.g.*, Kevin A. Carson, *The Desktop Regulatory State: The Countervailing Power of Individuals and Networks* (Tulsa, OK: Center for a Stateless Society 2016); Kevin A. Carson, *Exodus: General Idea of the Revolution in the XXI Century* (Tulsa, OK: Center for a Stateless Society 2021); David D. Friedman, *The Machinery of Freedom*, 3d ed. (n.p.: CreateSpace 2015); Edward P. Stringham, *Private Governance: Creating Order in Economic and Social Life* (New York: Oxford University Press 2015); and Peter T. Leeson, *Anarchy Unbound: Why Self-Governance Works Better Than You Think* (Cambridge: Cambridge University Press 2014).

128. Saint Paul's affirmation of the Roman Empire's legitimacy in Rom 13 contrasts sharply with the depiction of it as demonic in Rev 13. Saint Paul's approach presumably reflects his own experience as a Roman citizen (even one who would ultimately be executed by Nero) as well as a recognition of the pragmatic efficacy of avoiding conflict with Rome and an understanding of divine sovereignty as underlying the maintenance of the empire and other social institutions. He might also be read as assuming that the empire is (more or less) an agency of justice and that something like the empire is needed to maintain social order. The critique of state legitimacy I summarize here begins with the assumption that we should take seriously the experience not just of those, like Saint Paul, with frequently positive relationships with state power but also of those on whom the state's hand falls violently. It shares the view that violent conflict with state authorities can be destructive and dangerous and that there is no reason to offer excuses for violent crackdowns by such authorities. It assumes an account of providence like the one I articulated in chapter 2, in accordance with which God's will is often not done in the world, so that social institutions cannot be assumed without further ado to enjoy divine sanction. It highlights the consistent injustice done even by reasonably stable and reliable states—challenging the presumption that the empire and states like it should be thought of as deserving support in virtue of being sustainers of justice. (Compare the positions of conservative Calvinists who defended tyrannicide in the early modern area on the view that Rom 13 provided no cover for despots.) And it stresses the capacity of self-organizing networks and other social systems to provide social order without exercising monopoly powers. Thanks to Kevin Carson for emphasizing the need to discuss Rom 13 here.

The Worth of Networks

In today's international system, violence happens (in significant part because state actors face incentives to be violent that ordinary people don't); the current international system is hardly ideal. But it is no constant Hobbesian war of all against all. And yet there is no Leviathan, no world ruler, to maintain planetwide peace on earth. Rather, moral and pragmatic considerations make international cooperation between states and individuals possible without Leviathan. One way to think about the kind of network-based model of politics I'm describing is to think of it as paralleling the model of contemporary international society, from which any sort of Hobbesian Leviathan is absent, universalized.

Because they are consensual and voluntary, networks can be *peaceful*. By contrast, states—which exclude alternatives,[129] threaten the use of force, and impose demands on the unconsenting—cannot, even in principle. Affiliation with a particular network can follow a *person* whatever her location. Because people can thus switch from network to network without bearing the potentially high cost of relocation, they can easily exercise the freedom to exit. And their ability to do so would place substantial pressure on networks to embrace arrangements likely to attract and retain members. Similarly, the desire to avoid costly and potentially violent extended clashes would encourage networks to adopt conflict-of-law rules and similar norms designed to make disputes among members of different networks as easy as possible to resolve.[130]

Networks responsible for maintaining social order—providing law (doubtless often in ways enabling members to select from among legal rules for particular transactions and relationships), dispute resolution, and safety services—could

129. Kevin Carson notes that one can envision "decentralized, geographically-defined governance institutions that don't necessarily lead to a territorial monopoly of decision-making" (email message, Oct. 20, 2020). See Carson, *Exodus* 139–66, 259–96, 331–80 (discussing "Platform States" and "partner cooperatives"). (I take Carson's point to be that, for economic, cultural, or other reasons, consensual networks providing various sorts of services might function in a given geographic area, even though each was unable to exclude others. He has in mind, in particular, those responsible for geographically specific resources or infrastructure.) I tend to envision networks that intersect with each other in particular geographic locales but that may also operate in regions from which those with whose service areas theirs overlap elsewhere might be absent.

130. See, *e.g.*, Trent J. MacDonald, *The Political Economy of Non-territorial Exit: Cryptosecession* (Cheltenham, UK: Elgar 2019); and Max Borders, *The Social Singularity: How Decentralization Will Allow Us to Transcend Politics, Create Global Prosperity, and Avoid the Robot Apocalypse* (Austin, TX: Social Evolution 2018).

be expected to take multiple forms and to exhibit diverse characters. Some might build on existing systems of religious law (Catholic, Jewish, or Muslim, for instance), some might be worker or consumer cooperatives of various kinds, some might be not-for-profit service providers, and some might be commercial entities.[131]

By rooting legal authority in consent, expecting people to internalize the costs of their choices regarding legal rules, and making exit easy, a deterritorialized, network-based approach to governance would likely make politics in the narrow sense less intrusive, threatening, and dangerous. It could thus create more space for people to focus on the aspects of flourishing they preferred to prioritize.

As a result, a network-based politics would reduce the range of political (again, in the narrow sense) complications encountered by friends qua friends and the variety of political issues with which they needed to concern themselves, thus leaving them freer to focus on their shared interests. It would also increase background prosperity (by replacing costly monopolistic institutions and eliminating elite privileges that inhibit growth and the sharing of wealth). In so doing, it would reduce friends' economic worries and offer them more opportunities to interact with each other and otherwise pursue their (shared or individual) goals.

In some cases, people would likely influence their own circumstances primarily by exercising the freedom to exit; opportunities for influence over the contents of legal rules might be limited, for instance, in the case of networks upholding traditional systems of religious law. But people would, of course, be free to pick among networks that featured different institutional arrangements. And some people would undoubtedly welcome opportunities to participate in (say) consumer cooperatives featuring deliberative decision-making mechanisms.

There would be reasons for networks to be maintained at human scale. Diseconomies of scale affect large organizations, as I've already noted; small size can enhance organizational efficiency, even if it's not guaranteed to do so. In addition, networks could be expected to respond to the preferences of those interested in joining effectively in decision-making. And technology would often make it affordable for networks to be small. As a result, interested individuals could often be active participants in shaping institutional arrangements, and

131. See, *e.g.*, Chartier, *Anarchy* (esp. 241–62).

groups of friends could thus influence institutional conversations and outcomes as they did in the Greek city-state.[132]

Networked structures for order maintenance would also create opportunities for friendship groups to be politically significant because friends separated by geography could still participate in the same network. While proximity is important for friendship, friends are often unavoidably separated. A networked politics would enable friends in different places to work together to shape institutions in which they participated.

A decentralized, deterritorialized, political order would offer "possibilities of meaningful incorporation" into political life,[133] possibilities that must be available for significant communication about political questions to take place. Such an order would make it possible for friendship to be even more politically influential than it can be at present. Because at least in principle thoroughly peaceful, it would also replace the essentially violent state apparatus that inhibits the formation and maintenance of friendships and sometimes brutally ends those friendships—through war, incarceration, and restrictions on migration and other forms of movement, as well as through rules that reduce the space for friendship in our lives.

I do not mean, in arguing for the value of networks over states, to endorse any sort of naïve overconfidence in people's virtue in voluntary settings. Coercive institutions are not the only environments in which sin is painfully evident. But power presents obvious, and dangerous, temptations. The concentration of power creates exceptional opportunities for mischief; it also attracts those prone to mischief, reinforces their tendency to engage in mischief, and runs the risk of corrupting even those who seek to acquire it with benevolent motives—in part by encouraging them to embrace benevolent authoritarianism, overconfidence, and self-righteousness. And proximity to political power constitutes vital, and

132. Roderick T. Long, "Virtual Cantons: A New Path to Freedom?," *Formulations* 1.1 (1993) <http://praxeology.net/libertariannation/a/f11l1.html>, comes close to articulating a constitutional model for cooperatives of the kind I have in mind, though the approach he develops in his article still assumes the existence of a national-level state (an option Long himself regards as second best). Nothing about the general model precludes treating the virtual cantons as the only needed or desirable political entities, though, as I note above, there's no need to opt for a single model, not least because not everyone could be expected to *want* participatory structures—cp. the quip, widely attributed to Oscar Wilde, that "the trouble with Socialism is that it takes too many evenings." People's preferences and tolerances for meetings no doubt vary widely.

133. McFadyen, *Call to Personhood* 260.

troubling, divisions among social classes.[134] Distributing power widely and subjecting it to multiple checks thus seems crucial in virtue of the sinful penchant to abuse power.

In addition, in societies as in business firms, centralizing power is not only a source of temptation to abuse but also a way of ensuring that widely distributed information is not used effectively. Networks allow distributed knowledge to be employed effectively without being collected in a single repository. Hierarchies, by contrast, function well only if those exercising authority have access to all relevant data, which it's ordinarily impossible for them to do.

Relatedly, networks, marked by flexibility as well as by ease of exit, can experiment at much lower costs than states. Because they're consensual, networks will need to internalize the costs of mistakes. And those who wish to avoid what they expect will prove to be, or what already seem to be, mistakes will find it relatively easy to opt for alternatives. In this way, networks can help to minimize the bad effects not only of the sinful arrogation of power but also of well-intentioned ignorance.

Conflicts of Loyalties

As ideological conflict brewed in Europe, E. M. Forster noted that it might sometimes be unavoidable to choose between a state and a friend.

> Personal relations are despised today. They are regarded as bourgeois luxuries, as products of a time of fair weather which is now past, and we are urged to get rid of them, and to dedicate ourselves to some movement or cause instead. I hate the idea of causes, and if I had to choose between betraying my country and betraying my friend I hope I should have the guts to betray my country. Such a choice may scandalize the modern reader, and he may stretch out his patriotic hand to the telephone at once and ring up the police.[135]

Forster talks about a "country" rather than about a political institution or a set of political institutions. But I think it's clear that he isn't concerned with

134. See David M. Hart *et al.*, eds., *Social Class and State Power: Exploring an Alternative Radical Tradition* (New York: Palgrave 2018).

135. E. M. Forster, *What I Believe* (London: Hogarth 1939) 7–8.

land or people, including people networked and otherwise connected in a given society. He's concerned with a conflict between loyalty to a friend and loyalty to a *government*, a *state*. When loyalty to the state conflicts with loyalty to a friend, Forster urges us, in effect, to side with the friend.

Someone might respond that that was a deeply constitutive relationship between the citizen and the state.[136] But states are flawed in ways that might well prompt a reflective person to maintain critical distance from them. That's true not only because of the problems related to states that I've already noted but also because identifying states with the populations they govern also runs the risk of making it easier to legitimate the abuse of power. Similarly, a state is not best seen as the highest-level, most comprehensive organization of a given society. Understanding the state in this way is inconsistent with the recognition that states lack consensual legitimacy and are often predatory. And even someone who does affirm the importance of the state on broadly liberal grounds must recognize that the kind of state liberals might be inclined to affirm hardly deserves the kind of allegiance that it would be blasphemous to betray.[137]

One can recognize and celebrate one's connection with a *society*—with arrays of interdependent, cooperating people—quite apart from any stance one might take in relation to a set of *political* (in the narrow sense) institutions. Disregard for a society looks very different, morally, from disregard for a state.

The Status of States

Talk of "betrayal" suggests an underlying duty of loyalty that might sometimes be trumped—as, in Forster's envisioned case, when it conflicts with loyalty to friends. This is a common way of looking at the matter. And one might, indeed, think of a weak duty of loyalty to a state rendered null in a given instance by a strong duty of loyalty to a friend. But I think one can make an even stronger case for Forster's position than this.

If I'm right that we ought to be skeptical about states' claims, then there's good reason not to accord them loyalty, given not only their lack of consensual authority but also the degree to which they reliably engage in predatory behavior, cronyism, war, disregard for diversity, and the suppression of experimentation.

136. See MacIntyre, *After Virtue* 147. Always sophisticated, MacIntyre is too skeptical of states himself for it to be fair to attribute precisely this criticism to him; but I don't want to detour here into an analysis of the intricacies of his own position.

137. Clark, *Peace* 42.

Similarly, they don't deserve affectionate identification or symbolic expressions of devotion, and certainly not obedience—given that their claims to legitimate authority deserve to be questioned.

There will, of course, be pragmatic reasons to cooperate with states even though they are not entitled to obedience—as when doing what the state directs would not itself be wrong and when not doing so is likely to result in a significant penalty. Cooperating with a state will be permissible, perhaps even obligatory, when a state is using reasonable mechanisms to safeguard rights that are defensible quite apart from their definition by state authorities. And good faith state actors certainly might deserve gratitude in particular cases.

It is unreasonable to choose in a manner inconsistent with THE PAULINE PRINCIPLE. So even if the state threatens to subject you to a serious penalty if you don't do so, it still won't be right, for instance, to torture someone or purposefully kill anyone. However, while prohibitions of torture and purposeful killing follow from THE PAULINE PRINCIPLE, further norms follow from other requirements of love in action.

Just legal claims to physical things, for instance, are ones that reflect THE GOLDEN RULE.[138] In accordance with THE GOLDEN RULE, it is ordinarily unreasonable to take something that belongs to someone else (and a just legal system will seek to prevent you from doing so and will require compensation if you do). However, if the state commands you to steal from someone and threatens you with a serious penalty if you don't, it might be consistent with THE GOLDEN RULE for you to do so. It would be permissible for you to do so if you would be willing to accept a general, nonarbitrary norm that permitted others to steal in similar situations, even from you or your loved ones.

Friends and States

In many cases, then, when there is a conflict between the claims of the state and the claims of a friend, there will be good reason to side with the friend and little or no reason to side with the state. This will be true, in particular—at least in most cases—when the issue is one of obedience to a state command that doesn't embody a moral requirement that would obtain in the command's absence. Suppose, for instance, that a state diktat calls for a friend to relocate from one side of an arbitrary line to the other because of her immigration status: there will be no moral reason to cooperate with the state in such a case.

138. See, *e.g.*, Chartier, *Anarchy* 49–153; Chartier, *Life* 47–60; and Chartier, *Theory* 14–20.

Genuine conflicts between loyalty to a friend and any duty with respect to the state seem likely to arise only in a case in which a friend falls foul of a state-made law that upholds a genuine right and does so in a reasonable way. In this kind of case, one might act wrongly if one helped a friend evade legal responsibility. One certainly does not serve the flourishing of one's friend if one encourages her to ignore others' warranted claims: it is not in a friend's own interest, whether or not she acknowledges this, to act unreasonably.

Even then, however, there might be extenuating circumstances. For instance, it might ordinarily be right in a particular case to expect a friend to provide compensation for, say, an injury she's caused in an automobile accident, and so wrong to help her evade a legal system's demand that she do so. However, there might be a case in which public exposure of the friend's whereabouts in the course of a legal proceeding might yield significant social or physical risks to the friend.

In this case, one might (again, this would be a matter of respecting THE GOLDEN RULE) reasonably insist that one's friend provide the required compensation even while *not* demanding that she do so in connection with a legal proceeding and, indeed, while helping her to evade public scrutiny and the reach of the law. It would clearly be unfair to the person entitled to compensation to urge one's friend to ignore the duty to compensation or to help her to do so. However, the person entitled to compensation is not, at least ordinarily, morally entitled to receive compensation *in a particular way*—through the legal system rather than in some other manner. As a result, this person could not reasonably object if one helped one's friend evade liability for reasons like those I've contemplated, provided one also took steps to ensure that compensation would be provided.

If one is deciding whether to help a friend evade a state legal system's judgment, it would also be reasonable to ask whether the state's probable judgment in the friend's case will itself be just. She might, let us say, be guilty of theft; but her guilt would not settle the question whether just *any* response by the state—say, cutting off her hand—would be legitimate.

Perhaps Dean is confident that Chris is, indeed, guilty of a felony. He knows that, given the opportunity, the authorities will imprison her—constraining her liberty, offering no actual benefit to her victim, and putting her physical safety, mental health, and moral character at risk. Dean recognizes that there is no justification for retributive or deterrent criminal punishment or for forcible rehabilitation.[139] Suppose he also reasonably believes that Chris poses no ongoing

139. See Chartier, *Anarchy* 283–94.

threat to others. In this case, it might be appropriate for Dean to help Chris escape from the custody of state authorities in order to enable her to avoid being subjected to retributive or deterrent punishment—or, indeed, to benevolent reeducation—even though Chris has acted wrongly (and might, indeed, owe significant compensation to a victim even while in hiding from the authorities, compensation Dean should certainly insist that she provide).[140]

Questions like those Forster's words provoke cannot finally be answered in the abstract. But it is one's commitments, one's promises, and the vulnerabilities and kinds of reliance one has invited—in tandem with THE GOLDEN RULE and THE PAULINE PRINCIPLE (and the other requirements of love in action)—that will determine what kind of choice is appropriate. The fact that loyalty to a friend might conflict with loyalty to a political institution is not, per se, relevant, even apart from the fact that political institutions are not entitled to loyalty.

Friendship and Political Idolatry

While religious belief and practice are for many people increasingly unimportant, politics has come to take on a religious aura in our society. Political idolatry can complicate our friendships in various ways. We should firmly resist it.

The Dynamics of Political Idolatry

Today's political climate is marked by a concern with purity and a conviction of moral superiority.[141] The disturbingly sacral politics of the present moment exemplify just the self-righteousness, judgmentalism, and exclusivism typical of intolerant and fanatical religion. Whatever the associations of this kind of politics with overt religious doctrines and practices, whether or not it purports to promote religion, in reality it sidelines religious in favor of political orthodoxy. It is thus an instance of *idolatry*. It involves treating particular human projects as, in effect, identical with God's project in the world, regarding human beliefs and

140. See Jason Brennan, *When All Else Fails: The Ethics of Resistance to State Injustice* (Princeton, NJ: Princeton University Press 2019).

141. See, *e.g.*, Arthur C. Brooks, *Love Your Enemies: How Decent People Can Save America from the Culture of Contempt* (New York: Broadside-HarperCollins 2019); Joakim Book, "Can Enemies Be Our Friends?," *AIER* (Aug. 12, 2021) <https://www.aier.org/article/can-enemies-be-our-friends/>.

practices as absolute and untouchable, imagining that human sources of insight manage to deliver something like unalloyed divine truth.

There are many deeply troubling manifestations of this idolatrously religious sensibility. But I want here to note its toxic relationship to friendship. It is much less common today to respond with horror to the thought of a marriage or another form of friendship that crosses overt religious boundaries. But the religion of politics seems to make it profoundly difficult for people to envision and sustain friendships, romances, and family relationships that cross *political* boundaries.

Public Opposition

There are, of course, contexts in which it may be permissible or required to oppose a friend's *actions* in the public world when those actions arise from or embody political convictions. The most obvious of these contexts will be ones in which the friend's actions involve directing or engaging in the unjust use of force or the perpetration of serious lies to the public. Perhaps one's friend is affirming the reality of what one knows to be nonexistent weapons of mass destruction in a country targeted for military invasion or is seeking to arrest people for the noncrime of crossing an imaginary line in order to work without government permission. In such cases, the friend is engaged in conduct that constitutes or has a significant chance of leading to serious injury. It may be morally acceptable to respond vigorously—perhaps, indeed, in some cases wrong not to do so (THE GOLDEN RULE will ordinarily be decisive here, though COMMITMENT may also be relevant).

Opposing, even physically interfering with, a friend's unreasonable action may be an unavoidable means of protecting others. But, since acting unreasonably is injurious to the actor, seeking to prevent or end a friend's unreasonable action can also be a way of benefiting the friend herself—helping her not to injure herself by acting badly or come back from a self-destructive way of being she has already embraced.

One's opposition to her public actions may sometimes lead someone who has been a friend to cease being one. But one need not reject a friend oneself, even if she is behaving very badly. Despite her bad choice, there is no reason to ignore the invited reliance, the promises, the commitment, and the shared identity in virtue of which the friend is dear to one. And she may (whether she recognizes it or not) be especially in need of one's generosity of spirit at a time when she is pursuing an unreasonable course of action—not only because one can help her move past her unreasonableness but also because the knowledge of one's love at a time when she is behaving very badly may be deeply healing. The willingness to keep loving in such cases can powerfully convey one's openness to mediating God's grace along with one's rejection of political idolatry.

Fear and Rejection

The cases in which active opposition to a friend's public behavior is worthwhile, even morally unavoidable, are likely to be quite rare, not least because most friends do not occupy public roles. Political idolatry is evident much more frequently in the case of private ideological disagreement. Political affiliation becomes a kind of tenaciously grasped tribal membership; one insists on the political agreement of one's friends as a means of validating the conviction that one's tribe is superior.

When one has come to treat political convictions as foundational to one's identity, challenges to those convictions can be deeply unsettling. The intensity of the confident bluster with which one responds to such challenges is likely to vary directly with the degree to which one is aware at a deep level, perhaps without conscious acknowledgment, that one might be mistaken or that, even if correct, one's convictions (or their objects) don't merit the idolatrous reverence with which one is tempted to treat them. And the most unsettling challenges may be those embodied in the actions or expressed in the words of one's friends. *After all*, one may think, *if anyone understands why I'm right, my friends should.* So it may be especially tempting to reject them unequivocally when they disagree with one's politics.

The Illusion of Cruciality

In reality, outside the imaginative world fashioned by idolatrous devotion, private political disagreements have very little effect on the world. The firebombing of Dresden and the use of atomic weapons on the people of Hiroshima and Nagasaki were horrible injustices.[142] But suppose my friend Emma embraces, say, Joseph Fletcher's view that attacks on noncombatants in Japanese cities

142. On the morality of using nuclear weapons, see, *e.g.*, G. E. M. Anscombe, "Mr. Truman's Degree," *Collected Philosophical Papers of G. E. M. Anscombe* 3: *Ethics, Religion and Politics* (Oxford: Blackwell 1981) 62–71; and Finnis, Boyle, and Grisez, *Nuclear Deterrence*. On related historical and

could be justified as a matter of Christian love.[143] She is almost certainly doing nothing in the real world to make such atrocities more likely. She is simply not a danger to others. And that's true even if she votes for mistaken policies, since at the national or regional level, her vote is very unlikely to be relevant to any electoral outcome.[144] Her impact on actual events is likely, at least ordinarily, to be no greater than that of a drunken sports fan yelling advice to a coach through a television screen.

The policies and practices regarding which one's friend is, ex hypothesi, wrong may themselves be profoundly important. But her *beliefs* about them are not, because those beliefs likely have no influence on the real world. There is no moral imperative to oppose Emma in any active way any more than there is to argue with the inebriated fan—much less to reject her as a friend. Caring about her doesn't somehow involve me in endorsing the bombings (an intellectual mistake) or commit me to engaging in or authorizing similar bombings (a serious kind of wrongdoing). Our disagreement is simply a disagreement in *belief*, and there's no inconsistency between bare differences of belief on the one hand and love on the other. (We can, of course, love those whose actions are deeply wrong, even if we need to obstruct and resist them, but that's obviously a different matter.) Holding a view different from mine needn't itself be unlovely; and, even if it is, I can still love a person, just as I would want to be loved, despite moral and other flaws. (Obviously, it may in any given case be *my* belief which is mistaken. I'm simply noting that, even if one is clearly correct regarding a dispute with a loved one, that should have nothing to do with whether one loves that person.)

There may be some reason to try to educate a mistaken friend about topics regarding which she holds false beliefs, just because knowledge is itself valuable. Education may be valuable if it is undertaken for the friend's benefit rather than to reduce one's own cognitive dissonance and validate one's own beliefs. But the friend and the friendship matter more, far more, than the friend's coming to accept what one takes to be correct beliefs. There will thus often be no warrant for continuing a dispute rather than smiling and changing the subject.

---

strategic issues, see Daniel Ellsberg, *The Doomsday Machine: Confessions of a Nuclear War Planner* (New York: Bloomsbury 2018).

143. See Fletcher, *Situation Ethics* 98, 167–8.

144. Mancur Olson, *The Logic of Collective Action: Public Goods and the Theory of Groups* (Cambridge, MA: Harvard University Press 1971); cp. Jason Brennan, *The Ethics of Voting* (Princeton, NJ: Princeton University Press 2011) 13–42 (on voter efficacy and its implications).

Moral Excuses

When it does not flow simply from fear of the kind I've already noted, the rejection of friends (or others) with divergent views is perhaps most often motivated by two highly questionable impulses—the desire to punish and the quest for purity.

(*i*) The impulse to punish is deeply destructive. Even when it arises in response to actual injury, it does nothing to constitute or bring about a remedy to a harm that has already occurred. It adds further loss to the world without effecting healing for losses that have already taken place. It doesn't reestablish balance in the world, because one injury doesn't match, and so can't counterbalance, another.[145]

(*ii*) The desire to achieve purity by avoiding contact with putatively impure people (or things) is unwarranted and counterproductive. Talk about purity is an exercise in mystification. As I've already emphasized, there is no such thing as a moral purity that can be sullied, not by one's own unreasonable choices, but by contact with supposedly impure people.

Of course, this proposal is unlikely to satisfy political zealots of right, left, and center. There can be no fraternizing with the enemies of the revolution, or of God's coming commonwealth, or of the messianic realm.[146] This sort of censorious monomania can be especially attractive precisely when one thinks one is concerned with something truly important—environmental toxicity, war, the threat of nuclear annihilation. "People possessed by such passion tend to make the rest of us feel a bit guilty, as we simultaneously suspect that they are right and yet continue jealously to guard our right to take the time to enjoy a baseball game."[147] The zealots' posture is in fact "a form of totalitarianism and tyranny."[148]

Resisting the totalitarians is a crucial affirmation of the value of ordinary life, which must itself be acknowledged if concern with political issues is

145. This is entirely separate from the question whether playing tit for tat confers some sort of evolutionary or other advantage. Acting wrongly in particular cases may yield genuine benefits without its being the case that the benefits cancel the wrongness of the actions that bring them about.

146. My observations in what follows reflect insights I've gleaned from Stanley Hauerwas, "Taking Time for Peace: The Ethical Significance of the Trivial," *Religion and Intellectual Life* 3.3 (Spring 1986): 87–100.

147. Hauerwas 88.

148. Hauerwas 90.

ultimately to make sense;[149] for most of us most of the time, the value of politics lies, precisely, in its ability to safeguard and enhance our nonpolitical lives. We can't effectively push back against dominating, authoritarian, even totalitarian forces, like those potentially responsible for war or lethal pollution, if we embrace totalitarian attitudes ourselves,[150] if we seek to make everything subservient to the political. To test, say, a friendship by the demands of the zealots is to accept the logic which makes it conceivable that imperial warfare could be mounted, nuclear weapons used, our environment destroyed.

The Christian revolutionary who seeks, in the name of this or that putatively good cause, to sweep away the ties of friendship—at least friendship with the politically unsound—has confused his own imagined kingdom with the realm of God. And he has failed to recognize the nature of the flourishing which should be the focus of all Christian political and cultural activity. To rule out friendship in the name of Christian praxis is to miss the *point* of such praxis. It's hard not to be reminded of putative defenders of democracy who think the best way to promote it is by rigging elections, testing poisons on helpless prisoners, and assassinating inconvenient political leaders.[151]

Friendship isn't an instrumental good, and friends understandably don't want their relationships with each other instrumentalized.[152] Friendship is a way

149. Hauerwas 90.

150. Hauerwas 92.

151. The recent work of Stephen Kinzer has provided an accessible overview of military and intelligence agency interventions and their consequences: Stephen Kinzer, *All the Shah's Men: An American Coup and the Roots of Middle East Terror* (New York: Wiley 2008); Stephen Kinzer, *Overthrow: America's Century of Regime Change from Hawaii to Iraq* (New York: Times 2007). On interventionism more broadly, see, *e.g.*, Chalmers Johnson, *Blowback: The Costs and Consequences of American Empire*, 2d ed. (New York: Holt 2007); Noam Chomsky, *The New Military Humanism* (London: Pluto 1999); Andrew Cockburn, *Kill Chain: Drones and the Rise of High-Tech Assassins* (London: Verso 2015); Christopher J. Coyne and Abigail R. Hall, *Tyranny Comes Home: The Domestic Fate of U.S. Militarism* (Stanford, CA: Stanford University Press 2019); Daniel Ellsberg, *Secrets: A Memoir of Vietnam and the Pentagon Papers* (New York: Penguin 2003); Michael Swanson, *The War State: The Cold War Origins of the Military-Industrial Complex and the Power Elite, 1945–1963* (North Charleston, SC: CreateSpace 2013); Nick Turse, *The Changing Face of Empire: Special Ops, Drones, Spies, Proxy Fighters, Secret Bases, and Cyberwarfare* (Chicago: Haymarket 2012); Peter van Buren, *We Meant Well: How I Helped Lose the Battle for the Hearts and Minds of the Iraqi People* (New York: Macmillan-Metropolitan 2011); Scott Horton, *Fool's Errand: Time to End the War in Afghanistan* (Austin, TX: Libertarian Institute 2017); Smedley D. Butler, *War Is a Racket* (New York: Round Table 1935); and Tom Engelhardt, "A New Map Shows the Alarming Spread of the US War on Terror," *Nation*, Jan. 4, 2018 <https://www.thenation.com/article/a-new-map-shows-the-alarming-spread-of-the-us-war-on-terror/>.

152. See Hauerwas, "Taking" 95.

of flourishing, not, per se, a means to it (though of course friends may also help each other, and help third parties, to flourish). Friendship exemplifies and highlights what matters in a world worth contributing to.[153] Without assuming that everyone's political convictions are equally warranted, the Christian can recognize the value of the diverse actors on the political stage and rejoice that God has given some of them to her as friends, whatever their divergent visions of the good might be.

Political idolatry involves treating political attitudes as justifying the rejection of friends and the refusal to form friendships. Identifying this way of thinking, feeling, and acting as a kind of idolatry emphasizes that it is a spiritual malady. It isn't the only kind of spiritual malady that poses challenges to friendship. In chapter 6, I will examine some ways in which friendship might seem to be in tension with the quest for spiritual maturity as well as some ways in which, by contrast, it might help to constitute or support our spiritual lives.

153. See Hauerwas 99.

6

Spiritualities

In loving friends, we love God, whether we know it or not. And the experience of friendship can point people toward explicit recognition and love for God. So friendship has the potential to be a rich spiritual resource, a valuable element in a healthy spirituality.

I begin chapter 6 by evaluating an alternative style of Christian spirituality that can foster discomfort with friendship. I assess the conviction that we ought to avoid the love of friends in preference for the love of God because of friendship's supposedly unstable and transitory character. I go on to examine the belief that God and the created world are in competition for our love and that friendship is thus a breeding ground for idolatry.

Because of the unity between love for friends and love for God, I maintain, people can express love for God in friendship with others even if they don't believe in God at all. Building upon this conclusion, which challenges the spiritual barriers that have often separated Christians from those who do not share their convictions, I will explore some issues raised by religious disagreements among friends. Then, I suggest ways in which friendship can help invite a person to consider explicit love for God. I highlight the significance of the basic trust fostered in friendship for the formation of healthy religious convictions. I identify aspects of the experience of friendship that could encourage some people to reflect on the question of God. And I point to the significance of friendship for making possible dialogue about ultimate questions and the link between being open to dialogue and accepting one's identity as a creature. Finally, I reflect on the idea of friendship with God.

Friendship, Love for God, and Flight from the Transitory

Because human beings are finite and mortal and because they are not always dependable or loyal, some Christians have believed that it is better to avoid loving them at all. We should love God instead of other people, on this view, because God's love is the only love we can count on.

"The love of created things is deceiving and unstable," said Thomas à Kempis, "but the love of Jesus is faithful and lasting. . . . Love Him and hold him for thy friend, for He will not forsake thee when all depart from thee."[1] Saint Augustine articulated the same conviction when he said, speaking of his reaction to the death of a cherished companion, "Wretched I was; and wretched is every soul bound by the friendship of perishable things; he is torn asunder when he loses them."[2]

We accept vulnerability when we love. To allow another person to become part of myself is to subject myself to possibilities of torment and loss. Adhering solely to God can therefore be a means of deliverance from genuine dangers associated with friendship. And, of course, these dangers were much more real for the writers I've quoted than for most of us. Disease, distance, and political violence made it much more difficult to sustain close relationships.[3]

Further, while the temptation to avoid intimacy is common in our society, for many of our predecessors, the real challenge may have been to find individuality, to learn to hear their own voices more clearly. If so, differentiating oneself from others may have been a more spiritually significant task than it is now.[4] Still, shunning vulnerability (whether the vulnerability created by friendship or the vulnerability brought about by intense attachment to creative projects, social causes, or scholarly undertakings) seems likely often enough to impoverish our lives.

1. Thomas à Kempis, *The Imitation of Christ*, trans. William Benham, Harvard Classics 7 (New York: Collier 1909) 245. "He who cleaveth to created things," he adds, "will fall with their slipperiness; but he who embraceth Jesus will stand upright forever."

2. Augustine of Hippo, *The Confessions of St. Augustine*, trans. Edward B. Pusey (New York: Collier 1909) 50. Similarly, Saint John of Damascus urged detachment from created reality for the simple reason that whoever "has come to hate the world has escaped sorrow" (*The Ladder of Divine Ascent* [Boston: Holy Transfiguration Monastery 1978] 12, qtd. Margaret R. Miles, *Practicing Christianity: Critical Perspectives for an Embodied Spirituality* [New York: Crossroad 1988] 151).

3. A point emphasized throughout Miles, *Practicing Christianity*.

4. So Miles 152.

Friendship impels us to accept vulnerability and venture trust. And this aspect of friendship plays a central role in orienting us correctly toward God. Isolation may often render us more narcissistic, more turned in on ourselves—and thus less open to God—than participation in the social world, which may stimulate us to change and grow.

A strategy of flight from the world would represent a denial of the truth expressed in Christianity's central narrative—the story of Jesus of Nazareth. Christians have seen this story as underscoring the reality that God is willing to be affected by the contingency, vulnerability, and limitation of creaturely being.[5] Jesus was no Stoic sage, no detached philosopher. He accepted the vulnerability that all human beings experience; but, more than that, he entered passionately into the experience of being human, touching the heights of human joy and the depths of human sorrow. To be Godlike is not to escape the flux of human experience, not to cultivate a calm reserve about what happens in the world, but enthusiastically to enter into the richness, drama, and passion of being human.

In addition, hope in God can help make our losses less devastating. When we lose our connection with a friend, we may hope that God's grace will help to heal the wound our friendship has suffered. And, while we may lose our friends to death, we can hope that we will be reunited with them.

There is no way to receive the rich gift that is friendship while holding oneself largely in reserve. Refusing to be open and vulnerable will undoubtedly protect one from loss. But it is also likely to protect one from multiple constituents of a well-lived life.

There is a very real choice, then. It is a choice between lives of two quite different kinds.

One kind of life is marked by a flatness, a secure sameness. It is one relatively unscarred by the losses that afflict people who risk themselves. But it is also one from which many rich opportunities for flourishing are absent. The other is topsy-turvy, varied, diverse. It includes events that rightly occasion disappointment, discouragement, and dismay. More importantly, though, it is filled with varieties of fulfillment to which the more conservative are strangers. To bond with another, despite the risk of loss, opens up immense vistas of possibility that cry out to be explored and that offer rich rewards to those willing to venture within them.

5. See, *e.g.*, John Barton, *Love Unknown: Meditations on the Death and Resurrection of Jesus* (Louisville, KY: Westminster John Knox 1990) 13–25, 33–7.

Do Friends Distract Us from God?

Another reason people sometimes see love for friends as spiritually objectionable is the thought that there's a basic, unavoidable conflict between loving other people and loving God. I believe this view misconstrues the relationship between God and creation.

Fear of Friendship

For some Christians, God "is the only thing worthy of love."[6] Every other reality is less important, less valuable. Prayer and devotional practices (and perhaps various sorts of ministry) are the only genuinely worthwhile activities. We are wasting time and emotional energy when we focus our attention on intimate connections with others.

"Everyone should be chary about having to do with 'the others,' and should essentially speak only with God and with himself," Søren Kierkegaard wrote.[7] If we are to focus as intensely on God as we must, we cannot permit those who might seek to claim our hearts to distract us.

Along similar lines, Saint Francis de Sales argued that friendship "is the most dangerous of all types of love."[8] One can devote one's limited resources of time and emotional energy either to the love of God or to the love of persons. For the true Christian, the choice between the two must be clear.[9] And Thomas à Kempis declared, "If thou wouldst learn to put away from thee every created thing, Jesus would freely take up His abode with thee."[10] Except "a man

6. Simone Weil, "Forms of the Implicit Love of God," *Waiting for God*, trans. Emma Craufurd (New York: Putnam 1951) 212; cp. 210: "There is no final good here below."
7. Qtd. Martin Buber, "The Question to the Single One," *Between Man and Man*, trans. Ronald Gregor Smith (New York: Macmillan 1948) 50. In his essay, Buber advances a detailed critique of Kierkegaard's spirituality. See *Søren Kierkegaard's Journals and Papers* 3, ed. and trans. Howard V. Hong and Edna H. Hong with Gregor Malantschuk (Bloomington: Indiana University Press 1975) 45–6; and *Søren Kierkegaard's Journals and Papers* 2, ed. and trans. Howard V. Hong and Edna H. Hong (Bloomington: Indiana University Press 1970) 80.
8. Saint Francis de Sales, *Introduction to the Devout Life*, trans. John K. Ryan (New York: Image-Doubleday 1972) 17, qtd. Miles, *Practicing Christianity* 151.
9. Miles, *Practicing Christianity* 151.
10. Kempis, *Imitation* 245. See 210 ("Choose for thy companions God and His Angels only, and flee from the notice of men") and 224 ("The greatest saints used to avoid as far as they could the company of men, and chose to live in secret with God").

be freed from all creatures," Thomas asserts, "he will not be able to reach freely after Divine things."[11] Indeed, he envisions God as declaring, "Thou oughtest to be separated from thy acquaintances and dear friends."[12]

The Creator Is Not a Part of the Creation

If God were a creature, God might compete with creatures for our attention. God might inhabit only one district of experience or another. God might be present in some places or times or feelings more than others. But God is not a finite object competing with other finite objects for our attention. As Creator, God is present to and active in every aspect of created reality. At every moment of our lives, therefore, whatever else we are doing or thinking or feeling, we are interacting with God.

This does not mean that, as for pantheism, God and the world of finite creatures are the same thing, that God-talk is just another way of describing the world. The world is intimately present to God, but it is not God. God isn't a thing, an object, a bit of finite reality. God is qualitatively *other* than each of the things that make up the universe and *other*, too, than the array of finite things viewed as a totality.

We meet God in and through our experiences of things in the creaturely world,[13] not as another reality alongside finite things. "Creation is not a hurdle on the road to God, it is the road itself."[14] God doesn't live in church or synagogue or mosque or temple. Having pious feelings isn't the only way to be sensitive to God's presence (indeed, it may not even be an especially good way).

We cannot turn away from particular things in the world to know or love God better; all we can do is to turn from some finite things to others—from

11. Kempis 295.
12. Kempis 322.
13. John E. Smith, *Experience and God* (New York: Oxford University Press 1968) 52 ("Every alleged experience of God would also be experience of something else at the same time. If this is so, no singular experience would stand in analogy with a sensible experience of an object as evidence that God exists"); Rahner, *Foundations of Christian Faith* 83 ("If there is any immediacy to God at all, that is, if we really can have something to do with God in his own self, this immediacy cannot depend on the fact that the non-divine absolutely disappears"); Nicholas Lash, *Easter in Ordinary: Reflections on Human Experience and the Knowledge of God* (Notre Dame, IN: University of Notre Dame Press 1988); Nicholas Lash, "Human Experience and the Knowledge of God," *Theology on the Way to Emmaus* (London: SCM 1986) 157.
14. Buber, "Question" 52; cp. 54.

engagement with friends, say, to deliberately pious activities. Refusing to engage with other people, or to do so intimately and intensely, isn't a way to experience God without mediation. Trying to avoid attending to other finite things is just a way of focusing only on oneself instead of on the rest of the world. It's an expression of moral and spiritual solipsism, not a path to spiritual maturity.[15]

A God who could be a human friend's rival for our affections—even a *successful* rival—isn't really God at all.[16] "God is not an object beside objects and hence cannot be reached by renunciation of objects. God . . . is not to be found by subtraction and [is] not to be loved by reduction."[17] The Creator is not a competitor with any aspect of creation for our attention and love.

Friendship and Idolatry

As I've already noted, idolizing political causes, movements, beliefs, figures, or institutions can lead people to resist opportunities to friendship and to reject friends. But people who think God and creation are in competition for our affection may brand friendship itself and other creaturely loves as idolatrous. They may urge us to avoid loving other people too much. They may try to teach us to be on guard constantly to make sure we don't make idols of those we care about.

If we learn lessons like these too well, passion for our friends can become a source of guilt. We can become suspicious of delight in and desire for other people. We can begin to fear that God may punish us for loving too much or that God may call us to sacrifice our loves just because they are intense. "Why are we to be divided?" Charlotte Brontë asked her friend Ellen Nussey. "Surely, it must be because we are in danger of loving each other too well—of losing sight of the *Creator* in idolatry of the *creature*."[18] If we embrace anxieties like this, we may even envision a malicious deity playing spiritual games with us, testing us by calling us, like Abraham, to give up those who matter to us most to keep a jealous God "number one" in our lives.

15. Buber 52.
16. Buber 57.
17. Buber 58.
18. Charlotte Brontë, letter to Ellen Nussey, Feb. 20, 1837, qtd. Elizabeth Gaskell, *The Life of Charlotte Brontë*, 2 vols. (London: Smith 1857) 1: 166. Thanks to Alexander Nehamas for bringing this letter to my attention.

The Real Meaning of Idolatry

Real idolatry—the idolatry of the political, for instance—is a real problem. We can't treat any creature as if it were infinite—as if it were God—without falsifying the nature of reality. If we are to treat each bit of finite reality appropriately, then we can't allow any single constituent of the creation to trump the claims of all the others. We need to view and treat creatures *as* creatures, to put every finite reality in perspective and give each one its due. That's what it means to avoid idolatry.[19]

Recognizing God as God *does* clearly mean, then, that one can't act as if a friend is the only reality that really matters. The awareness of ourselves as creatures relativizes all of our particular loyalties. It puts each one in its proper place. Acknowledging God as Creator means not viewing any finite reality as *ultimate* in importance.

It *doesn't* mean, however, that we can't or shouldn't care deeply, intensely, about particular people and communities and things. Indeed, love for God manifests itself precisely in our love for and attachment to particular goods.[20] But we need to avoid treating the goods—in our own lives and in those of others—that we're not seeking to realize as if they weren't genuine goods by injuring them purposefully and instrumentally. We need to treat the people (and other creatures) our actions affect fairly, instead of dismissing those in whom we aren't interested or about whom we don't care as irrelevant. We need to allow our commitments to be relativized and contextualized in the light of the reality of creatures other than ourselves.

Idolatry is a fundamentally moral concept. It's wrong, then, not because God needs more attention from us, but because idolatrous action doesn't give each creature what *it* is due. "God does not stand in line waiting his turn at the wicket, not even at the head of the line. Rather, he brings this or that neighbour to the head of the line, and demands our best attention for him. And at another moment, perhaps, he closes the wicket, sends the whole line away, and demands to inspect our books."[21] Rejecting idolatry means letting our particular

19. See H. Richard Niebuhr, *Radical Monotheism and Western Culture, with Supplementary Essays* (New York: Harper 1970); Paul Tillich, *Systematic Theology*, 3 vols. (Chicago: University of Chicago Press 1951–63) 1: 13; and Langdon Gilkey, *Shantung Compound: The Story of Men and Women under Pressure* (New York: Harper 1966) 230–5.

20. See Adams, *Finite and Infinite Goods*, *e.g.*, 193–6.

21. O'Donovan, *Resurrection and Moral Order* 232–3.

loves take their proper places in relation to the other elements of created reality. So we refuse to succumb to idolatry by choosing to live morally responsible lives, not by forsaking life in the world.

It is not our job to replace God. We are not responsible for the universe. To act as if we were would itself be an especially pitiful and futile kind of idolatry. We can and should have particular, finite projects of our own, causes and relationships that matter to us deeply. Passionate desire, devotion, and care aren't idolatrous: they are appropriate responses to the irreplaceable and so immeasurably precious creatures human beings are.[22] And, obviously, if we care about some things, we will be able to devote less attention to others.[23] But we should still avoid idolatry by declining to treat the things and people *we* care about primarily as the only things and people worth caring about at all.

Idolizing someone—a friend, a lover, a leader—is bad for her or him as well as for others whose legitimate claims we may ignore because of our idolatry. Being treated as an irreplaceable source of meaning and value imposes an enormous responsibility on the idolized person for the idolater's well-being, one the idol is incapable of bearing.

Enchanted by the idolized person, she or he may give up freedom, agency, responsibility. She or he may find the failure of the idol to deliver the ultimate satisfaction for which she or he seeks profoundly disappointing. And the idolater's vulnerability may prompt her or him to try to manipulate or control the idolized person.

There is good reason to avoid idolatry. But we don't have to ration our love for our friends to make sure we've got enough left over for God. Any reality to which we could be loyal only as we turned away from God's creatures wouldn't be God at all. In fact, it would itself be an especially demonic idol.

Friendship, Religious Practice, and Idolatry

That's true even if the reality we treat as absolute is religious practice.

Sheldon Vanauken's compellingly beautiful book *A Severe Mercy* provides an especially poignant example of how such beliefs can play out in contemporary lives. The book centers on the love between "Van" and his wife, Jean, or "Davy," who shared an intense, passionate love for each other that began in an idyllic, pre–World War II South. After the war, Van and Davy, now married,

22. See Oppenheimer, *Hope of Happiness*; and Allen, *Love*.

23. See Adams, *Love* 200.

moved to England, where Van undertook graduate study at Oxford. The influence of C. S. Lewis led the two to become Christians, and they began to live out their convictions as part of a tight-knit group of Christian friends.

When they returned to the United States, the Vanaukens settled in Virginia, where Van began teaching at Lynchburg College. There, they ministered to Van's students and joined enthusiastically in the life of a local congregation. Then, slowly, a subtle rift began to develop between them. While both believed that Christianity must suffuse their entire life together, Davy desired God with a single-minded passion that Van feared was progressively impairing her relationship with him.

> When Davy wasn't reading the Bible to prepare for her class, she was reading it for her soul's sake. She was always reading it, or reading Brother Lawrence and other devotional works. I wanted to protest that it was too much; but how could I do that? It's not possible for one Christian to say to another: You love God too much. Nor to say: You are holier than necessary. I couldn't even *think* such thoughts. They would have been dangerous. . . . I merely *felt* a sort of helpless protest. I didn't quite like to see her poring over Isaiah or St. John. I think I'd have smiled to see her curled up with an Agatha Christie. I knew that everything had to be different now we were Christians—but *this* different?[24]

Van felt as if he and Davy had lost something. "What I wanted, emotionally if not intellectually, was the old Davy back along with the old love of life and beauty and poetry for their own sakes." But this desire "seemingly could not be reconciled with my intellectual commitment to Christ. Even less could it be reconciled with Davy's wholeness, both mind and heart, of devotion."[25]

For Davy Vanauken, finding God seems to have meant letting go of everything else. Loving God meant focusing on worship and the practice of the devotional life almost to the exclusion of everything else. And even though Van felt vaguely jealous of her relationship with God, he seemed convinced that in principle she was right: her single-minded pursuit of God was apparently incompatible with the lighthearted, enthusiastic involvement in the ordinary world that had previously marked her life. But the notion that living before God

24. Sheldon Vanauken, *A Severe Mercy* (San Francisco: Harper 1977) 136–7.

25. Vanauken 139.

is a *replacement* for living in the world rests on a misunderstanding of the function of formal religious practice and the nature of humanity's experience of God.

Engaging in overtly religious activities isn't, in any privileged sense, the way we love God. We relate to God—appropriately or inappropriately—during every instant of our lives, and each moment provides every one of us with a fresh opportunity to respond in love to God.

Further, our relationships with God are just as much *ours*—limited by our histories and identities and contexts and assumptions—when we do "religious" things as when we do anything else. Churches are human institutions. Doctrines are human constructs. Worship rituals are human creations. Religious feelings are inexplicable without reference to human biology and psychology and sociology. God is present and active in and through all these things. They're still *human* realities, though. They're still parts of the world. Attending to God in these ways doesn't enable us to bypass the limitations of creaturely existence. Those limitations affect our relationships with God in explicitly religious contexts just as they do in all the other parts of our lives. The only way to know God without limits is to *be* God.

Worship services and private spiritual practices matter not because they enable us to love God in some way that other activities don't. Instead, they help us to own our identities as parts of God's good creation so we can live flourishing, fulfilled, responsible, and joyful lives *in the world*. They can't and shouldn't *replace* our day-to-day life in the world. Recognizing God as Creator means rejecting the idolatrous claims of religion as much as the arrogant illusions of states and ethnic groups.[26] The god who demands that we forsake the good creation in order to focus on explicitly religious practice has been misidentified as the God who deserves our worship, our trust, and our love.[27]

Religion as an Idol

Thus, when "religion" distracts us from our creaturely loves instead of sustaining and enriching them, it may become an idol itself. Forsaking friendship in the name of a distorted spirituality may not only express but contribute to the idolatry of self or church. Friendships challenge us to refine our idiosyncratic, individual conceptions of God. In friendship, we learn to revise our views of God, ourselves, and the world. Alone, we no longer benefit from the implicit

26. Adams, *Love* 210–3.

27. See Adams 185–7.

and explicit correction our relationships with others make available. And so, ironically, choosing solitary religious practice in place of relationship is as likely to lead to distortion in our relationships with God as it is to enable us to experience greater intimacy with God.[28]

The Unity of Friendship and Love for God

To love God's good creation is at the same time to love God. We love God in particular (though not exclusively) as we love other people. Friendship can therefore be a form of love for God.[29]

Love as Spiritually Basic

Every genuinely moral choice is an implicit expression of love for God. For to accept a moral limitation on my being is to accept my status as a creature,[30] and one way to accept such a limitation is to accept the other *as other*.

With every moral choice I confront comes the requirement that I acknowledge or refuse to acknowledge that I am a *part* of God's *good* creation.[31] Every time I make a choice about some concrete, particular thing in the world, I am

28. See Lash, *Easter* 102.

29. I am especially indebted here to Karl Rahner, "Reflections on the Unity of the Love of Neighbour and the Love of God," *Theological Investigations* 6: *Concerning Vatican Council II*, trans. Karl-H. Kruger and Boniface Kruger (London: Darton 1974) 231–49. See also *The Love of Jesus and the Love of Neighbor*, trans. Robert Barr (Middlegreen, Slough: St. Paul 1983).

30. See Karl Rahner, "Atheism and Implicit Christianity," *Theological Investigations* 9: *Writings of 1965–67*, trans. Graham Harrison (New York: Herder 1972) 153; Keith Ward, *Images of Eternity: Concepts of God in Five Religious Traditions* (Oxford: Oneworld 1993) 177–8; John Baillie, *The Sense of the Presence of God* (London: Oxford University Press 1962) 79–87; and Jacques Maritain, *Approaches to God*, trans. Peter O'Reilly (London: Allen 1955) 84. See H. P. Owen, *The Moral Argument for Christian Theism* (London: Allen 1965) 36. Despite Owen's criticism of Baillie and Maritain (he's the source of the references here to their works), I think it's important to emphasize that not all knowledge is knowledge by description, nor is it conscious—it is not necessary that what one knows should be present to one's consciousness, should be "thematized," in order for one to know it. Knowledge may be tacit. We may know by acquaintance. And I think it is in *these* senses that nontheists may still, if the Christian doctrines of creation and inspiration are correct, be said to know God.

31. See Karl Rahner, "Anonymous and Explicit Faith," *Theological Investigations* 16: *Experience of the Spirit: Source of Theology*, trans. David Morland (New York: Crossroad-Seabury 1979) 55–6.

also helping to determine who I am—and I am challenged to ask, consciously or unconsciously, if my choices take the reality and value of others, and myself, into adequate account.

Our encounters with other people pose the basic moral and spiritual question with particular force and clarity. Will we exist with others in relationships of love, or will we sacrifice them—or ourselves—in relationships of abuse, domination, or neglect? Will we be open to the world, or will we refuse to acknowledge any reality beyond ourselves?[32]

In friendship and other close relationships, our bodies are involved, along with our ability freely to shape our lives over time and to define our identities by combining the disparate moments of our pasts into coherent narratives; our capacity to hope for—and dread—the future; our moments of disillusionment and moral despair; and our recognition of our finitude and mortality. Personal relationships call up, challenge, and engage every aspect of our humanness.[33] Interpersonal love is thus an especially important reflection of who we are.[34] When we love, therefore, we can help in important ways shape and express a basic orientation to the world—and so to God.[35]

Close friendship can embody and express the decision to accept oneself as a part of God's good creation in several ways.[36]

Friendship as Moral Demand

The claim of the friend is an especially insistent call to let go of who I have been and, in ways subtle and not subtle, to reorder my perception of my world

32. See Rahner, "Unity" 239–44; cp. Tillich, *Theology* 3: 40. See also Rahner, "The 'Commandment' of Love in Relation to the Other Commandments," *Theological Investigations* 5: *Later Writings*, trans. Karl-H. Kruger (London: Darton 1966) 456.

33. Rahner, "Unity" 242.

34. Rahner 243.

35. Persons and communities of persons are not the only sources of value in the universe. Other sentients also confront us with challenges that remind us of our creatureliness, as do inanimate objects and systems. However, persons present us with special challenges. They're not pliable in the same way inanimate objects, or even nonhuman animals, frequently are. Relationships with people at least sometimes require us more insistently to ask important questions about our identities than relationships of other kinds.

36. My analysis here depends on Lash, *Easter* 242–6.

and myself, to come to perceive and experience God's good creation more adequately.[37]

Being a friend means exhibiting a range of specific virtues, at least to some degree and in some contexts.[38] More broadly, it means acknowledging the claim of the friend as an independent other. It is to grant, practically if not always explicitly, that we are finite, contingent, vulnerable. It is to deny the possibility that we could ever exist on our own and thus to affirm that we are *creatures*. We recognize our dependence, even as we celebrate the grace on which we are dependent.[39] When we do so, we orient ourselves aright, even if imperfectly, in relation to God.[40] We choose openness to the world and thus of love to God.

Recognizing our responsibilities to our friends means being alert to the reality that we may fail in fulfilling those responsibilities in multiple ways. So in friendship we can discover how to acknowledge our clumsiness or wrongdoing, to offer amends, to seek reconciliation. In coming to grips with our brokenness, we learn, as friends, how to acknowledge that we are God's creatures—imperfect, fallible, in need of grace.

The same is true of learning to live with a friend's own brokenness. When a friend injures or wrongs me, I can learn how to abjure retribution, how to exhibit fidelity, how to love despite the fear of hurt and betrayal, in the way I'd like if I'd been the one who behaved badly. Again, in so doing, I stretch myself, I grow, and I accept my finitude by acknowledging my own imperfections, refusing to take on the role of an (imaginary) divine scourge of evildoers, and the temptation to let myself be defined by my resentment.

Friendship and Difference

Friendship requires *respect for otherness*.[41] My friend is different from me. And so—no matter how much I love her, no matter how much she is part of my self, no matter how much our interests may converge—I must recognize that she is still free, that she can surprise me, that our goals and needs may not always

37. See Luke T. Johnson, *Faith's Freedom: A Classic Spirituality for Contemporary Christians* (Minneapolis: Fortress 1990) 70–1.

38. See, *e.g.*, Casey, *Pagan Virtue* 186–7; and McClendon, *Systematic Theology* 1: 172–3.

39. Lash, *Easter* 246.

40. See Johnson, *Faith's Freedom* 82–3.

41. On this point, see Weil, "Implicit Love of God" 200–8. See Tillich, *Love, Power, and Justice* 24–34.

coincide. To take her seriously as a friend is to grant her the space to be who she is.

This is always difficult. Too often, we view other people as extensions of ourselves, as means to the fulfillment of our own desires and needs. Respecting the otherness of a *friend* is especially hard. A friend is someone with whom one is close, with whom—to one degree or another—one identifies. Indeed, if one has truly given oneself to a friend, truly bonded with her, one cannot but *need* her deeply and intensely. One's need for and vulnerability to her can make it especially difficult to grant legitimacy to her desire to be herself. It may be very easy to convince oneself that it is both necessary and appropriate that she should merge her identity with one's own—and thus to deny her difference from oneself. It is a minor miracle to grant a close friend freedom.[42]

Of course, if the identities of two friends truly merged, they wouldn't be *friends*. Love is so powerful, so profoundly moving, precisely because it is given *freely* by an *other*. A friend who is not *other* cannot really *love* me. The inner logic of friendship requires the maintenance of otherness, respect for difference, between the friends. But despite this pressure exerted by the relationship itself, allowing a friend to be herself can involve a delicate balancing act.

Friendship does not, of course, simply involve *respect* for difference. It must also, at the same time, feature a concern genuinely to *understand* the other in her particularity. Friendship draws us out of ourselves, then, not only because it prompts us to let the other be who she is but also because our own capacities are stretched when we confront the ways in which she is different. We have to learn how to listen, how to discover, how to be surprised. And in this way, too, our contingency is underscored, and we are prompted to live out our identities as God's creatures.

Learning how to be surprised can also mean learning how to be unsettled. A friend's differences from me can make me uncomfortable because they undermine my sense of the inevitability of my own way of being. Learning to accept a friend despite our differences can be a vital way of living as a finite, fallible creature.

I can also grow in friendship when I learn about myself by seeing myself through a friend's eyes—notably, when I'm surprised by what I learn from a friend about myself.[43] The willingness to see myself in new ways, both welcome

42. So Weil, "Implicit Love of God" 202.

43. On the role of friendship in fostering spiritual growth by facilitating self-understanding, see Matthew Hale, "Deification, Friendship, and Self-Knowledge" (MA thesis, Abilene Christian University 2015).

and unsettling, can result from both what a friend's words and behavior reveal about me and what my own reactions to a friend show me about who I am. This willingness can be an important way of declining to absolutize my own perspectives and of acknowledging the insights a friend helps me to gain—and so, again, of accepting myself as a creature.

Friendship, Dependence, and Grace

Another important moral and spiritual dimension of friendship is discerning the essentially *graced* quality of a life of which friendship is a part. Accepting friends and friendships as gifts; accepting a friend's ongoing, particular self-gifts; and accepting oneself as a friend's gift are all ways in which, as a friend, one owns oneself as a part of God's good creation.

As a Christian, I can suppose that God has been at work in and through the events leading to the formation of my friendships. In this sense, certainly, each friendship is a gift of grace. But it is possible to accept and respond to the experience of grace in friendship whatever one believes about divine providence. That a friendship cannot be planned or controlled confronts us directly with its character as a gift. Friendships come into being when we least expect them. The factors that predispose us to enter them are often unconscious; we often want particular people as friends for social, cultural, and psychological reasons we are quite unable to articulate. Seemingly random circumstances bring people together and give them opportunities to discover each other as potential friends. Thus, our friendships tend to be beyond our conscious control.

Whatever may predispose one to consider another as a friend, each of us is always free to reject an explicitly or implicitly proffered friendship. When someone I want to be my friend chooses to accept my friendship and to give her own in return, I have received a gift. She has not been *compelled* to be my friend by her genes or her environment or divine predestination. She hasn't chosen in a vacuum, certainly; many factors constrain all of our choices. But she *has* chosen, nonetheless, to give me the gift of her friendship. Indeed, she must continue to do so throughout our friendship's life—though her commitment to and identification with me as a friend obviously constrain the appropriate exercise of her freedom. That a friendship is a gift is not simply an accident; it is intrinsic to the value of friendship or any other love. Any seeming love that is not a gift freely given isn't a love at all but rather something else entirely.

The process of becoming and remaining a friend reflects the recognition that our lives are enriched when we connect ourselves with others, that we miss out on something valuable when we close ourselves off in isolation. As a friend, I accept that I need someone else if I want to experience a certain quality of life. And after a friendship has come into being, and I have bonded my life with that of a friend, I also need her if I am to be the person I am, to retain the identity I have achieved in relationship with her. In this sense, I am dependent on her.

As one weaves one's life together with a friend, one becomes dependent on her in other ways as well. A friendship itself is a gift. But gifts of various kinds may also accompany or result from it. Gifts of time, money, expertise, and emotional support may all express a friend's love. Receiving these gifts joyfully may sometimes be easy—but not always. Fearful of domination and abuse, we may flee dependence. But accepting gifts is part of what it means to be a friend. To let a friend know that she has something valuable to give by accepting her gift is a gift in its own right. And when we grant the reality of our dependence by accepting our friends' gifts, we affirm again our status as God's creatures.

To make another person a close friend is to make her part of oneself. Who one is, then, depends on who she is. One is always vulnerable, of course, to forces outside one's control. But in friendship one explicitly *owns and accepts* vulnerability. One chooses it. One agrees that one's identity will be affected by the actions of another. Realizing that her love has shaped and continues to shape who one is, one accepts that one's identity is a friend's gift. It is contingent on her choices and on what befalls her. "A friend is a part of my own being. If he is no longer there, then I have somehow died with him."[44] Thankfully to receive the gifts offered by friendship—rather than shunning it as a source of enervating dependence—is a way of choosing life as a part of the good creation.

Accepting that one is dependent on one's friends doesn't mean that one has to treat oppression or manipulation as appropriate. Not all dependence is good. But there's finally no getting away from dependence as such. In friendship, we can and should own and celebrate the fact that we are each other's gifts—accepting our contingency, our vulnerability, our need to rely. To do this is another way in which, because we are friends, we orient ourselves appropriately in relation to God.[45]

44. Ladislaus Boros, *Meeting God in Man* (London: Herder 1968) 57; cp. Lash, *Easter* 245.

45. See Lash, *Believing Three Ways* 54.

Friendship as a Participation in and Response to God's Love

In friendship, we love God when we appreciate God's goodness as it is reflected in the qualities of our friends. And we deepen our intimacy with God by sharing God's love for our friends.

To delight in and desire our friends is in an important sense to care about God. For, precisely in virtue of what it is we love about them, creatures reflect the image of God. God *is* the Good, the source and ground and primal embodiment of goodness. It is not that one cares about one's friends only because one also cares about God; one could be completely unaware of the reality of God and still respond appropriately to God's goodness as one encounters it in one's friends. But in responding to their goodness, one is forming a motivational structure marked by love for goodness—and so for God—whether one realizes it or not.[46]

In sharing God's delight in creation, including, in particular, one's friends, one grows progressively more like God—one of whose central characteristics for Christians has always been love for creation. Further, by analogy with human friendship, we can see that sharing God's love for our friends deepens our relationships with God. Becoming a friend involves, among other things, learning to enjoy what one's friends enjoy. Coming to love one's friends more, then, is part of what learning to be God's friend must involve, since God loves one's friends more than one does oneself. Again, this will hold whether one is consciously aware of God's presence or not.[47]

Being a friend reflects one's acceptance of oneself as a part of God's *good* creation. In friendship, one forms and expresses an appreciation for God's goodness and embodies God's love in the world. In all these ways, friendship is a form of love for God.

> To love love-*in*-someone is, by the courtesy of heaven, to love love and so to love God. It is to turn our eyes towards, to choose and desire the truth of all truth, the beauty of all beauty; to look and to hope in and to love and serve and know the Father, the Son, and the Holy Spirit, from whom and for whom everything in heaven and earth exists, even the cold, flabby, and fantasy-ridden hearts of human beings.[48]

46. Adams, *Love* 187–96.
47. Adams 196–8.
48. Rowan Williams, *Open to Judgement: Sermons and Addresses* (London: Darton 1994) 156.

Friendship can be a way of loving God for multiple reasons. It involves sharing God's loves, appreciating created excellences that reflect God's own, acknowledging the graced (and so creaturely) character of our lives, and recognizing and appreciating difference. In addition, the self-limitation that is integral to acknowledging moral responsibility and to forgiving and asking forgiveness is part of the experience and activity of friendship, which can serve as an expression of love as a fundamental orientation.

Friendship and Religious Disagreement

In addition to concerns about the transitory character of human love and the potential for loving creatures idolatrously, another spiritually rooted barrier to friendship is the worry that it's somehow wrong or risky to love people with significantly different religious beliefs.

People in today's world confront a dizzying array of religious options. And so it shouldn't surprise us that people we care about, people who care about us, disagree with us about some or all of the things that matter most to us.[49] It is spiritually vital that we learn how and why to love them anyway.

On Not Being Unsettled by Disagreement

Religious disagreement is a principal cause of conflict among friends.[50] We may find it disturbing, even threatening, when friends and other loved ones disagree with us because their doing so calls our convictions into question.

We may also find religious disagreement unsettling because we worry about the spiritual status of friends who disagree with us. Reviewing what he describes as "a photo album Mom made of my childhood pictures," Frank Schaeffer notes that adjacent to a picture of him "playing with a friend," his mother had written, "Frankie sitting with his friend, explaining Christian Basics." In fact, Schaeffer recalls, he "was doing no such thing."[51] As a child, though, he

49. This issue is sensitively addressed, though with explicit reference only to family members, in Karl Rahner, "The Christian among Unbelieving Relations," *Theological Investigations* 3: *The Theology of the Spiritual Life*, trans. Karl-H. Kruger and Boniface Kruger (London: Darton 1974) 355–72.

50. Haapanen, "Close Friendship," 161.

51. Frank Schaeffer, *Crazy for God: How I Grew Up as One of the Elect, Helped Found the Religious Right, and Lived to Take All (or Almost All) of It Back* (Cambridge, MA: Da Capo 2007) 112.

might well have wondered whether he should have been: "*Should* I have been explaining 'Christian Basics' to that friend? *Was* the only point of playing . . . to get to the moment in a friendship where I could try to convert him? If he didn't convert, was that *my* fault?" It was hard to escape the worry "that, whatever you were doing for the Lord, more was required. Normal life was just a series of interludes between bouts of evangelical zeal."[52]

This kind of anxiety converts friendship from a relationship valued for its own sake into an occasion for proselytizing. It robs us of the chance to focus on the flourishing of our friendships *just as* friendships. But it might seem inescapable if a friend's failure to share one's Christian beliefs means that she's floundering in spiritual darkness and destined for damnation.

But, while it may be useful to share one's own view of the world with friends who see things differently, the kinds of worries that can thoroughly unsettle us when friends disagree shouldn't actually prove as troubling as we might initially think.

Reasons for Relief

(*i*) God's presence and activity are universal (as are the realities—religiously significant at least for Christians who embrace belief in creation out of chaos—of the created world and the dynamic, creative activity of all actualities). This means that people with multiple religious and spiritual perspectives can be aware of and responsive to reality, to God's truth, despite differences in conscious belief. So we can expect people in a variety of settings to have gained genuine truths about God and the world.

(*ii*) Different people and communities will be well positioned to better understand different aspects of reality and to live out different *aspects* of the good. Thus, in particular, differences in behavior (including systematic differences in the behavioral recommendations of different traditions) may reflect the embrace of varieties of goodness rather than of genuinely opposed alternatives.[53]

(*iii*) We love God in and through our love for our friends, including friends who disagree with us. And they, in turn, love God in and through their love for us. Recognizing and respecting our friends' *otherness* is part of what it means for us to own our identities as creatures and thus to orient ourselves aright in

52. Schaeffer 113.

53. See Brian Hebblethwaite, "The Varieties of Goodness," *Ethics and Religion in a Pluralistic Age: Collected Essays* (Edinburgh: Clark 1997) 49–63.

relation to God. Receiving our friends' love as mediating, and as undergirded and inspired by, God's love gives us extra warrant for valuing that love. And understanding our own love for them as conveying and as rooted in God's love gives us further reason to offer our love to them.

(*iv*) Since none of us is infinite or omniscient—none of us is God—we all need to come to grips with the limitations of our own perspectives and the legitimacy of other people's. We should be deeply doubtful about any sort of spiritual or theological arrogance that treats our own views as *unquestionably* correct. We should not use the uncertain accuracy of our own convictions as the basis for rejecting the certain reality of a loving relationship that lies before us. To close oneself off to the challenge posed by a friend's disagreement—even (perhaps especially) for supposedly religious reasons—may be to indulge in an excessive self-confidence that represents a kind of idolatry, an implicit denial of one's creatureliness.

(*v*) Given our own finitude, fallibility, and sin, we always have things to learn from those who experience the world differently. They can help us understand God and the world better. We can learn new things in virtue not only of what disagreeing loved ones *say* but also of what they *do* as they put alternate understandings of life on behavioral display. One should *expect* to change in the course of sharing life with the people to whom one is close. Indeed, one should be disturbed if one does *not* change.[54]

> Most people assume that in a loving relationship individuals agree with each other. Many people, for example, become scared or shaken when their partner disagrees with them. Then they compound the mistake by trying to change their partner's mind. Yet on a personality level, two people are different in all respects and cannot be made identical in any way. There are no well-matched couples. Friendship is seeing differences, accepting differences, yet continuing to love and be happy.[55]
>
> If I actively look for differences and accept each one I see, I notice that my basic bond with a person is not threatened or even touched by our differences. Looked at this way, other people's differences become interesting and entertaining. They add to, rather than subtract[ing] from, the richness of the relationship. Interestingly, comfort with ourselves, not

54. See Jones, *Transformed Judgment* 85.

55. Prather, *Love and Courage* 90.

war, is the agent for change. And accepting another's personality is the starting point for an improved friendship.[56]

You don't have to be on the same spiritual path or any path at all; you don't have to work alike or play alike; you don't have to eat the same diet or vote for the same candidate. All you need is to share a vision of gentle understanding when you look upon each other's face. If you have this, the day will come when you will love every line and wrinkle you see, every inch of stoop in each other's walk, every creak in each other's disposition—because they will all eloquently sing to you of the effort that this dear friend has made for *you*, of all that your beloved has gone through, yes, all that your beloved has gone through [without abandoning you].[57]

(*vi*) We may find ourselves reacting defensively to disagreement because it calls into question the seeming inevitability of believing what we have so far believed. A challenger may be threatening because we sense that embracing our current convictions isn't unavoidable. And we may be so thoroughly invested in our convictions, may view ourselves as so thoroughly *defined* by those convictions, that the possibility that we've invested ourselves fully in beliefs that might be mistaken can be deeply disturbing. We need to find our security in God rather than in our status as people who accept particular beliefs *about* God. If we do, we can greet our loved ones' disagreements with equanimity, even curiosity.

(*vii*) It is quite possible that one may find one's own convictions essentially unaltered by a close relationship with someone who does not share them. But even then, one may well find that this relationship enables one to acquire a clearer understanding of just what it is one believes, what one's beliefs mean, and how important they are. Loving engagement with disagreement helps to clarify one's thinking whatever the outcome.[58]

(*viii*) Engaging with and learning from disagreeing loved ones can also be useful because it can help one to learn how to manage disagreement interpersonally

56. Prather 92.

57. Prather and Prather, *I Will Never Leave You* 164.

58. See Jones, *Transformed Judgment* 83; Stanley Hauerwas, "How My Mind Has Changed: The Testament of Friends," *Christian Century* 107 (Feb. 28, 1990): 213–4; Stanley Hauerwas, *Hannah's Child: A Theologian's Memoir* (Grand Rapids: Eerdmans 2010) 145; and Stanley Hauerwas, *With the Grain of the Universe: The Church's Witness and Natural Theology* (Grand Rapids: Baker 2013) 25n21.

and how to manage one's own emotions when one finds disagreement unsettling or threatening. We can grow as we learn better how to understand and accept those whose differences from us may make us uncomfortable, to disagree constructively and helpfully, and to recognize our own finitude and creatureliness. (*ix*) In addition, it can be a profoundly valuable exercise to learn how to explain one's disagreement with a cherished other in an attractive way. (*x*) In learning to do these things, we can model for others, including our children, our other friends, our neighbors, and our fellow congregants, how to deal with difference in a welcoming and loving manner.

(*xi*) Even if there are times when (while embracing the epistemological humility for which our finitude surely calls) we are warranted in being quite confident in our own beliefs, it does not follow that we should be unwilling to love and engage intimately with people who disagree with us. Their presence in our lives should be viewed as a gift to us, not as some sort of spiritual pollution. Believing them to be mistaken is quite compatible with loving them and celebrating the ways in which God's beauty and playfulness and joy are manifest in their lives. (*xii*) Obviously, in turn, we can offer ethically and spiritually important gifts to others whether they share our beliefs or not. Our ability to do so can make engaging with them very important—perhaps in some cases even imperative.

(*xiii*) One source of dismay for some people confronting religious disagreement may be a worry about the spiritual status of loved ones who disagree with them. What's most important here is, of course, God's own universally accepting love and continued work in the life of every person. But the dynamics of friendship itself are also relevant. Accepting the moral limits imposed by the practice of friendship is an instance of accepting oneself as part of God's good creation and thus of being in right relation to God. Friendship is, as I have argued, a sign and expression and instance of implicit trust in and love for God. Thus—whatever her religious convictions—a genuine friend, *in virtue of her friendship*, has given evidence of her fruitful relationship with God. Indeed, that she *is* a friend is an *aspect* of her love for God. By being a genuine friend, she has responded trustingly and lovingly to God, owned herself as part of God's good creation, gratefully accepted God's acceptance—acknowledged her identity as a creature.

(*xiv*) Suppose that, as the result of loving someone with whom one disagrees about this or that significant topic, one comes to change one's view of that topic and adopts a position which actually is, in fact, less correct than the position one embraced before. Provided one does not do so in a bad-faith, intellectually dishonest manner—adopting a belief in that sort of way always involves injuring oneself—one might well judge in retrospect, in view of all relevant information, that the good rendered to oneself and to one's friend by the relationship was worth this loss of a correct belief.

Religious disagreement need not be profoundly troubling. We can embrace it as an opportunity for growth in our marriages, romantic relationships, family relationships, and other friendships. And we can see multiple evidences of spiritual health on the part of friends who don't agree with us.

Whether one changes one's views or not in response to a friend's disagreement, whether a friend changes her own views, part of being a friend is acknowledging the otherness of one's friend, respecting her integrity, and learning to accept disagreement—including disagreement regarding things about which one cares deeply (perhaps *especially* this kind of disagreement).[59] It's important to come to recognize that one doesn't need to be right, that one doesn't need to convince others to accept one's beliefs, that one needn't be at all uncomfortable just because others, including loved ones, disagree. Letting go of the worries we frequently associate with disagreement is spiritually important: accepting one's own limitations in this way is one of the ways in which friendship is an instance of implicit love for God. Understanding and accepting the perspectives of loved ones who disagree with us and the reasons and motivations that lie behind those perspectives while learning to love them despite disagreement can be spiritually liberating and transformative. So can recognizing their love and ours as mediating God's own love.

Disagreement and Rejection

People who truly care about each other should usually be able to find creative, graceful ways of remaining close despite disagreements.

A true friend is another self. And this means letting her into the inmost core of one's being, being vulnerable to her, accepting that one can and indeed likely will change in relationship with her. So respect for a friend's otherness cannot mean keeping her at a distance. Being a loyal and compassionate friend means remaining in relationship with another despite stresses and tensions. The

59. Germain Grisez, *The Way of the Lord Jesus* 2: *Living a Christian Life* (Quincy, IL: Franciscan 1993) 743–4, allows for this possibility while expressing considerably more reserve than I do here.

occurrence of such stresses and tensions is no reason to forsake a relationship, nor is it any reason to see the relationship as unsustainable.[60]

We must extend acceptance, understanding, and respect to loved ones who disagree with us. And so we must resist the temptation to reject them out of self-righteousness.[61] (*i*) Self-righteousness is inconsistent with THE GOLDEN RULE—because I wouldn't want to be viewed or treated judgmentally or rejected because of my beliefs and because I wouldn't want people I care about to be treated in this way, I have good reason not to treat others in this way. (*ii*) Self-righteousness implies a kind of ethical and spiritual superiority to which, as a human affected by humanity's endemic brokenness, I'm simply not entitled. (*iii*) It is an obvious and serious barrier to building valuable close relationships. By contrast, (*iv*) viewing loved ones openly and acceptingly, and assuming the best about their motives and insights, substantially increases the likelihood that I will understand them properly. And (*v*) self-righteousness will also dramatically reduce my ability to assist my loved ones if their beliefs have negative consequences for their lives. Friends who disagree will encourage change on each other's part, if they do, not by threatening rejection or offering hectoring lectures but, rather, by putting their alternative visions of life on display. In addition, (*vi*) when I disagree about religious or related matters with loved ones, I need to recognize that accepting *my* differences with them may complicate life for *them* as much as accepting their differences does for me, and this should provide me with further reason for humility in relation to them.

When Differences Might Matter

Adopting different views need not always trouble us. Many differences are relatively unimportant. And, even when they are not, they ordinarily provide no reason for those who disagree not to love and engage. But disagreement might pose a serious barrier to love if loving someone with whom one disagreed necessarily entailed violating, or meant one was seriously tempted to violate, the requirements of love in action.

60. See John Gottman with Nan Silver, *Why Marriages Succeed or Fail* (New York: Fireside-Simon 1994) 23–4; John Gottman and Nan Silver, *The Seven Principles for Making Marriage Work* (New York: Three Rivers 1999) 129–55, 217–42; and Linda Bloom and Charlie Bloom, *101 Things I Wish I Knew When I Got Married* (Novato, CA: New World 2004) 90–2.

61. See Hunt, *Fierce Tenderness* 170: "People I want to be around do not subject their relationships to a standard of political correctness."

Sheer differences in ethical *opinion* need not pose barriers of any sort to love than, as I noted earlier, differences in political opinion. The dispute I envisioned in chapter 5 concerning the use of weapons of mass destruction by the Allies during World War II, an imagined controversy I framed precisely as a religious disagreement about the meaning of Christian love, can serve as a perfectly good example here too.

If loving someone with significantly different views *were* to lead to a situation in which one violated or was tempted to violate the requirements of love in action, the potential violation would most likely amount to either (*i*) choosing purposeful or instrumental injury to oneself or another or (*ii*) unjustifiably imposing unfair risks on third parties. Perhaps joining a friend for a religious ceremony could mean participating in animal sacrifice, for instance. One may on occasion have no choice but to say *no* to a loved one. But one should normally be able to do this while still loving deeply and loyally by adjusting relevant aspects of one's interactions with a loved one. Even though doing so may sometimes be challenging, the kinds of conflicts that require the sort of alteration I've contemplated may be expected to be relatively rare; dealing with them can be an occasion for growth by all those involved; and, in any case, that one must adjust one's behavior in these cases need not call into question one's continued commitment to friendship or any other sort of love. You can think about such cases using the approach I suggested for thinking about cases of potentially problematic moral influence in chapter 4.

Idolatry, Exclusion, and Disagreement

The conviction that God is the world's transcendent Creator, that God's truth is infinitely greater than our beliefs, that God's world is far vaster than our particular communities, should make us question any attempt to keep our beliefs or lives pristine, unchallenged, and unchanged. When a religious institution, claiming the sanction of God for what it does, prohibits or discourages relationships with "deviants" or outsiders, it may unwittingly be assuming the status of an idol for its members.[62] A religious community has come to exercise demonic power in our lives if we refuse to allow contact with those who resist its authority or doubt its doctrines to upset our orderly lives within it or our attachment to the beliefs it endorses, if we seek to protect our identities at any cost.

62. See Adams, *Love* 210–3; and Johnson, *Faith's Freedom* 65.

Any community must be open to challenge and change if it is to avoid idolatry. But Christians might be thought to have particularly strong reasons to seek to transcend the barriers that divide people. The ministry of Jesus and the teaching and preaching of Saint Paul were clearly designed to create inclusive community. Christianity was founded on the premise that boundaries that separated people and communities ought to be broken down.[63]

The ministry of Jesus stressed the importance of inclusion. Similarly, throughout his letters, we find Saint Paul wrestling with the question of how Christianity, with distinctive, particular historical roots, could become a truly universal community. His solutions and prescriptions are, of course, carefully shaped—albeit pragmatic—responses to the particular challenges he confronted. But the consistency with which they exhibit his commitment to inclusivity in the face of prevailing purity rules is both obvious and noteworthy.[64]

Shunning those whose views might unsettle us or challenge the convictions of our communities is a manifestation of idolatry and as such should itself be shunned, not embraced. Jesus and Saint Paul were committed to fighting both the idolization of human communities and the consequent creation of boundaries designed to keep outsiders at arm's length. Thus, a central Christian belief and a fundamental trajectory of the Christian tradition both militate against exclusionary attitudes.

63. See, *e.g.*, Borg, *Conflict, Holiness, and Politics*; and E. P. Sanders, *Paul and Palestinian Judaism* (London: SCM 1983).

64. Saint Paul addresses the question of community boundaries throughout his writings. The issue of eating with believing "gentiles" is addressed in Gal 2:11–7 (cp. Acts 15). In 1 Cor 10:27–30, he explicitly affirms the appropriateness of table fellowship with those outside the Christian community. The central importance in Pauline thought of the notion that the boundaries between the supposedly "pure" and "impure" are broken down is highlighted in Eph 3:4–6, which identifies "the mystery of Christ" with the fact that "the Gentiles have become fellow heirs, members of the same body, and sharers in the promise in Christ Jesus through the gospel."

With its call not to be "mismatched with unbelievers" and its injunction "touch nothing unclean," 2 Cor 6:14–7:1 might appear to be inconsistent with Saint Paul's general commitment to opposing purity distinctions. If it is not to be understood as a surd interjected in the middle of his argument, however, perhaps it might be seen not as representing a call to the Corinthian Christians to separate themselves in general from those outside the Christian community but rather as embodying a call—making pragmatic use of traditional purity language—that they refuse to give their loyalty to the opponents whose views Saint Paul implicitly critiques throughout the letter. See L. William Countryman, *Dirt, Greed, and Sex: Sexual Ethics in the New Testament and Their Implications for Today*, 2d ed. (Minneapolis: Fortress 2007) 322–3n25.

Friendship, Basic Trust, and Belief in God

People find it difficult to believe in a loving and empowering God for an enormous variety of reasons. But it is certainly unlikely that someone will be able to believe if she is closed in on herself—fearful, self-protective, or arrogant.

Friendship can help to make healthy religious belief possible for such a person. That's because it can contribute to the development of basic trust: the confidence that the universe is, despite its darkness, danger, and undeniable obscurity, a fundamentally friendly place, a place in which it is worthwhile to risk oneself in love.[65]

The person who feels detached and alienated is ill-disposed to rely on or be open to others. And, if our own identities are such that we cannot trust, then we will find it no easier to trust God than to trust other creatures.[66] Without a sense of basic trust, one's attitude toward God will be no different from one's attitude toward any other reality different from oneself. The only kind of God one will be able to imagine will be an object: an object to be manipulated or a competitive oppressor. One may thus distort one's picture of God beyond recognition or deny that God-talk refers to any kind of reality at all.[67]

If "the absence of human community . . . renders prayer well-nigh impossible,"[68] then only when such community exists will authentic, appropriate religious believing be viable for many people. This is obviously a societal, cultural, and political as well as a personal or interpersonal problem. However, as friends offer each other love and trust, they can begin to exchange fear for love and doubt for hope. When people learn to trust each other—and when, as a result, they come to experience the world more trustingly—they will find it easier to believe in a trustworthy God as well. Close friendship provides a setting in which people can acquire the sense of basic trust crucial to recognizing themselves as creatures, understanding creatureliness as empowering rather than frightening, and so embracing belief in God.[69]

65. See Pannenberg, *Anthropology in Theological Perspective* 220–42; Hans Küng, *Does God Exist? An Answer for Today* (New York: Vintage-Random 1981) 442–77; and Jack W. Provonsha, *You* Can *Go Home Again* (Washington, DC: Review 1982).

66. Lash, *Easter* 202, 213.

67. Lash 202.

68. Lash 202.

69. Lash, "Experience" 154.

If a person's social world has been shattered, or if it never cohered in a meaningful way at all, it will be very hard for her to see the world as anything but a place of threatening darkness. The experience of friendship can serve to light a candle in that darkness, to begin the challenging process of constructing or reconstructing a social reality within the context of which she can find it possible to believe.[70]

Friendship Raises the Question of God

Friendship can not only foster a crucial attitudinal prerequisite to belief in God but also encourage people to think about the question of God. The experience of friendship can nudge us to ask whether viewing the world as a self-contained, self-explanatory system with no ultimate purpose, meaning, or source of hope really makes sense as a way to live.

As Ronald Sharp observes, "It has become commonplace for us to regard friendship in what, from an historical point of view, can only be seen as a religious context."[71] The examples Sharp offers of the functions of contemporary friendship—consolation, confession, guidance—and of the rituals associated with it serve to substantiate his conviction: insofar as the disciplined shaping of the self is at all a feature of the lives of many modern persons, it is effected in and through the practice of friendship. In "many respects," Sharp opines, "we turn to . . . [our friends] as primary sources of meaning and faith."[72] Similarly, Andrew Greeley contends that friendship is "religious behavior in the primordial sense of that word. In the friendship relation we give *ourselves*, and such an offering of the totality of our being is so primordial and intimate that it touches the very roots of our existence and forces us necessarily to face questions of the ultimate."[73]

70. See Adrian Furnham, "Friendship and Personal Development," Porter and Tomaselli, *Dialectics of Friendship* 93. Thanks to Jeffrey Cassidy and Heather Hessel for conversations that have contributed to my understanding of this point.

71. Ronald Sharp, *Friendship and Literature: Spirit and Form* (Durham, NC: Duke University Press 1986) 113.

72. Sharp 113.

73. Andrew Greeley, *The Friendship Game* (Garden City, NY: Doubleday 1970) 17, qtd. Sharp, *Friendship* 114.

Our friends offer us consolation, guidance, and the opportunity for confession. They are "primary sources of meaning and faith."[74] Friendship can't be the sum and substance of the spiritual life all by itself. It won't meet contemporary people's spiritual needs on its own. But, in addition to providing the spiritual nourishment Sharp highlights, it can nudge people to reflect on the dynamics of existence. Thus, it can help to prompt conscious awareness and love of God.

Friendship doesn't make space for God in our thinking, speaking, and acting by serving as a premise in a knockdown, drag-out argument. Rather, it nudges us to see our world in new ways. It leads us to highlight certain aspects of our experience that we might otherwise overlook and to wonder about their significance.[75]

Trust and the Question of God

Viewed from a theological perspective, the basic trust that friendship fosters makes sense as a response to the way reality really *is*, a making real of God's sustaining and accepting grace. We may reasonably wonder whether this sense of confidence in the ultimate friendliness of reality has any validity. If the world is ultimately chaotic and pointless, if there is no overarching source of meaning and hope, then friendship's encouragement to experience the world trustfully is a call to self-deception.[76] The basic trust experienced in friendship dares us to believe that it is not. Friendship embodies a protest against contemporary trustlessness, inviting us to take the risk that trust really is warranted.

Friendship and the Need for Hope

We recognize that our friends may reject us or that, despite their intention to be faithful, they may die. So in friendship we need hope.

To begin with, we need hope for tomorrow. As one risks oneself in friendship, one looks toward a relationship that will continue over time. But our friends cannot secure us against fate.

74. Sharp, *Friendship* 113.

75. This and the following paragraphs detail an analysis dependent on Langdon Gilkey, *Naming the Whirlwind: The Renewal of God-Language* (Indianapolis: Bobbs-Merrill 1969) 305–470; Peter L. Berger, *A Rumor of Angels: Modern Society and the Rediscovery of the Supernatural* (Garden City, NY: Anchor-Doubleday 1970) 49–75; and David Baily Harned, *Grace and Common Life* (Charlottesville: University Press of Virginia 1970) 27–9.

76. See Berger, *Rumor of Angels* 56.

One hopes that a friend will not desert one—but, even more fundamentally, that she will not die.[77] Of course one knows that she will someday die; and still one blunders on in hope. If this life is all there is, then such hope is simply denial. On the other hand, if one's hope *is* meaningful, if it is not simply a futile projection of one's passion against the void,[78] then its source must lie beyond the realm of our ordinary experience. It is too much to say that only belief in God will justify such hope. But only in the context of something *like* belief in God, some overarching—and thus essentially religious—structure of meaning, is such hope likely to make any sense.[79] The conviction that providence can help to restore a broken relationship, that there is reason to hope for life beyond death, can help to warrant the hope we embrace as friends.

Friendship as Play and Protest

There is clearly a playful quality to friendship. Friends may sometimes (though not always) approach shared activities with the light touch that might make us describe them as "play." But a friendship is always, to a greater or lesser extent, gamelike—featuring a distinct world shaped by its own rules and proceeding in accordance with its own inner dynamics. During play, ordinary time seems to be suspended; events are located chronologically with reference to events that form part of the game. Similarly, the experience of time in friendship is shaped by the friends' implicit adoption of a timescale internal to their relationship, their use of aspects of their shared past and common experience to mark time. There is a "dialectical movement between objective and personal time in friendship." The experience of "the past, present, and future each molds and is molded by the other dimensions of lived time."[80] The playful world of friendship, in which space is reidentified and ordinary clocks and calendars superseded, delivers another protest against the meaninglessness and death that mark the ordinary world.[81] This protest may be foolish. But our "play" with friends may call us nonetheless to hope that it is not, to look for a "final

77. See Boros, *Meeting God* 57, 61.

78. A variant of a phrase I owe to Stephen Donaldson. See Stephen R. Donaldson, *Epic Fantasy in the Modern World: A Few Observations* (Kent, OH: Kent State University Press 1986).

79. See Berger, *Rumor of Angels* 61–4.

80. Becker, "Phenomenological Explication" 151–2.

81. See Berger, *Rumor of Angels* 58–60.

vindication of childhood and of joy, and of all gestures that replicate these"—including those integral to friendship.[82]

Friendship and Ultimate Meaning

If one can touch the lives of one's friends, then perhaps that's all that really matters. One makes a difference in their experience, at least. Couldn't one just be content with that? For some people, the answer is obviously yes. The world of one's loved ones becomes the only real world. Such small-scale worlds often seem like the only manageable ones left us. In reality, however, the difference one makes in the lives of one's friends may seem just as fleeting as any difference one might make in the wider world. One's investment in one's friends can appear as pointless as investment in politics or culture or industry.

So friendship may raise the question of meaning with particular poignancy. One may not expect that the consequences of one's actions in the public world will be visible, tangible, immediately present in one's own experience. But one does expect to see the results of one's love in the lives of one's friends. By the same token, however, one is sufficiently close to them, sufficiently exposed to the particulars of their lives, to see their failures, their losses, their deaths, and how ineffective one's efforts on their behalf sometimes are.[83] Thus, the desire to be sure that what one does and who one is will *count* in the grand scheme of things may be especially pronounced as one considers one's relationships with one's friends. So friendship can inspire one to long for the assurance that there is an overarching order within which one's actions and experiences make sense and which will guarantee that one has not wasted one's life. In this way, too, friendship raises questions to which God may be the answer.

Friendship and Perfect Love

In friendships and other love relationships, we experience the quest for more than we could ever possibly have. Our behavior suggests that we want these relationships to offer, not merely deep and committed love, but a kind of love that is absolutely unswerving, that is always available, and that assures us unequivocally of our profound value.[84]

82. Berger 60.

83. See Gilkey, *Naming* 336–41.

84. See Diogenes Allen, *The Path of Perfect Love* (Boston: Cowley 1992).

Our friends cannot provide us with this kind of love. But even as we realize this, and struggle against it, we confront the demand within ourselves for something that can. Again, we might conclude that this striving for perfect love is futile and foolish. But we must at least acknowledge that it expresses a desire for more than the reality we confront with our senses, the reality of ordinary life, seems on its own able to deliver, which raises the question whether that world truly is all there is.[85]

Friendship and the Desire for Total Acceptance

Just as we seek perfect love, we seek total acceptance. Friendship provides us with distinctive opportunities for evil as well as good. The vulnerability to which we commit ourselves in friendship gives us the opportunity to do each other profound harm. And the vulnerability we exhibit when we open ourselves to friends creates the opportunity for devastating rejection.

If our moral failings are especially evident in our friendships ("You always hurt the one you love!"), and if we are especially exposed and therefore vulnerable, then these relationships challenge us with particular intensity to seek acceptance. And, while a friend from whom one has become separated can accept one anew, while a friend who finds one puzzlingly and off-puttingly odd can nonetheless embrace one, we may want more—an acceptance that covers, not merely this particular failure or peculiarity, but all possible wrongs and oddities, past and future. Such an acceptance must represent an affirmation of who one is in one's totality, without illusions—otherwise, what would it be worth?[86]

How can we find such acceptance? Our desire for it can seem finally unrealistic. But those of us who continue to search for this kind of acceptance can at least be pardoned for finding their quest an anomaly with which a vision of the world of finite things as self-contained is arguably ill-equipped to deal.

The impulse to find deep acceptance is one of several features of friendship that perhaps fit somewhat uneasily within the confines of the world as contemporary people may instinctively understand it. Christian theology discloses friendship as a form of *implicit* love for God. But a theological analysis can perhaps suggest ways in which aspects of our experience of friendship can point to discontinuities within our day-to-day experience of secularity, discontinuities that might spur us to raise the question of God *explicitly*.

85. Gilkey, *Naming* 316–33.

86. See Gilkey 402–7.

Friendship, Creatureliness, and Dialogue

Being a friend helps to make one a certain kind of person. Friendship expresses and reinforces a basic commitment to be in the world *dialogically*, to attend to the surprises with which things and other people present us, to relativize our own perspectives and projects as we listen—literally and figuratively—to others. Attending to what is other than oneself, allowing one's preconceived notions to be challenged, is essential if one is even to consider the possibility that a religious interpretation of reality might be appropriate.

This kind of openness is necessary if dialogue about religious questions is to get underway. But it is not simply a prerequisite for discussing belief in God; it is to a significant degree the *goal* of the dialogue as well. A healthy belief in God is expressed, crucially, as one opens oneself to the rest of reality, recognizing one's inherent finitude and fallibility. And this is precisely what the kind of openness required for dialogue is about.[87] One can offer implicit love to God without being overtly religious. But one cannot be overtly religious in a healthy way without adopting a basic stance of openness to the world.[88] Such a stance, characterized by readiness for dialogue and respect for otherness, can be both generated and sustained by the experience of friendship.[89]

Friendship with God

To answer the questions friendship raises by affirming the reality of God may be the first step toward intentional friendship with God.

87. Such openness matters in friendship whether or not dialogue about religious matters is a feature of the friendship.

88. On the possibility that the structure of a person's family may play a greater role in shaping her religious convictions than the explicit content of the beliefs taught her by family members, see Anderson and Guernsey, *On Being Family* 132–6. *Whatever* its religious or antireligious orientation, a warm, accepting family that provides each of its members with a sense of order, meaning, value, and purpose is more likely to foster the religious development of its members than one marked by chaos and authoritarianism. It is reasonable to assume that structural features of other intimate relationships, including friendship, would have similar consequences for personal religious experience.

89. See E. D. H. "Liz" Carmichael, "Friendship and Dialogue," *Journal of World Christianity* 7.1 (2017): 28–46.

Because God is Creator, all of our talk about God requires qualification. It's drawn from our experience of ourselves and of things in the world. Our minds—finite, fallible, sinful—are incapable of grasping the reality of God with finality and precision. Our thoughts about God are unavoidably inadequate, so any language we select to express the insights they reach is likely to be yet more inadequate.

The use of the language of friendship to characterize human relationships with God is a long-standing feature of more than one spiritual tradition.[90] While it can be worth employing, we need to be sensitive to its limitations.

(*i*) Human relationships with God don't involve the kind of dialogical interchange that's so important to friendship between creatures. Austin Farrer puts the point nicely as he describes the spiritual struggles in which he engaged early in life:

> I thought of myself as set over against deity as one man faces another across a table, except that God was invisible and indefinitely great. And I hoped that he would signify his presence to me by way of colloquy; but neither out of the scripture I read nor in the prayers I tried to make did any mental voice address me. I believe at that time anything would have satisfied me, but nothing came: no 'other' stood beside me, no shadow of presence fell upon me.

Farrer moved beyond his angst and puzzlement when he rethought how God interacts with us.

> I would no longer attempt, with the psalmist, "to set God before my face." I would see him as the underlying cause of my thinking, especially of those thoughts in which I tried to think of him. I would dare to hope

90. Among many treatments, see, *e.g*, Paul Wadell, *Friends of God: Virtues and Gifts in Aquinas* (New York: Lang 1991); Sallie McFague, *Models of God: Theology for an Ecological, Nuclear Age* (Philadelphia: Fortress 1987) 157–80; Moltmann-Wendel, *Rediscovering Friendship* 10–6; and Raphael Joshua Christianson, "A Thomistic Model of Friendship with God as Deification," *New Blackfriars* 100 (2019): 509–25. Mark Zhakevich argues that the idea of friendship with God receives little biblical attention: Mark Zhakevich, "The Compensatory Benefits of Discipleship in the Gospel of John" (PhD diss., University of Edinburgh 2018) 150–2. Zhakevich suggests, however, that considerable attention is paid in the Fourth Gospel to what he labels "royal friendship" with Jesus (145–95).

> that sometimes my thought would become diaphanous, so that there should be some perception of the divine cause shining through the created effect, as a deep pool, settling into a clear tranquility, permits us to see the spring in the bottom of it from which its waters rise. I would dare to hope that through a second cause the First Cause might be felt, when the second cause in question was itself a spirit, made in the image of the divine Spirit, and perpetually welling up out of his creative act.
>
> Such things, I say, I dared to hope for, and I will not say that my hope was in any way remarkably fulfilled, but I will say that by so viewing my attempted work of prayer, I was rid of the frustration which had baffled me before. And this is why, when Germans set their eyeballs and pronounce the terrific words "He speaks to thee" (Er redet dich an) I am sure, indeed, that they are saying something, but I am still more sure that they are not speaking to my condition.[91]

The kind of dialogue Farrer was led to expect seems likely to require a kind of divine action that it is probably not reasonable to anticipate given the constraints on God's activity in the world suggested by the problem of evil. A seeming experience of explicit dialogue seems likely, rather, to be shaped by the finite subject of the experience, even if it involves genuine awareness and responsiveness to God's presence and activity.

(*ii*) While God is present and active in and through all of the events of our lives, we can hardly assume that we are *aware* of just what God is up to in particular circumstances. The history of my life is always and unavoidably a history of interaction with God, but that doesn't mean that I will be able to point to just what God's intentions were in particular cases and whether they were realized.[92] So not only will I not be responding in the course of a conventional dialogue; I also won't be reacting to God's actions qua divine actions.

(*iii*) Interaction with God is always a dimension of our interactions with creatures—or, indeed, with any aspect of the creaturely world. Because God is present wherever we are and is aware of all of our thoughts, all of our feelings, and everything that is going on in our bodies and in our unconscious minds, there is no point at which we are not interacting with God. And this means, in turn, that the finitude which limits our interactions with creatures doesn't affect

91. Austin Farrer, *The Glass of Vision* (London: Dacre 1948) 7–8.

92. See Lash, "These Things Were Here" 150–63.

our interactions with God. We have to choose between interacting with one friend and engaging with another, but this isn't the case with God.

(*iv*) In more than one way, loving creatures is at the same time also loving God. So authentic friendship with creatures is a way in which we participate in friendship with God.

(*v*) On the other hand, because God is fully aware of what we do and think and feel and are, our choices and experiences make a difference in God's own life. They introduce novelty into God's own experience and present new realities in relation to which God acts. Of course God is fully aware of all *possibilities* at all times, but God knows contingent events, like our free choices, as they occur. "God is the great companion—the fellow-sufferer who understands."[93] And God is responding to our choices and the events in our lives as they occur, even if divine action is constrained by creaturely freedom and the integrity of nature and even if we cannot often discern the movement of providence. So our interaction with God isn't one-sided.[94]

(*vi*) If talk of friendship with God is to have any cognitive significance, however qualified in light of our limitations, one thing that follows is that we cannot envision created persons as simply absorbed into the divine life or into any sort of boundaryless collective. For friendship essentially involves otherness, the gift of another's presence and engagement. Any sort of eschatology that envisions creaturely friendship with God must thus be an eschatology that incorporates belief in the preservation of personal individuality and agency, even if it also anticipates greater openness, permeability, and responsiveness to God and to other creatures. The image of life beyond death as resurrection, of life beyond death as *embodied*, helps to capture and underscore this sense of creaturely particularity as persistent even in a future glorified state.[95]

There are substantial differences between friendship with creaturely persons and our relationships with God—not least that our relationships with God are not alternatives to and cannot displace creaturely friendships. We can use the language of friendship with God metaphorically, however, to emphasize that

93. Alfred North Whitehead, *Process and Reality: An Essay in Cosmology*, ed. David Ray Griffin and Donald Sherburne (New York: Free 1978) 351.

94. See, *e.g.*, Oord, *Nature of Love* 91, 114–6; Oord, *Defining Love* 71, 189–200; and Ward, *Sharing in the Divine Nature*.

95. See Reinhold Niebuhr, *The Nature and Destiny of Man* 2: *Human Destiny* (New York: Scribner 1964) 296–7.

God loves us, that we can make a difference in the divine life, and that our relationships with God can be marked by mutual delight.

As God delights in us, so God delights in our friends and our friendships. That's one of several reasons that loving friends is neither irrelevant to Christian spirituality nor a distraction from friendship with God. As a form of love for God and an inspiration for basic trust and explicit Christian belief, it can play an important role in Christian living. That friendship is a way in which divine love is shared and experienced and nourished gives us good reason to celebrate it as a rich divine gift.

Conclusion

Friendship matters. It helps to enrich our lives, sustain our institutions, and mediate divine love. Our friendships help to shape us, and friendships and friends are partly constitutive of our identities. Our friends are entitled to our loyalty, and we to theirs. And it is perfectly reasonable to invest ourselves and our resources in initiating and nourishing friendships.

Meeting Challenges

Most of us instinctively acknowledge the significance of friendship in our lives. Social attitudes and theoretical stances with the potential to undermine our appreciation for friendship and our loyalty to our friends can and should be resisted.

Recognizing that we're essentially social and relational helps us to say *no* to pictures of ourselves as detached atoms. Our friends and our friendships help to constitute not only our well-being but, indeed, our very identities.

While friends may share all sorts of interests, it matters that they create and maintain space for intimate disclosure and mutual discovery. Friendship is finally about the friends themselves and not just about any interests they might share, so it can persist when interests change, and it can rightly involve intimate communion and not just common activities.

Friends may be drawn together by many different things, including each other's moral excellences. But mutual love is not about seeking moral purity or praising each other's virtues. People can be loved whether or not they live up to our moral standards. (The inherent dynamics of friendship itself help to constrain friends' moral characters, since being a friend at all requires a capacity for openness, loyalty, and other positive moral qualities—even if not all the virtues one might want oneself or another to exhibit.)

Despite what we might like to think, none of us is a little (or not-so-little) god, a god who could or should be friends with everyone. Our active, positive loves are necessarily particular. Part of loving is treating those affected by our actions fairly—nonarbitrarily. But, at least ordinarily, it's not arbitrary at all to choose to invest in relationships with friends and in the activities and undertakings we share with them.

Relationships often evolve in slow, circuitous, surprising ways. Dependencies and vulnerabilities and attachments can emerge unexpectedly and without being consciously acknowledged. There might be value in the public celebration of friendship; but friendship, even very deep friendship, can come about without such celebration. Friendship can be a tacit rather than a formal institution. But it need be no less morally weighty than if it *were* formalized, not least because reflective, communicative friends can identify their responsibilities to each other without appealing to the agreed-upon feature of any public role.

Commitment to a friendship, an invitation to a friend to rely on one, and promises to one's friend can rightly limit one's options. Accepting the limits that flow from friendship is an inherent part of realizing the goods internal to friendship. And doing so leaves one free, even as one accepts the limits friendship naturally imposes, to reject a friend's attempts at domination or manipulation. As sinful human beings, friends can sometimes engage in such attempts, but nothing about friendship—in general or with them in particular—requires one to acquiesce. There are good reasons to qualify one's own autonomy by choosing relationship; but one can acknowledge those good reasons without submitting to another's arbitrary will.

To own one's ties to a friend is often, at least, to give one's friendship with her a priority higher than the ranking one assigns to ascending a corporate hierarchy or exploring a new geographic setting. Obviously, it may be economically inescapable to accept a new position or to move to a new location. But taking friendship seriously means recognizing the impact of career and geographic changes on one's connections with one's friends and giving one's friendships due weight in one's deliberations about transitions. It also means supporting (*i*) institutional changes that reduce economic pressures on the stability and depth of friendships and (*ii*) social norms that help people to resist such pressures.

We should feel free, much of the time, to choose our friends over our governments. And we have every reason to reject idolatrous understandings of politics or ethics that seek to swallow up our time and energy and leave no room for friendship. The goods we can (sometimes) achieve through politics (in the narrow or the broad senses I have distinguished) are real. However, given the qualitative differences among categories of well-being, as also among individual instances of flourishing and fulfillment, those goods can't (absent individual commitments) trump or purport to outweigh the goods to be realized in friendship (or any number of other pursuits). We should be skeptical of our own pretensions to political infallibility or righteousness. And even when we are right and our friends mistaken, even when they are quite horribly mistaken, and while this may require us sometimes actively to oppose them (when doing so makes a tangible difference it would be unfair to ignore), putatively mistaken beliefs on their part give us no reason to stop loving them.

Friendship and liberalism can support each other by reinforcing regard for individuality, personal and institutional and cultural diversity, experimentation, and freedom of choice. The adoption of liberal policies, especially in tandem with liberal challenges to prevailing cultural norms, can undermine barriers to friendship created by contemporary workplaces and economic dynamics and encourage the formation of friendship in the face of traditional barriers.

The classical understanding of friendship as politically significant can remain viable insofar as friendship can help to shape people's capacities to participate in public debate and nurture their readiness to engage in dissent. We have good reasons quite apart from the significance of a network-based political order for friendship to seek this kind of decentralized political order; and, in such an order, the friendship group could be significant (in workplaces and deterritorialized political institutions) in something like the way it was in the classical era. Networked politics—deterritorialized, consensual, voluntary, peaceful—can provide opportunities for human-scale political involvement, including involvement by friendship groups, while reducing the pressures states, predictably captured by elites, tend to place on friendship and other aspects of our flourishing.

There is no need to ignore friends in order to focus on engaging in certain kinds of spiritual practices. (Indeed, because it prompts us to recognize ourselves as finite but valuable creatures, because it encourages us to open ourselves to surprise, because it challenges us to love in the face of difference, because it is a school for loyalty—for all these reasons, friendship itself is a vital spiritual discipline.) It's a mistake to suppose that God is in competition with creation for our attention. Being friends with creatures can happen at the same time as loving God; it is, indeed, a way of loving God.

The quest for purity, whether in politics or in religion, is deeply problematic, not least when it is understood as involving separation from morally or spiritually or politically impure people. Association with or love of people who differ from us doesn't make us impure (nothing does). Even if it did, given the value of the relationships the pursuit of purity could lead us to shun, many of us would have reason not to strive for purity. Because none of us is flawless, seeking purity conceived of as entailing the rejection of supposedly impure people would ultimately mean excluding everyone from our lives. And of course others in search of purity could be expected to exclude us, too.

To a significant degree, "our need for friendship is bound up with the sharing of our vulnerability and our wounds."[96] But it is easy to worry that friendship will actually *increase* our vulnerability, expose us to multiple risks. These potential risks include not only the risk of losing a friend but also the risk of losing one's freedom. It might well be wrong to insist that "freedom's just another word for nothin' left to lose."[97] Nonetheless, an attachment to another is, unavoidably, a self-embraced constraint on freedom. Friendship involves the relinquishment of the moral (and sometimes the psychological) ability to do things it would be otherwise perfectly possible to do. That's part of what it means to accept a friendship. One can, to be sure, seek to avoid the moral and emotional constraints friendship generates. But to do this at least runs the risk of denying that friendship is a genuine good or pretending that the value of freedom can outweigh the worth of friendship. One can certainly choose reasonably to invest oneself in goods other than friendship, but only if one acts in view of the genuine value that friendship retains whether or not one selects it as a priority.

Embracing Contingency

Worries about freedom and vulnerability are very much in view when Walter, one of the interlocutors in Ælred of Rievaulx's classic *Spiritual Friendship*,[98] puts to the abbot the opinion that those may be right

96. MacIntyre, *Dependent Rational Animals* 164.

97. Kris Kristofferson and Fred Foster, "Me and Bobby McGee," side 1, track 3, on Kris Kristofferson, *Kristofferson*, Monument 1970.

98. On Ælred, see, *e.g.*, Carmichael, *Friendship* 70–100.

> who say that friendship should be avoided, on the ground that it is a compact full of solicitude and care, not devoid of fear, and even subject to many griefs. For since it is enough and more than enough for anyone to bear his own burden, they say a man acts rashly in so tying himself to others, that he must needs be involved in many cares and afflicted with many evils. . . . Therefore they judge it safer so to love others as to be able to hate them at will, and in so relaxed a manner to hold the reins of friendship that they may be tightened or loosened at will.[99]

Flight from the contingent is a characteristic feature of much discourse about friendship,[100] one of the features that links the concerns and convictions of many of those whose views have been considered here. Many modern friends profess uncritically to desire a utopia in which they can maintain flourishing friendships while regularly giving first priority to their own plans and projects. Thus, it seems, they hope to escape the consequences of linking themselves to others in relationships influenced too much by factors outside their control. It is unsurprising, then, that some people argue that there is no such thing as moral responsibility in friendship.

Another way of seeking to tame the contingency of friendship is to attempt to define the relationship in such a way that the bodily, the natural, the passional are absent from it. By declaring that friends ought to focus their attention on some reality external to their friendship, this approach implicitly provides an anchor that might seem to render friendship safe(r) from the risk of loss.

Consider the effort to free friendship from bondage to vulnerability by urging that it be understood as focused on a common quest for *the good* so that a relationship between friends is treated as concerned with moral virtue or personal excellence rather than with ties between the friends themselves. Or consider a less rarified approach, one that sees friendship's focus as on the ordinarily attractive qualities of the friend rather than the friend herself (even if the qualities are embodied in a distinctive way in the friend's life). On this sort of approach, one is justified in ending a relationship that has been transformed by the contingencies of circumstance. And if the qualities are the only things that matter, one can always find a replacement if a friendship sours. Ignoring

99. Ælred, *Spiritual Friendship* 2.45–6.

100. I suspect that my initial attention to the role of contingency in discourse about friendship reflected the influence of Martha Nussbaum's early work, to which my attention was directed, in turn, by a 1989 letter from Stanley Hauerwas.

the difference between friendship and church membership can also be a way of disregarding the contingent particularity of individual friendships (even if not a way of making us safe despite their contingency).

So the Stoics and their successors, whose views Walter repeats to Ælred, were by no means alone in their concern to avoid "the perils of friendship."[101] The unpredictable ambiguities and tensions of our lives encourage us to understand ourselves and our relationships in ways that provide us with a measure of security, either as self-sufficient individuals or as members of self-sufficient collectives. But such self-sufficiency is an illusion. We are socially, historically, and relationally formed. Particular interactions—unavoidably contingent ones—are the means by which we are shaped by our societies. Each of us contributes individual elements of novelty to those interactions as well, elements that only increase the distinct and unrepeatable character of our stories and situations.

Like all social interactions, interactions with friends help to form our identities. But because they are more extensive and more intensive than most of our other relationships, and because they are marked by a freedom from social expectation that allows our individuality to display itself, and because those with whom we unite in them become, in an important sense, parts of our identities, our friendships play especially important roles in determining who we are. Friendship is a prime instance of the factors that contribute to the contingent formation of our lives.

Ironically, the recognition of friendship's contingency is one of the things that can help us to respond to its apparent perils. Acknowledging the permeable boundaries of our selves will allow us to view the vicissitudes of friendship as challenges to which repair and healing, not recrimination and vengeance, are the proper responses. A bond with a friend need not seem like an alien imposition. It may rather appear as a natural outgrowth of a desire for personal integrity, given the roles of our friends and friendships in making us who we are. And it is the specific, contingent histories we share with our friends, rather than their abstract attitudes and qualities, that individuate our friendships and ground our attachments to our friends, even as our free, and so contingent, commitments to relationships with free and unpredictable others help to shape our identities.

The appreciation for contingency can help, also, guard against another of the dangers to which one might be prone in friendship—namely, to absolutize it. Crises occasioned by friendship can, in fact, serve to relativize not only the relationship but our lives generally, helping us discern better our place in

101. Moravcsik, "Perils of Friendship" 132–51.

the universe, our identities as God's creatures. The self-sufficient person may attempt to guard herself against such experiences of contingency, but the friend can find in them a disclosure of one of the "dimensions of ultimacy."[102]

To open up the self in friendship is to make possible the creation or reinforcement of a sense of basic trust. Here, too, a recognition of contingency is important. Self-sufficiency may warn against such a risk. But to venture in this way is to render oneself receptive to God's grace. To close oneself off, adopting the stance of an isolated ego, is to reject that grace—not because one has offended God but because one has opted for a self-dependence that is ultimately illusory. Someone's action, Barth observes, "might seem to be very noble but it is not human if he really thinks that he can be self-sufficient. . . . In this very likeness to God he becomes inhuman. In this apparent nobility he falls into the abyss."[103]

Our moral and political formation takes place in the course of our interactions with a range of people and groups and institutions, some engaged in ongoing conversations, the terms of which are set by particular traditions that shape our practice, our thought, our experience. It is perhaps not incidental that philosophical positions that have appeared especially suspicious of our situatedness, and thus of the contingency of our formation, have often also seemed inhospitable to friendship. But, if we embrace our particularity at the social and historical levels, we ought to be free to do so at the interpersonal level as well. Conversely, if we have discovered the significance of the contingent in our friendships, we may be better equipped to discern its relevance in other contexts. A relational understanding of the self, therefore, provides important resources for understanding friendship. It grounds the integration of friendship with spirituality. And it enables us to understand friendship's link with moral—and thus political—formation.

The "vulnerable co-creation"[104] that is friendship is a divine gift—given, we may believe, both in the creation of our natures and in the providential ordering of our individual lives and social interactions and institutions. It makes a distinctive contribution to our selfhood. And it has its own reality apart from all the other relationships—institutional and personal—in which we participate. Both in the demands it makes of us and in the contingency it displays, this

102. For this phrase, see Gilkey, *Naming the Whirlwind* 305–413.

103. Barth, *Dogmatics* 3.2: 263.

104. Carol S. Becker, *Living and Relating: An Introduction to Phenomenology* (Newbury Park, CA: SAGE 1992) 159.

relationship brings us into contact with God. It reminds us of our creatureliness. And it provides us with opportunity to love God in and through our love for creatures partly in virtue of its moral claim upon us—a claim of fidelity and love. Friendship's claim and invitation reflect our vulnerability to each other (in virtue of which we need each other and are obligated to each other), the bonds that arise within that vulnerability, and our commitments to love despite our own vulnerability and the contingency of the factors that affect our relationships. As an affirmation of a pattern of flourishing embodied in social structures formed by God's providence, as a medium and reflection of God's own particular and faithful love, and as a response to a divine gift, behaving responsibly in friendship is an outworking of our responsibility as flourishing parts of God's good creation.

That responsibility is exercised in the public and political worlds and not merely the private one. While those other worlds cannot devour us, cannot deny legitimacy to our friendships, still those worlds sometimes provide arenas for common endeavor with our friends. A political order in which the friendship group could play a role as significant as that which it occupied in the polis would contribute notably to the rehumanization of politics; but even now groups of friends can touch the wider world in diverse ways.

So this fragile gift finds its place in our lives as God's creatures. Its contingency is no bar to its dignity. Were we to deny our contingency *here*, where this relationship is concerned, it would still haunt us in the midst of our imagined self-sufficiency. But we gain nothing by ignoring the vulnerability that is, indeed, an inescapable element of our humanity. As Ælred's Gratian responds to Walter,

> Let us leave the opinion you have spoken of to the man who wishes today's love to be such that it may turn into hatred tomorrow; who wishes to be the friend of all without trusting any; who praises today and reviles tomorrow; who flatters today and criticizes tomorrow; who today is prepared for kisses and tomorrow is ready for reproaches. The love of such a man is acquired at a small price, and at the slightest offense it disappears.[105]

We are contingent, and our friends and friendship are contingent. But that doesn't mean that we are somehow relieved of the challenge to be loyal. It is, indeed, the contingency of our selves and our relationships that makes

105. Ælred, *Spiritual Friendship* 2.47.

trustworthiness matter: if we weren't vulnerable, if we didn't change, fidelity might be relatively effortless. But the fluctuations in our behaviors and circumstances and capacities and attitudes make the call to loyalty in friendship vital, perhaps sometimes even heroic, certainly a compelling expression of God's own love to us. Recognizing contingency doesn't mean treating disconnection, betrayal, and abandonment as unavoidable or beyond our control. Instead, it means acknowledging the genuine difficulties posed by the circumstances that *seem* to make such responses inescapable while learning to be the kinds of people who can surmount those difficulties and remain faithful.

Accepting our contingency, we become free to accept what friendship has to offer. We do not gain the whole world, or anything so grand as that, for friendship cannot pretend to carry the weight of the cosmos, or even to secure on its own the worth or meaning of our lives. But we gain access to one of God's simple gifts,[106] a gift we may hope to cherish in the course of an everlasting future.

106. Diane C. Kessler, *God's Simple Gift: Meditations on Friendship and Spirituality* (Valley Forge, PA: Judson 1988).

Index

About the Author

Gary Chartier is Distinguished Professor of Law and Business Ethics and associate dean of the Tom and Vi Zapara School of Business at La Sierra University in Riverside, California. He is the author, coauthor, editor, or coeditor of nineteen current or forthcoming books, including *Flourishing Lives: Exploring Natural Law Liberalism* (Cambridge University Press 2019), *Public Practice, Private Law: An Essay on Love, Marriage and the State* (Cambridge University Press 2016), and *The Analogy of Love: Divine and Human Love at the Center of Christian Theology* (2d ed., Griffin 2017). His byline has appeared over forty times in journals, including the *Oxford Journal of Legal Studies*, the *Anglican Theological Review*, the *Heythrop Journal*, and *Religious Studies*. He is a member of the American Philosophical Association and the Alliance of the Libertarian Left, a member of the board of the Molinari Institute, and a senior fellow of the Center for a Stateless Society.

After qualifying for a BA in history and political science from La Sierra (1987, magna cum laude), he explored theology, theological and philosophical ethics, the philosophy of religion, Christian origins, and political philosophy at the University of Cambridge, earning a PhD in 1991. He graduated with a JD (2001, Order of the Coif) from UCLA, where he studied legal philosophy and public law and received the Judge Jerry Pacht Memorial Award in Constitutional Law. The University of Cambridge presented him with an earned higher doctorate, an LLD, in 2015 for his work in legal philosophy.

A proud southern California native who wishes he had attended UC Sunnydale, he shares a slowly improving 1920 home in Riverside with his wife, Alicia Homer, Willow Rosenberg the Kitty, and Rupert Giles Feline. His hobbies include film, long-arc television, biography, genre fiction, spicy food, politics, human psychic and social dynamics, interminable conversation, and the esoteric, the quirky, and the arcane. His motto is E. M. Forster's "Only connect." Visit him online at <http://www.garychartier.net>.